TIGERS WAITING TO BE TAMED

HOW I FOUGHT MY WAY OUT OF VANCOUVER GANG LIFE

Jake Louis Hodgson

© 2017 Jake Louis Hodgson

Cover art courtesy Laura Zerebeski ©2015   lzerebeski@gmail.com

This book is dedicated to my three gifted, kind and beautiful daughters - they are my definitions of true success - and to my mother, who did the best with the cards she was dealt. Also to my editor, Danuta, who pushed me to finish. Thank you all. I hope I've set a good example and lived up to your expectations.

Table of Contents

Foreword 1

Chapter 1 A Blast from the Past 4

Chapter 2 Tigers in Training.. 10

Chapter 3 Living Below the Radar 13

Chapter 4 The Indoctrination... 28

Chapter 5 Learning the Rules of the Jungle....................... 32

Chapter 6 Steal from the Rich and Give to the Poor…Me 42

Chapter 7 Angels Come to Party 46

Chapter 8 The "Uncles" 52

Chapter 9 Playground Politics 58

Chapter 10 Tough Lessons for a Young Entrepreneur 69

Chapter 11 First Time in Jail 73

Chapter 12 Trying on Religion…Catholic School............................ 79

Chapter 13 Taking the Kid Out of the Hood or Taking the Hood Out of the Kid?... 84

Chapter 14 Department Store Sleepover............................. 88

Chapter 15 Flirting with Pyromania and Serving Up Some Payback 98

Chapter 16 Double Bounced... 108

Chapter 17 Sleepless in Vancouver 120

Chapter 18 There's No Place Like Home… Unless It's a Warehouse for Wayward Youths... 139

Chapter 19 Enter the Cowboy... 149

Chapter 20 Life in a Northern Town................................. 158

Chapter 21 Home Alone 164

Chapter 22 Braving the Elements 170

Chapter 23 Escape to the Army…the Salvation Army...................... 175

Chapter 24 Tilly the Hun to the Rescue............................ 180

Chapter 25 Back to School 187

Chapter 26 First Love...She Was Cool, Blonde, and Her Daddy Had a Rolls-Royce... 192

Chapter 27 The Cowboy "Reloaded" 196

Chapter 28 Leaving ...on a Greyhound 203

Chapter 29 Ward of the Court... 208

Chapter 30 Last Year of High School.. 219

Chapter 31 Odd Jobs and Trying to Stay Out of Jail 228

Chapter 32 Blood Is Thicker Than Water.. 239

Chapter 33 Night on the Town with My Old BFF............................ 254

Chapter 34 "Do Not Pass Go...Go Straight to Jail." 261

Epilogue It's Been a Long Road.. 271

Foreword

I was the runt of the litter and the last of five, entering this happy planet the usual way at a fighting weight of five pounds. I started out in the small town of Haney, British Columbia, soon to be raised by a single mother because my biological father couldn't cut the mundane tasks of fatherhood. One stormy West Coast night, my mother, a slender strong-willed English girl with jet-black hair and sparkling blue eyes, decided there must be more to life than being shackled with five kids and a deadbeat ex who resided way too close for comfort. With nothing to lose, she corralled her children onto a Greyhound bus and headed for the big city of Vancouver, exchanging soft green pastures for cold hard concrete. This was incredibly brave and a desperate move for a small town girl, but in reality she felt she had no choice. Besides being faced with the proximity of the deadbeat, she was shunned by most if not all of her family and the community for having had a baby (my oldest sister), out of wedlock. So she left the secure little hamlet her father helped homestead and headed to the city.

As she emerged from the Vancouver bus station, kids in tow, the stark reality of her somewhat impulsive decision hit her like a slap in the face on a cold Canadian winter's eve. No smiling faces to greet her, just street people looking for a handout, and the howl of the blowing rain. So began my inner city tale of living below the radar on welfare with my older brother and three sisters, often wearing clothing from the Salvation Army. No Norman Rockwell painting of my childhood for me, even though years later I was to find out that my father's family was among some of Britain's wealthiest elite, owning steel mills amongst other holdings while occasionally hobnobbing with some of the Royals.

In retrospect, my childhood in East Vancouver (known affectionately or otherwise by locals as "East Van") was no picnic, but at the time it was fun. Now I see the dark reality for children in that way-too-common situation, the worst part being monsters wearing human skin. Yes, the never-ending abduction attempts by predators that know the pickings are easy and the harvest is plentiful in the land of single mothers, unwatched children and wayward fathers. As for scars, I have some good ones from my journey thus far, including being poisoned and drugged, but among my favourites is the dubious badge of honour awarded via an eleven-inch butcher knife plunged through my back at age nine by a disgruntled six-year-old neighbour. That one made the papers. Another was having a buddy I lived with sucker-punch me, breaking my nose one night, and then, in the fight that followed, driving a sharp brass-tipped walking stick into my stomach.

As for encounters of the police kind, let's just say before I was granted a full pardon I garnered a rap sheet that made a U.S. customs officer exclaim, "Holy shit!" after he pulled my name up on the system. No one expects much from a guy with a history that included being charged with two counts of attempted murder and whose regular activities involved armed robbery, B&Es, high-speed police chases, shoplifting and gang fights.

The epiphany that I should not have made it out hit me many years later and made me ask out loud, "What if the lifestyle change I made is something worth sharing and can help others to push on?"

All of the above now seems like someone else's life as I travel the world, having earned the keys to the executive suite along the way. Starting off selling vacuum cleaners door-to-door, then shoes, vending machines, elevators and everything in between, included getting fired at least five times. But like they say, what doesn't kill you makes you stronger, so I never gave up, and along the way I won a multitude of sales and marketing awards with various multinationals and got the money that came along with it. I also earned black belts in karate and jiu-jitsu while training with legendary instructors Ron Sitrop, Al Chad and one of Bruce Lee's original students, the late Pat Thue. I pioneered the concept of vending routes for sale, started a bodyguard company with Mr. Chad that went international, obtained a student pilot's license, had a one-on-one chat with Mother Teresa and attended intimate talks with Buckminster Fuller and Margaret Mead. Plus, I had Howard Hughes's chauffeur as my foster dad for a time.

No question, my life could be summed up by saying, "If you see a turtle on a fence post, you know he had help getting there." Help came from school teachers, social workers, family members, and both intelligent and ignorant criminals. I thank them all. I bought the mayor's house, was married for 22 years, and put my three girls through private school. No. It was never easy but I guess I was just too stupid to quit or I just had the secret ingredient of all successful people: grit.

My philosophy and values today are the following:
I believe I am the product of the idea taught to me by one of my early mentors, Zig Ziglar, who said, "If you help enough people get what they want, you will get what you want".
My credo: "Never forget where you are, and always remember where you're from.. In my case, that is East Vancouver.

My ethos, pathos and logos: "Don't be a success in the corporate world and a failure at home; if you do that, you leave a loser's legacy for the world to clean up."

- JLH

Email me at: tamingtigers.ca@gmail.com

Twitter: @JakeHodgs1
https://twitter.com/JakeHodgs1

Facebook: Jake Louis Hodgson

Chapter 1

A Blast from the Past

It's just after 9/11. I'm standing in the security lineup at Vancouver International Airport underneath a patch of sun, and, beneath my Armani suit, I'm starting to sweat. My boss is already on the other side, and I know he's getting impatient. He needs to discuss our big meeting with the A-List client we're flying to meet in Boston. But all I can think about is what I'm going to say when the customs officer looks my name up on the computer. Interpol loves names and birthdates, and I smile as I think about how casually most people dispense their data to anyone who asks. After all, they've got nothing to hide. But I know Big Brother isn't going to look down so kindly on me.

A swarm of Chinese cruise ship passengers are ahead of me; my stress level is rising, and I wince as their grating tones pierce the air. A handful of families with noisy kids make up the rest, along with one or two super-sized Americans. We're moving at a snail's pace. I try to control the butterflies in my stomach and harness my racing thoughts. Finally, the guy ahead of me passes through like he won a lottery ticket and the officer absent-mindedly beckons me over. Already I feel like I'm back in the paddy wagon wearing handcuffs, out of breath from the struggle. My heart gallops as I stride up to the counter with a smile on my face and an air of confidence. I hand him my passport and ticket.

"Where are you heading?" He's a burly man who doesn't smile much. His uniform looks too tight, and I can see it's been a long day.

"Boston." Keep it short and simple, and keep smiling, I'm thinking. He punches away at the computer, stares at the screen, and then his eyes widen.

"Are you Jake L. Hodgson?" he asks.

"Yes."

"What does the "L" stand for?" he asks suspiciously.

"Louis," I say, as if this is such a common thing to be asked, a lump in my throat trying to choke the word from my lips.

"Spell your middle name."

I spell it, but can't help think that even an ESL student could spell my name.

"What's your birth date?" As if he doesn't have it on the all-seeing eye of his black screen.

I tell him.

"Holy shit!" he suddenly exclaims as he leans back in his chair, clasping his hands behind his head while staring at the monitor. "Do you have a criminal record?" I feel fifty pairs of eyes burning a hole in the back of my head trying to get a glimpse of why he is asking me this. A bead of sweat trickling down the length of my spine causes me to shiver like someone just walked across my grave.

Naively, I say "Yes." Take-away point: Don't guess what they have on their screen. Error on the side of innocence. Just my opinion.

He clasps his hands behind his huge sweaty neck and leans back in his chair. "What happened?" he asks with genuine curiosity.

"I got into a fight," I say. Nothing more; nothing less.

He pauses, looks back at the screen again, and continues to read.

"Well, you're going to have to visit INS. Immigration and Naturalization Service."

He pecks at his keyboard, then gets down off his chair and motions to me to follow him. I do it like a whipped dog. The old fight-or-flight urge comes over me like a rush of ice water. I swear under my breath as I pick up my briefcase and decide to risk a quick check of my cell phone. I see my boss has called three times and I assume he's waiting in the bar. No need for him to see me get tasered and tackled by security while I piss my pants, or something equally embarrassing. All I know is if I miss this plane, I'll lose my job. These days it's the game of one strike you're out, not three, since the West has bought into the Chinese philosophy of behind every able man are a hundred able men. Loyalty is only a marketing line these days and seems to have no place in business other than expecting it from your clients and debt-ridden employees. Goes without saying, I need this job like a junkie needs a fix. New twin babies, sixty days behind on my mortgage, and a mountain of debt. Disney is dead and I'm living a Tim Burton nightmare of my own design.

The INS office is stuffy and full of agitated, sweaty foreigners with unhappy faces. Twelve chairs line the glass walls, and six cameras are watching every move. An African woman wearing a bright smock yells at an officer, "I will miss my plane!" He loses it for second (so much for the advertisement behind him saying, "We are the face of America.") and snaps back, "I don't give a crap if you miss your plane, lady! You wait for the process or you go back to Canada."

"This looks promising," I'm thinking as I take a seat. Twenty minutes pass before a stocky no-neck officer with a healthy beer gut and an oily, pock-marked face finally calls my name. I look down and catch a flash of the neon lights dancing off the polished steel of his H&K semi-automatic patiently waiting to be released from its leather jail. All the power is in his hands. I make no attempt at small talk and I maintain eye contact as I stand before him like a child about to be scolded by his teacher. His fat fingers clatter away on the computer keyboard as I follow his school ring with my peripheral vision. He then begins to rattle off a series of open-ended questions. I smile and remind myself of the advice of a past mentor, cool heads prevail, as I lower my blood pressure and answer away, never breaking the ever-searching eyes of the U.S. border agent who was certainly taught that the eyes are the windows to the soul.

Bam! Within seconds, I'm right back in my past life, re-living vivid scenarios as they flash through my memory at lightning speed. I see the glint of my German-made blade as it slices through the flesh of two thugs who mistakenly thought I was someone else as they cornered me in a dark alley. I feel the agony of having a 120-pound police dog dragging me by my balls, its eyes wild with excitement over the scent of my blood. I hear the hollow sound of my baseball bat connecting with the Asian gang leader's head and see the slow-motion arc of his blood against the pale blue summer sky. I hear the scream of the neighbour fearing for his life and the clang of the steel doors slamming, and the roar of my hammering heart on that first night in a maximum security prison.

I have no idea what events in my colourful past are showing on his screen, but, like a prize fighter, I bob and weave, deflecting questions and giving as little information as possible, leaving my face as blank as a Texas Holdem champion's. I don't try to be buddies, and I certainly don't give him my life story, but am very thankful they don't yet do brain scans as part of the screening process.

Then the officer abruptly disappears through a door that leads to the big two-way mirrors that I watch my reflection in, purposely leaving me to my thoughts. I look at my phone and swear again. My shirt is soaked beneath my jacket and I long to change into my track suit and pour a sweet glass of the distraction I call Jack. Still I'm waiting. I've mentally prepared myself for another latex encounter, which from personal experience beats police dog interaction hands- down, and thinking my job is toast. Chubby saunters back with the swagger of Daniel Craig and stands in front of me for a second, looking into my eyes as he searches for my soul. Then, without a word, he slams the big stamp onto my passport and dismisses me with a wave of his hairy leg sized arm.

After hesitating in disbelief for a beat, I turn and bolt out the door just in time to hear the loudspeaker crying out, "Final call for passenger Jake Hodgson...Jake Hodgson, please come to departure gate 45, the doors will be closing in five minutes." I'm sprinting now, doing the classic O.J. Simpson run down the mile-long airport hallway. Heart pounding; teeth gritting: Note to self: Restart work out regime. No time to look cool, I can do that later. I come flying up to the check-in counter and hand the constipated-looking bald, gay guy my boarding ticket. He smirks as if he has a secret showing the fashionable gap in his bleached white teeth.

No time for a "moment". Boom! I'm past him as his eyes seem compelled to watch my skinny butt propel me down the gangway as if it were a security threat. Sweating profusely by now - I am a fatty! Shit! I gotta start working out. At this point I'm a total soup sandwich. What a mess. My dark hair is pasted against my head like I just got out of the shower, my laptop case is cutting all circulation from my hand, fingers bone-white and tingling.

I finally arrive at the plane door and stop cold. The flight attendant, weathered and aging, a remnant of the glory days of jet planes and pilots that earned real money, glares over her thick glasses as she impatiently contemplates my next move. I pause and look at her just long enough for her to break contact, assuring her I couldn't give a rat's ass about her schedule as there is no way in hell I'm walking on that plane looking like I just outran a van load of terrorists looking for YouTube footage. No. I close my eyes, entertain a quiet thought and take a long deep breath and hold it for fifteen seconds and let it out as I count to ten, a little technique I learned from my new book mentor, Anthony Robbins. This calms me as I open my eyes and walk onto the plane like I own it. And of course, who would be sitting in first-class sipping Champagne with a look of disguised interest? You guessed it, my boss with his bright red face, 46- inch waist, Rolex Daytona, ridiculous dyed hair and matching moustache. Can you say ladies' man? Perhaps gold digger's man is more appropriate.

I barely make it through the doors when I feel the plane lurch backwards, confirming to all that I held up the flight. As I make my way towards my seat in the deepest part of cattle class, I know I'll find at least seven hours of peace because my boss is not sitting with me. I ponder the question he is sure to ask, "What the fuck's wrong with you? If we missed that meeting, your ass was grass." He was a real charmer, no question. So I would just lie. Blame it on another passenger, computer glitch, etcetera, anything to detract the heat.

Finally, I settle in to the dreaded window seat, the land of those who don't pee or have no control of travel. I get out a book to take my mind off things. As soon as I'm allowed, I unconsciously order a double Jack, but seconds later change my order to club soda, my hands shaking as I imagine the sweet stinging smell rising up my nostrils and the satisfying burn on the back of my throat. It's been ten years since I've had a drink and I'm not ready to traverse that slippery slope; too much to do and too many people depending on me. My head slowly leans back as I stare through the double-glass window, foggy and scratched, making the billowing clouds look like something from a Monet painting. I start to relax, and my mind disengages from reality as we rocket high above those earthly troubles. I slowly drift into a restless coma with Technicolor dreams of my childhood jungle and the battles for survival and ambitions of significance.

Chapter 2

Tigers in Training

"We were wild, brutally pure in our thoughts and actions. No conscience, just a heightened sense of awareness of our surroundings, which with no attachments or future gave us an edge. We were products of our environment with no choice but to attack or be attacked. There's no status quo in our little jungle. Sometimes I feel my childhood was me looking at the one I wanted through a dirty window."

- JLH

It wasn't until I was nine or ten that I began to realize that it was not normal to live in a housing project with no dads to be seen. We used to joke about being in a safe place because the police cars were always there to catch the strays our moms missed because they were often pissed by noon.

I guess me and my pack of Perros Callejeros [Spanish for street dogs], all of us between five and ten years old, could be looked upon as baby tigers waiting to be tamed - cute and cuddly, but with claws and teeth and the strength of those with nothing to lose. Looking back some forty years now, I realize that, with so many of those kids now dead or in jail, we could be caged but never really tamed. Just ask Siegfried and Roy.

Act first, think later was our motto, which gave us lightning-fast reflexes that came with the added bonus feature of no concern about the consequences. And yes, this came with its fair share of pain. It's not that we weren't aware that our actions had consequences; we just weren't intimidated by them and ultimately didn't give a shit since there was no reason to. School was pretty much optional, and most of the kids didn't go or, if we did, skipped out and went looking for adventure. Why read about it in textbooks or be taught it by some nerdy teacher whose big life adventure was deciding what university to go to? No, we were going to make our own.

Our surroundings were ever-changing. This kept us engaged and looking out for the next event or situation, which was normally right around the corner. If not, no problem; we would make it happen. Light a school on fire; roll a parked car down a steep hill into fast-moving traffic; sneak into the movie theatre; pull a fire alarm. It didn't matter to us, and nothing was off limits; just as long as we never had still moments to contemplate the shit-storm we were living in. Besides that, it was fun! Living life like six Saturdays and a Sunday.

My jungle was the Projects, the Slums or Skid Row - whatever you want to call it. It was the terrain of marginalized children, single mothers and new immigrants who - and this is a scary thought - still thought it was paradise compared to where they came from. Yeah, I was in my own way a member of the so-called Lucky Sperm Club, as opposed to the land of Slum Dog Millionaire. We lived in a zoo of sorts, and like all zoos it was designed to keep the animals in a safe and well-identified location. This has always allowed the civilians to sleep peacefully, knowing the jungle had order to it.

The real dark side for children of this grungy little world was the never-ending abduction attempts by predators who knew the pickings were easy in the land of single mothers. These aliens (they sure as hell aren't humans) are cautious, calculating, strategic and as systematic as a MacDonald's; after all they don't want to get caught any more than a tiger does. They prowl the slums of the world where there are plenty of unwatched or unwanted children to choose from. I was lucky enough to escape my opportunities to have my face plastered on a milk carton or the back of some dirty semi-truck trailer racing by you on the highway with the words last seen under my photo.

But strangely enough, I have fond memories from my childhood. Not that certain risks didn't come with the territory, because they did. The upside was that the many gang fights and car thefts had some twisted educational perks, like the importance of being a team player, or always wearing your seatbelt and turning into the skid when involved in a high-speed police chase, and my favourite: If you're not the lead dog, the view never changes.

Years later, while watching the movie City of God I came to the realization that even my floor was someone else's ceiling and how lucky I was not to be born in some third-world country where my life would have been worth less than a few cigarettes or six-pack of Coke.

Chapter 3

Living Below the Radar

"The only thing stronger than fear is purpose, so make your purpose strong and live each day like you will be killed tomorrow." - JLH

December, 1965

By the time I was five, my mother, a slender and strong-willed English girl with jet-black hair and bright blue eyes, was fed up with her deadbeat, philandering husband, known around the small town her family helped homestead in the 1930s as the Drunken Milkman. Don't get me wrong, he had lots of potential, but that just means he hadn't done anything yet other than being married four times previously. Interestingly enough, he followed her from England after World War Two as a cameraman for Paramount, actually landing a then-rarely-seen airplane with his camera crew on the main streets of that small town. It's no excuse, but in retrospect, he left home at thirteen, and on the day he did it, he jumped off the roof on top of his father as he was leaving for a meeting and beat him senseless. Why? For many reasons, including being such an ass that his wife (my dad's mom, a nurse), dying from complications of a botched self-abortion, said to my dad, "I will not give this man any more children." She was going to have twins. So he never had a role model to show him what it meant to be a true "man of the house" and stand fast to whatever storm comes your family's way. No, he bailed when the clouds turned dark and made the rest up as he went along, following in the footsteps of many a wife-beater-shirt- wearing man of the times, including his father.

So late one night, my mother corralled her five kids onto a Greyhound bus heading for the Coast and left the memories of her little hamlet in search of a better life in the big city of Vancouver. It was a desperate move and a brave step for a small-town girl, but she was more afraid of what her life would be if she stayed, painted as the black sheep by her family brush.

As she emerged from the city centre bus station in the early hours of the morning, the stark reality of her impulsive decision chilled her to the bones like a blast of cold northern wind. No smiling faces to greet her, just the address of the Salvation Army's women's shelter, street people with tombstone eyes ever searching for their misplaced lives; the relentless blanket of Vancouver's not-so-advertised winter trademark of cold rain bouncing off the heartless pavement. This was the beginning of my inner city tale, one of living below the radar, a family on welfare, and Christmas presents courtesy of strangers and Good Samaritans.

I'm not sure where we lived when we first got there, but I do recall staying in a basement suite for a bit and possibly the Salvation Army women's shelter. Regardless, after a while, as God/luck would have it, a space became available in her sister's place, a hundred-year-old four-storey wooden rat trap down by the docks of East Vancouver, Franklin Street, which was wild then and doesn't seem much different now than it was forty years ago. The sick part about it was it is just a stone's throw from the heart of what has often been labelled as Canada's poorest postal code (V6A a.k.a. the Downtown East Side a.k.a. the DTES), and another short hop to the most expensive condos.

My auntie Gerty (my mom's sister), had one or two kids of her own (J.T. and K.T.) by then and lived in the upstairs apartment/attic. She was a doll, by far my favourite relative, a cool lady with a good attitude, but unfortunately she too was yoked to a deadbeat husband/dad. Sorry to say he died some years later from internal injuries after being beaten by some punks outside a 7-11 five blocks away from that very house. No charges were ever laid.

The house we shared was either too cold or too hot, with the old-fashioned radiant heating banging and clanging at all hours of the night. The set up was simple: when he was home I shared a bedroom with my brother, Wayne, who was three years older but acted like he was 20 years old; my three "snisters" shared a room; and my mom had her own small room, all on the same floor. The unfinished rat-home basement was a jungle of junk left by a multitude of previous renters: boxes, an old water tank (the water tank fell on me cracking my head open during some Spiderman training sequences), trunks and you name it . Oh, and did I mention rats? They can make good pets or good food I've heard; that is of course depending on your circumstances. I personally didn't care for the pushy little bastards and hunted them relentlessly.

After we settled in for what was sure to be a long cold winter full of puffed wheat, PB&J sandwiches and Kraft dinners, the Ukrainian landlord changed his tune and became obsessed with our heat and power usage, which at the time was included in the rent, so to cut costs he would routinely show up and somehow shut the power off. This went on for as long as we lived there and like a plantar wart, we seemed to get used to it. Now, I can't take credit for this, but on a couple of occasions he did find his car, which he stealthily parked down the alley, with a flat tire or a broken window. I knew this because he would come banging on the door in a rage yelling in some foreign tongue and my bro would be laughing in between puffs of his stolen Black Cat No. 7 cigarettes (Same ones my mom smoked ... hmmm?).

My new barrio was a mosaic of poverty-stricken characters: First Nation single mothers by the truck load, Chinese immigrants, hookers, tramps, drug addicts, stumblebums and thieves. A plethora of danger and playground for the absorbent mind of curious, unsupervised five-year-olds looking for adventure and NBFs. The surrounding area was a dying mix of old garment factories, sawmills and decrepit wooden houses. A few doors down from us was a commercial bakery, which wafted mouthwatering scents. Next to it were a chicken-processing plant and a cleaning supplies manufacturer. The streets were red cobblestone bricks that were paved over in some distant past but now were worn clean by years of heavy truck traffic.

After the peace and quiet of our farmhouse in the shadow of the coastal mountains, I couldn't get used to the hum of my new world, especially the lumber mill across the street and the clashing of trains splitting the silence of the night. Many nights, we were woken by sounds of screams and shouts or the occasional pop! pop! of what I assumed was gun fire echoing off the distant dock warehouses. My lullaby seemed to be squealing tires and wailing sirens as red and blue police lights flashed through the dirt-caked windows of our new home. It never really bothered me; as a matter of fact, I loved it. I would imagine what was going on out there and come up with vivid scenarios of how I would blast onto the scene and handle the situation, and that would get my pulse racing until the wee hours of the night. Like a baby tiger, I embraced my new surroundings and began learning the rules of this jungle.

My aunty Gerty and a friend of hers bought me one of the best Christmas presents I can ever remember as a child - a red miniature Mustang bike, my first bike. All the rich kids had them, and now I did too. This was my first love. That is probably why I still have an infatuation with Mustangs in general and have had a couple of the macho Fords, including a burgundy 1968 and a new factory custom convertible, black-on-black Eleanor-looking baby. The real high was that I was mobile. That changed everything, and my dirty little world got a lot bigger. I ventured out daily, riding through the bumpy streets of the undesirable side of town. I can say that I took in every sight, smell and sound of the landscape, including the ever-fascinating local red-light district. An average day would reveal a panorama of sights, such as heroin addicts shooting up in filthy doorways; drunken or (who knows?) dead bodies lying in their own vomit and piss-stained pants. If I didn't know better, I would have thought I was an unwitting extra in a really bad horror movie. The smart ones steered clear of the needles and stuck to the haze of sniffing model glue, gasoline, nail polish remover and the nonstick cooking spray called Pam. The classy ones would smell good by sweating out the Old Spice aftershave they would drink after straining it through bread, a twisted way to sip the nectar of their low-class gods I suppose, but what the hell? As always, I thought it was awesome! I never got too close to these unpredictable zombies. We did, however, antagonize and mock them at any given opportunity and occasionally knock them down on a dare or just to feel the adrenalin rush and almost getting caught as we did it for sport and fun, streaking by them on our powerful steeds. I think the Apache Indians of the U.S. called the game something like "Counting Cue." They, however, played it by laying a spear at the throat of a Buffalo running at full speed - not killing it, just proving they could.

My mom did the best she could to keep the family together, despite the stress of having five kids to look after, no support from her ex-husband and a constant lack of money. That's on top of living in one shit-hole house after another. I mean, no matter how many coats of paint you put on a dump, it's still a dump. I don't remember her ever complaining during that time. She was always caring, affectionate and eternally optimistic. She earned money when she could, including taking care of my aunt's daughter and son in exchange for free rent. Once I hit about five or six years, she started taking on chambermaid jobs at two-star motels, and then she did some in-home care/nursing (she was a nurse for a while when she returned from England after the War, working at Riverview and Crees Clinic psychiatric hospitals) for those stubborn elderly types who, to the disappointment of their kids, refused to die and/or sell the home and be farmed out to one of the warehouses. The jobs paid next to nothing and were thankless. I'm not sure how one can get jacked about cleaning up stained bed sheets and unflushed toilets, but she did what she had to with the cards she was dealt.

Food around our myriad of homes was a constant flow of puffed wheat, powdered and evaporated milk, PB&J sandwiches, and mac and cheese with some cut-up hotdogs and ketchup as a treat. Dessert was usually the left-over rice in a bowl with evaporated milk, some raisins and brown sugar. I loved it! Oh, I still love my mac and cheese but now, thank God, it's available at the better restaurants and bars. Mom was a good girl for the most part, then occasionally having the odd drink (she was a two-beer-wasted gal, often referred to as cheap date) to help her deal with the stress of her life. It was way too much work for her to handle on her own, and almost impossible to stop the destructive paths my siblings and I had begun to take. So I put it out there that I hold no ill will against her and I respect all single mothers this world has to offer and say, "Shame on you, deadbeat males who (temporarily are able to) hide from the privilege and responsibility of raising a family."

Within a few months, the negative influence of our environment started seeping in to our dysfunctional family unit. The bacteria-infected mouths and rotting teeth of life's dragons bit my brother first. He turned fast, like something from a vampire movie - pale skin, and dark black circles under his sunken eyes. He loved it, as far as I can tell, drinking the sour elixir and false wisdom of the local gangs who peddled it like candy. Young men with no other male role models flocked to it like the ice cream man yelling free ice cream. Yet nothing is free, so he soon learned that running with the local boys (some in their twenties) he had to earn his stripes. This included an initiation of arson, stealing cars, B&Es, drugs of all sorts and people that needed a good beating for some reason or the other. He was working nights, I guess you could say, but the flow of young females giving it up for a beer, snort, and toke was a great perk, he once told me. The badge of honour was to steal a cop car, be a second-storey man, win a knife fight or drag down the street some old lady who was too stupid or too stubborn to let go of her purse. He was like a rabid dog, and it must have been a living hell for my small-town mom, especially with the police knocking on the door every few days and her son not coming home for days at a time. When he did show up, he was usually dirty, drunk, high or bruised and beaten. I remember one night jolting out of what was a rare sound sleep to the sound of my mom screaming bloody murder at the site of my bro showing up with a stab wound the size of a dollar coin in his stomach. I honestly thought he had a second belly button, but my mother's face told me otherwise as she collapsed on the floor next to my bro, his blood forming a little pool on the cracked yellow linoleum. He was twelve at the time.

Next step for him included going to Juvie (Juvenile Hall) several times, then a work camp on an island for wayward youths, which he managed to escape from a couple of times by walking, hitchhiking, then sneaking onto a ferry boat back to the Mainland. He actually showed me how it was done. This lack of remorse eventually got him kicked up early to adult court and big-boy prison.

I'm sure my sisters were relieved he was temporarily gone because, as bad as our situation was, he made it 10 times worse. Weird that my brother loved women and was polite and charming to them, just not to my sisters. They hated each other. I remember him beating me up once for some unknown reason, and my oldest sister pouncing on him to protect me. So how did I repay her act of bravery? I hit her over the back with a steel chair. Why? I have no idea, other than she was beating the crap out of him, and I thought I needed to protect him. He never thanked me, just scrambled to his feet and ran out of the house as she lay on the floor in the little living room crying. I watched her for a few moments in some kind of detached interaction, pondering why I had done that. She never protected me again, nor did she ever forget it.

My sisters were no angels. They fought each other constantly and were, in their way, just as hard to keep track of as my bro. They had their moments like when one of them got caught selling or buying (not sure) drugs to an undercover cop. They all had boyfriends who were in local gangs, so by default they ended up being part of girl gangs.

As for me, fun in those days couldn't get any better than going hunting for rats under the docks. Armed with homemade slingshots, rocks and small clubs with some nicely positioned nails pounded through them. We rarely got them, since they can be fearless when cornered. and besides the obvious germs they carry, they got sharp little teeth and can jump really far, an amazing sight to behold when you're six years old and three feet tall.

If you wondering, yes, I was the runt of the litter, which comes from a nice combo of a momma who smoked and minimal protein and no steroid-injected fast foods, I suspect. This, as it turned out, was compounded by being born at the end of the year. In your twenties or thirties, ten or eleven months don't make a big difference in your growth chart ranking, but at five or six? Yeah, the other boys born at the beginning of the same year had inches and pounds on me. Not real good for the self-esteem of a young male when the school and other sports team put kids of the same age together. I learned that lesson when I tried out for the soccer team but it was really driven home by joining a boxing club. Fun times for sure. Oh well, I compensated with a big attitude and some God-given street smarts. What else could I do, entering this world at a whopping five pounds? It didn't take me long to realize being small had its advantages - like all my sisters' friends loved to pick me up and squish me against their breasts. Also going on adventures like sneaking onto the cargo ships and cruising through them looking for whatever I could find, or jumping on the back of buses holding on to the trolley hubs, or hopping on a train car and getting a free cool ride downtown. Pretty harmless stuff compared to my brother, but then again I was just a tiger cub in training. Another challenge of my own making: I had a big mouth, a razor-sharp tongue and a brain with no filter. A big mouth and a small body weren't the best combination. But God compensates and gave me a pair of skinny but ever-so-fast legs, which got me out of many sticky situations that my mouth walked me into. Road Runner and Speed Gonzales (fastest mouse in all Mexico) cartoons were my favourites.

Along with the rest of the family, I started getting into my own mini brand of trouble, including fights, shoplifting and grabbing (or should I say attempting to grab) the odd purse. For the most part, I kept it simple and stuck to dumpster diving. You just never know what you're gonna find in a Saturday-morning-full garbage bin. That was living the dream that was one man's junk is another boy's treasure. In addition to the bottles I would collect and take to the Chinese store, I found coats, plates, knives, and even a bike or two. This so-called fun had to come to an end, and that day came after finding a cool looking bottle labeled "Formula 44." Nothing ventured nothing gained they say, so my gnat-sized brain thought this must be a formula for success and I took a nice long swig of that bitter sweet nectar of the almighty rat gods. The liquid seared my throat, leaving a blistering path down to my stomach, and in a flash of brilliance I knew I was screwed. I scrambled over the edge of the rusting sky-blue Smithrite bin and hit the ground running, still clutching the bottle as best I could. Easier said than done, as I seemed to have gone blind about that time and the unpaved alley was full of pit-bull-sized pot holes. I hit my face a couple of times and tore the skin of my lily white palms, finally bursting through the back door of the old house, choking out an inaudible cry for my mom to save me. I collapsed on the kitchen floor and began vomiting uncontrollably. My mom came running into the kitchen and started yelling, "What happened ? Tell me what happened!" I managed to puke out some words that she understood to mean I had poisoned myself. Yes, there is hope for you! Not sure what you would have done, but she seemed to panic and to this day I'm not sure why she didn't call an ambulance that time either (didn't call one when water tank squashed my pumpkin; called a doctor who came and gave me stitches) I can only guess that she probably thought it would cost money and we had none, so she picked me up and half carried me to a bus stop. That was a ride from hell for my mom and me as well as the unlucky rush-hour passengers, with me having to get off the bus before, after and during the unpleasant act of dry-heaving my guts out. The ride took over two hours to get to the hospital. I can't remember a lot of what happened after arriving at the hospital other than the stuffing of a tube down my throat and having my stomach pumped. I guess it worked, since I am still here. I would like to say this taught me a life-altering lesson, but other than "don't drink from strange bottles you find in garbage cans" - nothing. I needed to be hit by life's steel club many more times before catching on. That was, from what I can remember, my first but not my last brush with an early departure from the blue planet. I will cover some others in later chapters.

Franklin Street, (renovated…did not look like this when we lived there) where we first lived in Vancouver; two block from the docks.

Building next to old Franklin Street house.

It wasn't until years later that I would discover my father's colourful history. His family was among Britain's elite, or should I say Wales's elite. While rummaging through my mother's private cabinet, I found a newspaper clipping with a photo of an old, well-dressed man who was ice-skating. The caption read "Oldest Skater in Canada," and I saw his name: Jake L. Hodgson. He was my grandfather on my dad's side, whom I had been named after but never met, and knew little about. Apparently, my father came from a rich family in Cardiff who owned the distinguished steel mills of Jake L. Hodgson & Sons (hmmm, that's my name), and then learned we were direct descendants of the famous or infamous Oliver Cromwell. Cromwell was a real shit disturber of his day and usurped the throne, helped establish Parliament, and beheaded King Charles, which is the only time in the past thousand years the Royals were not in power. Not so interesting is that he was very harsh, to say the least, on the Irish. This piece of our history was cool for a kid, but I got really supercharged when I found the below picture of my uncle with King George VI, strolling through our family steel mill. Wow! I was spellbound with visions of knights and bloody battles on the rolling green hills of England's countryside Not to mention a damsel or two in distress needing to be saved. Years later while walking around London, I came upon the Parliament buildings and. to my surprise, outside them was a statue of Cromwell.

Photo below from the JLH Quarterly 1955; my uncle is on the left of the then King of England [Colin Firth played him in The King's Speech] on the right.

"...the company was honoured in 1921 by a visit from his late Majesty King George Vl"... Interesting coincidence is that he too was born on December 14th as I was.

When I asked my brother why we lived in a dumpy row house when our family was so rich, he replied, "That's because you're a pimple on my ass and they don't give a shit about us. They don't even know we exist." He paused, then continued, "Look zipper-head, (he loved to call me that) rich people only hang out with rich people. The rest wash their cars and clean their shitters." From that day on, I thought of myself as different from the other street kids, because I had a secret, and one day someone from my dad's side of the family, would find me and say, "There's been a terrible mistake. You're not supposed to be here. No, no, no! You need to come with us to the castle immediately. Jump in the back of the Royals Royce Wraith. There's pop in the ice chest, young sir." Never happened, as you might have guessed, but I decided that I would somehow one day be rich and then track them down. This was a simple thing to do for a kid who still believed in dreams like average parents might tell their offspring when asked. "Yes Jake, you could be the prime minister or an astronaut, it's a free (they should say fee) country." So for some reason I began the practice of what is commonly known as autosuggestion, and began seeking and cutting out pictures of big houses, exotic cars and yachts and private jets. These precious gems I kept in a secret scrapbook hidden from dream vampires; you know, those well-meaning, be-realistic family members, school teachers, counselors and friends, who are with you as long as you are losing. Start to win or get ahead of them in some way, they either vanish like a David Copperfield trick or take the slow road and poison your thoughts over time. Also let's not forget the well-meaning friends, parents, cops and lawyers. Oh, yeah, your biological parents who don't know what they don't know, so they perpetuate the cycle of losers. Call them what you will, they all have the same agenda: to make themselves feel better about the missed dreams and shitty situations of debt and yearning for the better house or car or younger man or woman etc., by raining on your words of possibility and good things to come. Disappointing as it is, many live to suck the living colour from dreams until only greyscale remains, along with the faded memory of what could have been as a child. If you look closely, you may still catch a glimpse of it shrinking into the setting sun of the jaded middle-aged man or woman with an acute case of hardening of the attitudes sailing east and west into bitter seas looking for a sunset. Such was supposed to be my fate, that of a wayward youth growing up in a Canadian ghetto but I (and God) had other plans. We was going to kick butt and take names!

On the surprisingly many occasions my biological dad came to visit us, he usually made it a fun time for me and whichever of my sisters wanted to come along. He would always say we were going on safari, and for a six-year-old boy that was good enough. I had always hoped we would someday make it to Africa so I could meet Tarzan and ride a cheetah but have yet to check that off my bucket list. My brother seemed to miss most of those outings as I recall. As for my dad, he seemed like a fun guy and cool dresser - suit, tie and fedora. My mom didn't think so, and in reality, he was a textbook deadbeat dad with a history of drunkenness and a splash of cruelty thrown in for good measure, topped off with reputation of being a flimflam man - a con man of sorts. To those who didn't know he had at least six kids, five living on welfare in the slums, he was a classic gent. Well dressed, driving shiny new cars, a jingle of coins in his pocket and a ready hand to offer you a licorice-flavoured breath freshener lozenge called Sen-Sen. I thought he was rich, as he always bought us stuffed animals, and occasionally real ones like my dogs, Smooky and Chico;No idea how my mother tolerated him (speaks volumes on her character as wanting us to at least know we had a father) or, come to think about it, how he tolerated himself. I guess when you start your day looking through the bottom of a shot glass full of that golden nectar called C.C. or Canadian Club whiskey, the rest of the day looks pretty damn rosy. But he was my dad and I loved him in some way.

Last time I saw him, lying in some shitty cot at an old human storage facility, he gave me a glimpse into his past and one of his biggest regrets that certainly played a role in his life choices. It went like this: ***Picture this: Second World War is not going that well, a young rouge soldier in his uniform getting on a ship leaving London, England for a long awaited 2-week furlough in New York. His job in the war was to take pictures and make "Newsees". He slings his duffle bag over his shoulder and heads for the big swinging doors that lead to the gang way when he hears some one calling his name. He pretends not to hear it and walks a bit quicker, the voice gets loader. Other people are looking around to see who is being hailed. Then just as he gets to the doors a hand touches his shoulder. "Sir, this letter is for you. You are not to get on the ship and are supposed to report to HQ by 0800 tomorrow." "You have got to be kidding me". He says. "What the hell is this all about"? I don't know sir I am just an air force courier. With lightning fast reasoning he says to the courier "how would you like to make the fastest $50.00US dollars in your life?" {that's a lot of cheddar in 1944} Ya who do I have to kill the courier says smiling". No one. Just turn your bony but around and pretend you never saw me." Deal? You got it Sir. You slap the money in the kids hands an your off.

Some days later you find out that the orders where for you to film the "D-day" landing at Normandy. You live, many of your buddies don't. You go on to marry five different women and sire a number of children including Jake.

Below: On the left, a photo of dad's 400-square foot Chinatown apartment. Years later, I found out that the best man at my wedding had his father taken from him at the end of a robber's blade outside that building while my dad lived there. On the right, the Chinese store across the street where he would send me to get his mix for his C.C. afternoon cocktails. He always said, "Take your time getting there, but hurry back." I slept on the floor there for six months while in high school.

I can say back then there was no need for things like Facebook as there was rarely a dull moment around those wrong-side-of-the-tracks houses we lived in. My mom had to deal with continuous bombardments of situations and incidents such as car theft, stabbings and arson, all brought home by me, my sisters or worst of all, my bro, W.A.W., a.k.a. Lemo, with his jailhouse FTW (Fuck The World) and Bisco Cross tattoos on his wrist. After years of police visits and the never-ending battles with the marginalized of skid row, my mom decided we needed to escape this wasteland and find a safer neighbourhood. She thought she'd won the lottery when she applied and then got approved for us to move to B.C.'s first (built in 1954) and one of Canada's largest, housing project called Little Mountain. As of 2016, only one building remains. All low income residents and families have been sent packing, casualties of Vancouver's incessant need to tear down all things old to make way for certain cultures who only buy all things new.

Looking back as I do now, it seemed like a good move, but in reality it was out of the frying pan and into the fire.

Chapter 4

The Indoctrination

"Never underestimate the predictability of stupidity." – Snatch, the movie

The Little Mountain Housing Project, (Vancouver's oldest), was a sprawling series of dark, run-down three-storey walk-up apartments and dozens of barrack-style row houses built in the 1950s. Although many had sheets for curtains, boarded-up windows and cracked cement sidewalks, the surrounding area had plenty of grass and open fields - just what the doctor ordered for single moms with handfuls of kids sired by various fathers known and unknown. I loved it as a kid, hot long summers of running with a pack of wild boys through the grassy fields. All fun and games, that was, until I stepped on a broken beer bottle or a bee, which pretty much ended that illusion.

The noise of this new jungle was equally disturbing, although different than the rattle of the trains. Drunken single mothers and a parade of weekend "uncles" would gather at different apartments or row houses for a kind of newcomers' club party and the occasional swinger fest. This was a slippery slope and the beginning of a downward spiral for my mom. The sounds of summer were parties and '60s music while we kids ran free until the wee hours of the night, unwatched and in need of old-school male role models. But unfortunately for most of us, they were about as abundant as dodo birds. There were the older gang members and occasional lucid and cool deadbeat dads who visited once in a while and were quick to dish out their brand of Old Spice logic with some authentic pearls of wisdom, which we grabbed like starving peasants fighting for a loaf of bread. The unlucky kids would be scarred for life by falling prey to trolling pedophiles wearing the costumes of men, as they played the daddy or uncle role until they garnered the trust of both children and mothers, but never staying too long for fear of being discovered.

When in Rome do like the Romans, they say, so even my mom started bringing around a series of new "uncles." Fortunately for me, they were only alcoholics and not the other variety. I began spending a lot of evenings alone while she went out "to see a man about a dog." Oh boy, I thought. We're getting a dog! Never happened, and it didn't take me long to clue in to what that really meant. Going to the Legion, getting pissed and looking for a father to take care of her and her five offspring. Everyone has to have hope; that is all that keeps many going, not to mention it has helped many an army persevere beyond reason. As Napoleon said, "Leaders are dealers of hope." I guess I was looking for a leader, as was my mom. Yes, I did get eventually get a dog, or should I say mutt, called Chico, part Chihuahua and part something else. I loved him, but that too was a short-lived dream as I watched him get liquefied into the oil-slicked street by a car that never even stopped after a project kid thought it was funny to call him. What would you expect for an untrained dog being managed by an untrained boy? That outcome was inevitable and could have just as well been me - and it almost was, a couple of times.

We all began the indoctrination process once again. My brother was out of the scene for the first few months while he was in jail again for stealing a car. My three sisters were pretty much ruling the roost when my mother wasn't home, which in between her chambermaid jobs (which did result in the odd lemon meringue pie coming through the door in her hands) and her drinking binges, was often. For me, being the baby of the family meant playing up the innocent little boy with no front teeth role whenever it was to my advantage and enjoying the action of the nightly cat fights between my snisters over the bathroom, boys, booze, you name it. It got real ugly sometimes: hair-pulling, screaming, scratching and plenty of F-bombs. I would do my version of an intervention when it suited me, depending on who I liked that day. But let's be honest here, I could only do so much physically, weighing in at a whopping 47 pounds, so I had to use my mouth, which included some rather sharp baby teeth and some well-placed hair pulling. Then, like I say, do what you do after hitting a wasp's nest - run like the wind. Upside? I learned really young how to manage girls (handy - considering I was blessed with three daughters), and the importance of having multiple bathrooms.

As an example of how wild it could get, there was the time one of my sisters was about to slap some peanut butter on the last piece of Wonder Bread (now, that's real white bread!) in our tiny 1950s kitchen (yellow linoleum, turquoise table with matching chairs and a fork/spoon clock on the wall). I was hungry and wanted it too. I've heard that possession is nine-tenths of the law but I was too young to be charged, so it wasn't my law but physics that played a role, and there was no way of muscling it away from her. Asking politely to share was not our tribe's way, so I took the psychological approach and calmly observed, "No wonder no guys want to go out with you. You're a fat bitch with strawberry zits!" and ran for it, thinking I could lead her away from the prize and then double back and grab it off the counter. Not so, as it turned out. I knew there was no way she could catch me, and apparently she knew that too. So instead of chasing me, she simply turned cold-faced and let fly the peanut-butter-laden knife. Grinning as I turned the tight corner through the eating area while heading for the TV room, I caught sight of her arm pointing at me. Odd, I thought in my pea-sized brain. Then a small flash of the dull kitchen light showed the truth - a shiny metal blade flying through the musty kitchen air. So much for a clean getaway. The knife stuck in my bony lily-white butt cheek; it felt like a bite from a two-pound wasp covered in peanut butter. My knees buckled as I simultaneously tripped over my pajama bottoms and did a classic face plant on the threadbare green British Woolen. I, of course, began to scream bloody murder, but no one was home, just me and sissy. Kids are resilient, as they say, so I was up and running in a split second. No need to hang around and risk another knife-dodging exercise; besides I could always get her when she was sleeping. Out the front door I fled, glimpsing the streak of blood on my hand as I held my butt cheek. The sound of my twelve-year-older sister laughing like a hyena rang through the August air. Life lesson: you can't outrun flying knives, bullets or police radios. Fail to Plan, Plan to Fail. Plan accordingly.

Life at home quickly became bedlam. There was no mom, dad or any other real guardian figure around most of the time, except of course my sisters' guy friends or my bro's teenage heroin-pounding, cocaine-snorting and glue-sniffing pals. Yeah, that was great mentorship all right, especially the time Ken, the leader of the park gang, took me and four of my buddies up to Little Mountain for some training. This included going into the bushes where he said he wanted to talk to us about a new gang he wanted to start – "Peewee Gang," he called it. I passed on joining after he persuasively explained the initiation started with sucking his cock. From what I heard, some of the weaker kids joined his new gang and were his punks for years. He never forgot me though.

Years later at a party in East Van, he sucker-punched me following a fight I won with one of his gang. He would have been fifteen years older than that kid. To his surprise I didn't go down. I also knew better than to take him on. As they say, you don't bring a knife to a gun fight. As for Ken, last I heard he was doing life in prison for rape and murder.

My mother, who until that point had resisted the lure of heavy partying, began drinking to fit in with her NBFs. I can even remember the first time hearing her swear; it shocked me. I am pretty sure it was because of something I had done. I remember running out of the row house, down the three back cement stairs, hightailing it across the grass. She shrieked at the top of her lungs, the sound echoing amongst the project apartments, "You fucking little shit!" and slammed the door so hard it shattered the single-pane window of the cheap red paint-chipped door, glass crashing to the small sidewalk in front of the door. That was the real beginning for my mom; one of the milestones on the way to the dark side with the local welfare moms. I don't hold it against her. In that kind of environment you can't help but become a product of association; there was no way to avoid it. I'm sure one of the reasons the building of so called "Projects" has disappeared in North America is because it was simply compounding the negative, breeding generation after generation of welfare-dependent families.

"Those who seek to get ahead by riding the back of the tiger soon end up inside it."

- John F. Kennedy

Chapter 5

Learning the Rules of the Jungle

Our new neighbourhood had its own tricks for survival, and we learned them fast. Gangs were just the way of life, and the rules were clear: be in one or be the target of one - schoolyard politics across the globe. Each and every one a mini Lord of the Flies waiting to happen. You had little choice, in my perspective and experience. Say what you want but there is no questioning the fact there is strength in numbers; Belong or be cast out..." (lyrics of the Canadian band Rush). And who at that age, if you have choice, wants to be a loner? Not likely unless you are a sociopath or alien from some distant galaxy wearing the skin of our blue planet's dominant insects. That's not to say there weren't benefits of being in the fold, since there were always kids (girls included), that came from across the tracks - the quickly fading so-called normal two-parent homes, one of each gender, where the mom in most cases didn't go out to work. That's long gone today. Normal now is blended, split, single, gay, married to an attractive Shetland pony that has rights. But even then I would gravitate to like-minded kids - a kind of magnetic pull that could not be identified, but was a true north of its type for all who were so inclined in their conscious or subconscious. Like attracts like, I guess, and if that was the case for me (following in my big brother's footsteps - and why wouldn't I?), You could say I was a mini shit-magnet. Yet, to my pleasant surprise, some of the kids I bonded with (in most cases, ever so temporarily), were living in worse situations than I was, like the alcoholic, drug or barbiturates parent, one or both; or my personal favourite, the stepdad (they always seem to get the bad rap - like lawyers). Unfortunately, many who earned that badge always seemed to be caught doing something despicable to women, children or dogs, while wearing the now-fashionable wife-beater in the form of a Beater-T, ready for action), or the new "he is so good with kids" pedophile boyfriend, or pseudo-uncle who just wants a hug or to give you a back massage! Yeah, there is a special place in Hell for those monsters. Enjoy the heat, roast a marshmallow or two for me on your bubbling flesh.

The common denominator we were looking for was simply attention from those we looked up to and a sense of belonging; a micro-community, which really meant a nation within one, which also comes bundled with power and respect; every young male's right, don't you know? Politicians call them "gangs," and the Encyclopedia Britannica defines them as "A group of people, usually youths, who share a common identity and who generally engage in criminal behaviour. In contrast to the criminal behaviour of other youths, the activities of gangs are characterized by some level of organization and continuity over time...some gangs have strong leadership, formalized rules and extensive use of common identifying symbols...associating themselves with a particular geographic area and/or type of crime." I prefer a more sporting analogy like "team," but I guess it all depends on your perspective. No matter how you want to swallow it, the fact is that for those people it provides the nectar that tries to quench a primeval thirst that is as real today as it was a millennium ago, which in the book, Risk, equates to about three seconds in the history of the planet. Real or imagined, twisted and delusional, we didn't care. We sucked it back like there was no tomorrow.

The well-documented mob mentality can show up in any group or situation for that matter. Just look at the 2011 hockey riots in Vancouver or the London summer of fire a few months later: good people getting caught doing bad things through planned or unplanned association.

We saw it as harmless excitement, just pushing (for some of us, eventually cutting through) the boundaries set by parents, guardians, schools and churches, not to mention the screwed-up siblings we idolized and their equally messed-up friends. Oh yeah. Just a bunch of gangly uncoordinated, hormone-pumping, zit-faced, peach fuzz-faced boys, wandering the neighbourhood alleys stirring up trouble to prove we were men, or at least males. But in hindsight we really weren't that special. We were all just like the frog that gets cooked in the pot, thinking this is nice and warm as you doze off into a coma and the faint smell of burning flesh lingers on your tongue. I liken it to training jumping horses; you start with low fences, and before you know it you're leaping walls of reason, and inhibition is a childhood memory.

If we were unlucky enough to be born in one of those distant third world countries, only real in movies, I suspect we would have been targets for any number of things, including becoming child soldiers or unwilling organ donors. There are many definitions of dangerous, but one thing is for sure, a twelve- or fourteen-year-old boy with a knife or gun is definitely one of them. Consequences for your actions? That doesn't mean much when you're sleep-deprived (can't spell it) and haven't eaten in a couple of days.

Just baby tigers teething with chipped fangs and bloodied gums, gnawing on the cold steel reality of North America's contribution to the world's "bottom one billion". I guess it was good training for life's battles yet to come: and those that have [a.k.a. members of the global lucky sperm club] find it hard to understand why so many don't seem to fit in and be satisfied with the life fate has dealt them: The reality of today's Hunger Games.

I can say one thing: in my experience, it's better to be the boss than have one. And there was a big difference between joining a gang and building one. Like starting a business or buying a franchise, in either case you inevitably have to fight to keep your position or territory; expand and grow, or wither and die. Like a stolen car rolling down a hill, it is either gaining speed or losing it. There are no statues in the jungle, not even in our little quagmire of misdirected punks. I wasn't the only one who clued into the understanding that when you want to infiltrate or join a new group that was organized to some degree, you usually had to usually get a formal introduction from an existing member in good standing. It could take hours, days or months to be accepted and become what some call an "applicant." It took time and the patience of a stone in a cool stream: Cool heads prevail. "Entertain quiet thoughts," as my older sister once told me, "and plan accordingly."

If you were unlucky enough to be a scrawny little bone-rack like I was, you had to leverage what God-given talents you had; cunning over force was a given when you're born at the shallow end of the gene pool. Something you are taught in Aikido is a must: use the opponents' force against them whenever possible, plan (fail to plan, plan to fail) ahead, outsmart, conspire with their friends and enemies and when all else fails, ambush your way to position, stability and so called significance. Fighting dirty is a term used by the losers, because there is little honour in losing. Most history is written by the victors, who seem compelled to eradicate those who oppose: twenty million-plus silenced in Russia, for example. Burn the books that spark questioning; get rid of the prophets, teachers and sages. I thought actions get lost like smoke in the wind, but in truth the impact is like the ripples in the pond after the stone is tossed, or the currents in the air caused by the butterfly's wings; a hint of prey floating in the breeze perceptible to few like the sound of a gunshot to tigers and wolves. They stand vigilant in the hunt for weakness or trace of danger.

My version of the Golden Rule back in the day…a cliché I know, do unto others, before they do unto you, seemed the safest bet; act first and apologize later, but only if you absolutely have to, as in when your feet are being held to hot coals.

During the tight quarters of the project years, my little gang fluctuated in size depending on who moved in or out, or who broke one of our codes:

- No stealing from each other
- No running from a fight
- No ratting out if caught by the cops or store dicks, parents etc.
- Share the loot and candy

We called ourselves 'The Bull Dogs'. Seemed fitting as I had a British background and a cool British flag with a bull dog on it. There were usually around six to nine kids in my gang depending on who moved in or out of the Projects. I was best friends with Eddy (he was convinced we should have called ourselves the Sultans), who was one of a family of five brothers known as the "Mental Brothers." They lived up to that name on many occasions, including when his younger brother, Tommy, about six at the time, plunged a butcher's knife through my back for taking a piece of his toast. The Mental Brothers lived in the block of row houses directly across a grass field that had an unmaintained blacktop basketball court in the middle of it. Their biological dad was a steel worker and biker, but he didn't live there much. Their mom was cool biker chick who stood about five feet tall and made up for her size in pure fire. Her boys towered above her but were scared shiftless of her. So was I. She liked to smoke pot and drink Captain Morgan's Rum. She was good lady in her way and did the best she could at being a mom; basically no different than all the other single moms in the project. Then there was also "The Dale." He liked to refer to himself in the third person for some reason. I later learned it was because he was a sociopath, a psycho; in other words, he was just not wired properly. Basically the kind of kid who wouldn't lose a minute of sleep over hitting someone in the back of the skull with a ball peen hammer then covering them in a flannel blanket, dousing it with lighter fluid, and using the blue and yellow leaping flames to roast marshmallow and warm his hands as he hummed a tune to match the shrieks of horror. You get the picture. Better friend than enemy, if you know what I mean. He was a tall skinny kid with Prince-Charles-type ears, black haircut like he put a bowl on his head and cut around it (imagine Jim Carrey, Dumb and Dumber), blue eyes and a slightly creepy grin on his pale white (never go in the sun) face. Then again, who was I to judge? He was great fun and never said "no" to anything, as he had no fear, no conscience, and no brains and was looking only to fit in. He had come to the right place because we served up belonging and mentorship by the bucketful. As he lived about twenty feet away from me in a row house, we utilized the old home-made walkie-talkies: string and cans on both ends pulled tight between our bedroom windows. Not sure it worked well, but we imagined it did. I can't remember his dad being in the picture, but then again who needs a dad when you have plenty of uncles to choose from?

Ricky, another core member, lived across the alley from the Projects in his own house. He had a yard and a tree house and a dog - the picture perfect goal for us living on the other side. He was small kid too, but had the fortitude to stick with boxing lessons, so no one messed with him twice. A good-looking kid who attracted attention of the girl kind, which, as young as we were, always made for a different kind of fun. His mom was dead, so his dad took care of him and his brother. I never really got to know his dad but recall him being a fair man and a strict disciplinarian. After an altercation or police incident he would ban him from hanging round with us, but it never lasted long. I think I was jealous of Ricky as he seemed somehow different than the others - more solid and confident. I would say he was the only kid in our crew who never followed me blindly. If he didn't like what we were doing, he would just walk away. Next time we saw him it was like nothing had happened. We just picked up from where we left off, just like kids do.

We had a call sign or signal that everyone had to learn in the event we got separated or something like that. It was a cross between a really loud hee-haw and a Canada goose honk. Don't ask me how we came up with that one, but it was unique and came in handy more than once.

Just like any gang, we had our turf, which was the Little Mountain, actually in Queen Elizabeth Park. We felt we owned this spot, and it was our job to defend it any time a group of stray dogs wondered into our patch. There was this one occasion just around twilight during the dog days of summer when a rival gang from the other side of the mountain, West Side tough-acting rich kids we had heard about, came looking for adventure and we gave them some, along with a couple of scars tossed in for good measure. From one of our secret hiding spots, we spotted them coming up the hill They passed by us and we could hear them bragging about some poor nerdy kid from school they'd just beaten up and how funny it was to see him looking for his glasses as he wiped his bloody nose. They laughed and punched each other, kicked and joked as they headed towards Welfare Heights.

We were outnumbered and they seemed bigger - or maybe they were just better fed? Regardless, I gave the signal and we came screaming out of the trees like wild banshees, hurling rocks and eggs. They were caught off guard and instinctively ran for it. We were laughing and calling them chicken-shits and then stopped chasing them, certain of our victory. But, to our surprise, they also stopped running, re-grouped and turned back toward us. My boys were a bit freaked out by this sudden show of courage and so was I. That wasn't part of the plan - assuming we had one.

I could tell who their lead dog was: some black-haired jock type in shorts (why do they always were shorts...I mean even in the winter, you're joking right?), who took the lead as they confidently marched back towards us. My pulse jumped to fight-or-flight status as I reached into my special rock pouch. I picked a nice golf ball-sized round stone, felt the weight of it in my skinny fist, stepped back, and let it fly. Bang! It hit the lead jock boy on the top of the head. He fell like a sack of potatoes, clasping his head and wailing like a pigeon in the claws of a falcon, blood trickling down his forehead and messing up his confident smile. His buddies started swearing and throwing rocks (they had their own stash, which was also a bit surprising). We stood our ground, the rocks flew, but none came close to their mark. They ran out of rocks and picked up their blood-stained leader and headed west over the mountain to their Brady Bunch families and the detached home with crystal-clear swimming pools and multi-car garages.

We wallowed in our victory, whooping and hollering with high-fives for all as we headed back to our hideout - a large open cave-like area hidden under an impenetrable canopy of a series of thick giant prickly evergreen hedges that touched the ground. There we were safe, invisible and dry from the rain with our weapons, stolen sleeping bags and pirate booty.

A pack of wild boys left to run free, loving their inner-city world and what it has to offer. Yet, as the Lord of the Flies novel - based on the true story of a group of boys stranded on an island after a plane crash - proved, a garden will grow weeds if not attended. A classic example of my own was played out nicely one afternoon with my BFF Eddy's younger bro. We were hanging out in front of his row house, and for some reason Eddy went inside to get something. I followed him into the standard yellow kitchen we all had and stopped in my tracks, scenting the sweet aroma of freshly-made cinnamon toast with real butter. Mmmm! Yummy! Well, Tommy, Eddy's younger six-year-old bro, had just put the toast on the counter and cut it in half. So, as he was just a little punch and there were four halves just sitting there, I thought, "I'll eat one of those delicious, hot, golden brown babies." I nonchalantly grabbed half a slice and headed back outside to enjoy my snack. Well, that didn't exactly work out the way I had planned, since before my lips touched the golden brown crust, little Tommy drove an 11-inch butcher knife into my back. I felt the fiery sting of the blade flash through my body, momentarily paralyzing me where I stood, no words leaping from my mouth. Tommy's childish laughter dancing off the smoke-stained ceiling, I stumbled down the dirty grey cement steps as my voice broke free from the pain. I ran falling and screaming for my mom, as kids do. I needed the protection and shelter of my mother and our house. She and everyone else on the block came out to witness yet another bit of free entertainment and acquire more fodder for the following days of gossip over cheap gin and Old Style beer served up in stubby bottles. Then my mom, realizing I was the source of the screams, yelled, "Oh my God! What happened...what happened?"

I was heaving and babbling uncontrollably. She grabbed a dirty tea towel from the counter as I collapsed on the floor of our postage stamp-sized kitchen. She put pressure on the gushing wound while someone called an ambulance. I was sped to the hospital where they stitched me up and told me that two things were positive: 1. the blade got wedged in my shoulder blade, which saved my life and, 2. I was lucky he didn't do the multiple stabbing "Psycho" scenario, because the odds of a second or third jab failing to miss a vital organ would have been unlikely. All good, and now I have a cool scar to brag about.

The view I would have seen running towards my "Home" 123 Grouse Walk from Tommy's Fun House of Cinnamon Toast and Butcher Knives

Can't relate? Picture this: it's dusk on a hot summer's eve in an inner city project. This one is lucky enough to have several green grassy areas that, to an eight-year-old boy, looked like massive fields of hope that went on forever; the sound of other kids laughing in their bronze skin and music of the late'60s floating in the rich summer air; this tranquil scene is cracked to the sun by a shrill of some screaming, skinny, white kid streaking across a small patch of grass, his feet barely touching the summer-warmed black ash vault of the neglected basketball court, translucent droplets of blood spraying from his scrawny back as he sprints to the protection of his little hobble and the healing touch of his mother's arms, his life's essence making a crimson mist of fairy wings with the setting sun dancing off the stainless steel blade of the 11-inch butcher knife lodged securely in his narrow back.

Well, I made it past that hiccup and lived to play, lie, cheat and steal another day - or years, to be accurate - but revenge, they say, is best served cold. And I was cold-hearted as I tormented little Tommy for years to follow, making him pay for his so-called childish outburst. His punishments included an occasional unexpected shit-kicking, starting with the standard snap kick to his little balls; and setting him up to get caught by the police for something we did; or leaving him behind if he was being held down and beaten up by someone.

Eddy was somehow tolerant of my actions, within reason that is. But sometimes he would side with his little brother and to my surprise, leave with him. No question I had a demon edge, and little conscience to go with it. But such is youth. I would have been a poster child soldier in some Blood Diamond state in Africa or an Eastern European civil war situation. Come to think of it, Tommy would have done all right himself.

My row house just before they were torn down; displacing low-income families to make way for high-income ones...or more likely wealthy Asians and Grey-Heads.

Observation point: Beware of what my friend Mike called the Prick the Veil strategy commonly used by males of low self-esteem and poor character, con artists the works of them. The idea is to set the stage for control, and it works more than you think but is easily identifiable. Once you know the technique, it is generally used during your initial contact with the punk. It goes something like this: for women, it will be a negative comment about their appearance, actions, accomplishments etc., followed immediately with a smirk or smile and

40

direct eye contact. This seems to work especially well if the women (girls) are deemed by society at large to be attractive. Not sure of the psychology behind this, but it could be they just are just not accustomed to being told they have flaws…a.k.a. Princess syndrome = easy target. Another example is that business people fall for this trap when they begin interaction with a new supplier, prospective customer or existing client. It works like this: they will usually have approached you with a plausible business reason and working knowledge of your industry, but are too busy for details; they are on a tight schedule for some reason. So they push fast and professionally hard out of the gate, promising high (units to buy, money to be made etc.) and then when you question them on some logical point, they take immediate offence and turn the table by implying you couldn't deliver if you got the deal or you or your company are not financially sound, basically putting your integrity in the spotlight and you on your heels. This often causes the business person to want to please them both, or they may even hang up or leave the meeting only to re-engage after they have calmed down.

The situation deifies logic but is known to be effective.

Chapter 6

Steal from the Rich and Give to the Poor…Me

"Never manage your numbers…manage your behaviour." - JLH

Our hidden tree cave on the hill was one of our favourite hangouts. I'm sure if any of us had ever been invited to a "normal" kid's tree fort, we would have set it on fire. We were more like pirates in our little lair than kids in a tree house, that's for sure; keeping our loot hidden from the prying eyes of would-be thieves like us. We had a painting, a few posters of the black light velvet variety (I still have the Wolf Man in my trunk), candles, flashlights, candy, knives, pop, rocks, eggs, bikes, clothing, a fleet of Hot Wheels, sleeping bags and a battery-powered Easy-Bake oven. Not that we did much cooking, but you never know.

We accumulated our booty over many "shopping" sprees, or "Voyages of Acquisition," as I liked to call them. While people were in the mall shopping, we'd be in the parking lot doing our own brand of shopping; rummaging through their cars, stuffing what we found in pillowcases and swinging them over our shoulders like kids collecting Halloween candy. We would of course round off the day with some in-store collecting as well. We would just glide through the stores with ease. If anyone asked me what I was doing, I'd simply say, "I'm looking for my mom," which worked every time. Keep in mind there were no RFID tags or magnetic clips, and very limited video cameras, so shoplifting was for kids, as it were. One of my favourite techniques was to have one of the gang distract the usually chubby sales clerk with some random diversion, like "Where's the bathroom?" or "I can't find my mom" that was guaranteed to play on maternal heart strings while we would grab what we were looking for. Since we generally took a bit of time picking things out and had more than we could carry, sometimes I would set up a central depository of sorts. Basically it was a place to stockpile our stuff and decide how to move it out of the store without getting caught by the clerks, not that they could catch us, or store "Dicks'. We knew most of them, but they were tricky rabbits, always switching it up to keep it fresh. Since we are mainly talking about large department stores, there was an abundance of places to stash our goods, like locked bathroom stalls that we would climb under and out of again and again; there were also the false ceilings in the bathrooms. One of us would keep watch at the door while the other climbed the bathroom stall and pushed a ceiling tile up and to the side, placing our catch on the one beside it. Those tiles could even hold a 47-pounder like me in a pinch. There were boiler rooms, floor level air vents, the very bottom of fire exit stairwells etcetera, but my own preference was the ever present skirted table; 2' x 4' or 2' x 6'. All worked, but the bigger the better, especially in the luggage department. The stores always stashed stock under the tables which made for a great buffer zone between us and the public. Getting out of the stores required us to all use different exits. Generally, this was not a problem unless they were on to us. That means that we had been spotted during the day by multiple store detectives or staff, but they couldn't find us as we were many times lounging in our in-store loot lairs enjoying our new toys and chowing down on some hard-earned candy.

I guess I could say the entrepreneurial spirit was with me from the beginning, and this eventually led to a small little business of trading and selling what I picked up. Nothing too extreme, but it did add a level of business to shoplifting, which I thought was cool. I would barter or sell Hot Wheels, candy, toys, Barbies, anything Warner Bros., Scooby Doo articles, anything Disney. The word got out on the playground that I could get stuff. and our cave was my warehouse. Shoplifting was pretty much a way of life for me and the boys. None of us had much of an allowance; some of us didn't have any. Steal from the rich, give to the poor: that's us, we figured. They had plenty, so what was the harm in sharing?

The first time I can remember stealing was when I was with my mom at a five-and-dime store on Main Street. I was about six at the time. There was a little Matchbox car sitting on the shelf, looking at me, so scared and needing a warm pocket to hide in. Without a second thought, Poof! Like magic it was in my pocket, no one the wiser. I'm not sure if I even understood if it was wrong or not, I just knew I wanted it, but when I got outside and started walking back to the Projects with my mom, I had a disturbing thought . Where would I hide it? Suddenly my gnat-sized brain ran wild with scenarios of my mom randomly asking me to empty my pockets when we got home and the store owner doing inventory in that section just after we left. I think she was on to me. So I panicked and tried to discreetly drop it in the gutter as I nonchalantly lagged behind my mom.

But wouldn't you know it? I dropped the little cream-coloured Rover right smack dab on top of a discarded White Rock Cola pop can. The car and the can made a nice loud clack clack and, as we were on Main Street, my mom whirled around thinking the worst and instantly spied my precious car lying beside its new friend, the pop can. Her blue eyes flashed in my direction as she said, "Jake! Where did you get that?" I was hoping she would have asked, "Where did you get that crushed pop can," but it was not to be. In one swoop she grabbed me by the ear and my car from the road and we were off, my short little legs trying to keep up with the long strides of a furious mother. No idea what she was yelling at me by this point as I was doing these giant hops to try and stop from actually being dragged by my ears, which were for some reason at that age far too big for my head and could be likened to Prince Charles or Will Smith. She burst through the weathered wood-and-glass double doors with their faded and chipped forest green paint and asked to speak to the owner. My heart was pounding so hard I couldn't focus; I was guessing this is something like a trapped animal might feel, my mind racing with plans, scenarios and thoughts of escape, like a caged dog that knocks the dog catcher on his ass when it springs from the back of the truck as the door is carefully opened. My eyes were wet at this point, fat tears rolling down my freckled face. I was screwed! A few moments (or was it hours?) later, in walked a portly beehive-headed lady wearing a pair of black-framed Buddy Holly glasses secured by a gold chain dangling from the sides of her chipmunk cheeks. Her head seemed disproportionately small for her tree-trunk stump of a neck and Volkswagen-sized body. She, like many fat people, looked jolly and resembled my vision of what Mrs. Claus would look like. One thing for sure, like many fat people who have a secret and an artificial view of what they see in the mirror each morning, if investigated that secret is mostly likely a Twinkie in their purse. My mom wasted no time in telling her of my deed. As my mom told her tale, the portly owner looked down at me with a look more of pity than of anger. Perhaps she guessed what I'd be in for when I got home. Sheepishly I reached up, trying my best to look like a wounded puppy, huge eyes looking for compassion, and put the tiny British-made Corgi car in her hand. "Thank you," she said. She paused, looked deep in my eyes, then took a deep breath and calmly let out, "Now, we won't be doing that again, will we?" To which I of course said, "No," but my cheeks flushed ruby red, giving away my inner thoughts, like a stop light shining through my eyes, since I knew I would be Bach and she would be Beethoven.

One thing was for certain. I didn't want to leave the store because I knew what was coming when I got home; my momma was gonna open up a can of whoopass, never mind being beaten with the can-opener first. As soon as we passed through those old wooden doors and stepped on the street my mom smacked my butt, lifting my 47 pounds of pure joy about two inches off the dirty cement sidewalk. "Don't you ever do anything like that again! I can't believe you would do that!" she screamed. Her face going somewhat purple, which looked rather nice with her jet black hair and bright blue eyes. She had a full head of steam going, so she continued, "Do you know how embarrassing that was?" as she smacked me on the back of the head. This kept up all the way home. She was pissed, to say the least. After all that my brother and sisters had put her through since moving to the Projects, I guess I thought this was fairly trivial. I was wrong. When we got home, she sent me up to my room, and I knew not to push her on anything for now. But as I sat there contemplating what had just happened and why I had tossed that beautiful car into the gutter in the first place, I kept coming back to the same conclusion; if I can't buy it, what was wrong with taking it since they had lots of those cars and I only wanted one? This could only mean two things: 1. "They" were greedy 2. I had to get smarter.

Needless to say, this first failure didn't put me off what was to become a regular habit for years to come. We'll talk about that more later.

Chapter 7

Angels Come to Party

"If success is measured on a scale of zero to 10 [success being defined in many ways, but for this point let's say monetary and social acceptability] and you have fifty years to make it [without the help of starting off at a six due to family lineage] then that is a level playing field when you're smacked on the butt for that first rude awakening and the doctor says, 'You're not in Kansas anymore, Dorothy." But if you start off below zero and it takes twenty years to get to where the others started -zero - then the race isn't exactly fair. Knowing that, one may feel it's justified to even the odds by illegal and/or immoral deeds. The history books are full of these short-term success stories." - JLH

There were always bikers around the Projects coming and going at all hours of the day and night, the sound of their Harley Davidsons echoing off the pee-yellow walls of the row houses and apartments like distant thunder. I loved it ... as a kid it sounded like Thor's Hammer; no wonder I have had three of them so far. To a kid they were all really cool, but the ones that stood out and made everyone take notice when they rolled into our little world, all had black vests on with skulls on the back that said "Hells Angels." They didn't come often, from what I can remember, but when they did, it was always an awesome spectacle.

I remember walking home this one particular night during what was later called "The 'Summer of Love" after a full day of getting into my own brand of trouble with my pals, when all of a sudden I started to hear the sound of All Along The Watch Tower by Jimmy Hendrix rattling through the neighbourhood. It got louder and louder the closer

I got to our row house, along with the whoops and yells of people having a good time. As I turned the corner I saw them: bikes and bikers bigger than life and - wouldn't you know it? - they were at the unit a few doors down. This is going to be fun, I instantly thought. As I walked a bit faster, I could see the music was blasting from some speakers sitting on the window ledges, and the dim street light on the alley made their Iron Horses sparkle like jewels in the night. It was one of those surreal moments that imprint on your memory forever. Crowds of teenagers and people were hanging out on the tiny porch and sitting on the grass, laughing and swearing. There were about twenty of them in total, all smoking grass and passing around jugs of wine, cheap Five Star whisky and bottles of Southern Comfort.

As I walked past the party house I could smell the wondrous essence of burning meat on a charcoal barbeque. The thick smoke bellowing across the small patch of green grass and into the red sky. Then an epiphany flashed across my rabbit-poop sized brain. Hmmm I haven't eaten since this morning. My mouth watered at the idea of a thick juicy steak. Unlikely, considering I hadn't had one in maybe a year but who knows, maybe a hotdog? I went into stealth mode, trying to casually blend into the towering crowd, who for the most part consisted of spaced-out hippies standing around, young leather faces destined for row houses or trailer parks and multiple tattoos sagging into unrecognizable blobs of blue as the unstoppable forces of time and gravity took their toll. No one cared about me, this little Hobbit navigating between their long scrawny legs.

I saw that the guys were older and somehow more hardened than my brother's crew. Instinctively I also felt they were also much more dangerous. Maybe it was because basically all of them were wearing black, thick-soled boots, ripped jeans, leather vests. They seemed darker more serious, not sure why. but it definitely went beyond their cavalier attitudes, unshaven faces and pirate grins. I locked eyes for a split second with this one dude; he said nothing, but if the eyes are the window to the soul, then no wonder the hairs on the back of my neck stood straight up. It sent a shiver down my spine like fingernails on a chalkboard or maybe more like someone walking across your grave. As bikers go, he was bigger than most; a giant by my standards, wearing a chrome timing chain belt with a huge lion's head belt buckle the size of a hub cap. If my boys were there, I knew they'd be thinking the same thing as me: When I grow up, I want to be a member. Not a cop or fireman…no. Just lucky enough earn a 'full patch' and be a Hells Angel. These guys were legends with bad ass celebrity status, and I wanted some. If you think about it (and you may not be able to relate), what were my options? Join daddy's company? Have my parents pay for college? Not. It was more like, join a gang or join the military. That's about it. Those both seem to have a level playing field for those in my socioeconomic climate. Okay, sure there is also getting some excellent labour job like working in a lumber mill or on a fishing boat or maybe construction. Well, as it turns out I did all three and they sucked. So this seemed as good a goal as any.

That night was young, and action seemed everywhere: one girl crying and being consoled by three others; some guy heaving his guts out by the big blue garbage bin; two stray dogs fighting; and the neighbours sitting on the steps watching the spectacle and knowing for sure that it couldn't last too long as the cops would come sooner or later. Until then, crack open another Old Style or Black Label beer. I kept my distance, but as I was a kid I could get close without much risk; that is unless someone decided to have a bit of fun by holding me down and pouring whisky down my throat or pinching my nose and making me inhale some weed.

One pretty feather-haired brunette in skin-tight jeans yelled, "Fuck you, you fat bastard" at this tall dirty blonde dude who reflexively went to backhand her but stopped and began laughing, then slapped her on the ass of her bellbottoms. And so it went, they were all having their version of fun. What I didn't like was when some guy thought it would be fun to shoot a sleeping pigeon with a pellet gun. The shot went right through the eyes as the unsuspecting fbird fell to the cracked pavement making this noise that sounded to me like crying. Forgetting any sense of danger, I ran and scooped up the flailing bird, its wings flapping wildly as it did a death dance. Those who noticed laughed, thinking this was great sport and fit in perfectly against the backdrop of the clear night sky and dark rhythmic pulse of Led Zeppelin's Immigrant Song.

I ran like I was on fire, (a few years later I was actually on fire; got the scars) the pigeon's (flying rat's) blood seeping through my no-longer-white hands. I took the bird to our house a few doors down and burst in the door screaming for my mom. She was sitting in the front room having drinks with a few of the local ladies, my brother and sisters nowhere to be found.

"Mom, mom!" I yelled. She turned to look at me, not sure of what I had in my hand or whose blood it was. Empty bottles of Old Style beer covering the coffee table (should have been called liquor table), the ashtray overflowing with cigarette butts, the filters stained with red lipstick.

"What happened?"

I showed her the bird. By now the tears were rolling down my ruby red cheeks.

"Someone shot him," I spurted out. "You have to save him or call the ambulance to come and get him."

"What? Who got shot? Slow down. Stop heaving."

Slowly she sat upright and took a minute to adjust to my so-called emergency.

"Oh my god, what is that? Don't get it on the carpet! Take it in the kitchen!"

I ran into the kitchen and frantically looked for a box.

"Are you calling the doctor?" I yelled.

My mother mumbled something from the living room. I heard papers rustling, things falling on the floor. "Shit!" she breathed, thinking I didn't hear her.

"Where's the phone book?" she asked.

The bird was still flapping in my hands and the blood was all over me and the linoleum. I grabbed a box from the garbage outside and plucked handfuls of weeds and grass from beside the stairs. I put it in the box, building my version of what a nest might look like. Gently, I placed him on the cool green bed and tried soothing the dying bird by softly whispering to it that it will be okay, knowing in my rapidly beating heart that this was not likely. My mom was on the phone by this time speaking to the "hospital." "Yes, my son found a bird that's been shot. Can you come as soon as you can?" An hour later a white

49

van actually came from the SPCA and picked up my box with the pigeon, which for some reason was sitting quietly in it. In shock, I guess but nevertheless I did what I could. When they left, my mother hugged me and said, "He'll be okay. Don't worry."

She told me I should go to bed, but I told her I was starving. She searched through the cupboards and found a box of Kraft Dinner. I scarfed it back and took my glass of powdered milk mixed with water and went upstairs to my little bedroom. Luckily, I had the room to myself for a while as my brother, W.A.W., was still in jail on Vancouver Island and my three sisters were out, and I can say I hadn't seen them for a couple of days, so I lay down in bed and thought about what had happened. I figured the pigeon was probably in surgery by now and envisioned a team of white-robed doctors yelling, "Scalpel, Clamp, and Swab!" to nurses wearing aprons splattered in crimson-coloured pigeon blood with bandages wrapped around his head. I looked up at the dirty brown blinds that made a clacking sound in the summer breeze and at the street light, yellowy brown through the dusty single pane window. The music was still pumping outside, but it seemed to be blended with sirens and soon the red and blue lights were pulsing across my poster-filled wall.

I stood up on my bed and peeked through the blinds like they were maybe thinking, Hey, while we're here let's pick up the Hodgson kid. Save some time since if he hasn't been caught for something, he will be eventually. Two guys with cutoff jean jackets were being handcuffed and half dragged towards a big black and white paddy wagon. The neighbours were out on the porches; this was better than TV, especially since only a few in the Projects had cable. My eyelids were heavy, as though a team of midgets were hanging on them, each with a wine bottle in his stubby fingers. I laid my head on the windowsill and drifted off for what seemed like a second, only waking to an empty alley and the sound of the legendary Charlie Pride coming from the turntable downstairs. I fell asleep and dreamed of flying away from this place with my pigeon as my wingman.

The next day there was a buzz about something that happened at the party. No one was sure if it was fact or folklore, but it involved one of the girls having what they called "a train pulled on her." We figured out what it meant but didn't find out who the girl was. I was secretly glad my sisters weren't there, even though I had little use for them other than when they did some cooking. That house never had another party for as long as we lived there.

Chapter 8

The "Uncles"

> "You can't fight, but only manage, many things, including time, aging, gravity, oxygen, love and community."
> - JLH

The various 'uncles' that came to visit our house never lasted long. In retrospect they were all weak or lost men. My mom was a good lady, but maybe that's all she could handle or attract, considering that she had no education and that five lovely, but wayward, kids were part of the package. The men were usually labourer types who drank daily and came in all sizes and shapes; quite a few had beer guts they'd invested a lot of time and money into. Clothing was usually polyester pants and wrinkled t-shirts, but for the first date they'd show up in a tie and take off for a big night at the Legion.

Interesting how the brain recalls things. I watched a Discovery Channel show about the brain and they had the top of this dude's head opened up like a can of Campbell's soup. Not sure why, but there he was, and, oh, he was awake and talking to the doctors. I guess it was an experiment of sorts, since they were using some type of small electric metal rod which they were probing parts of his brain with. They were asking him questions mainly about what he was feeling, smelling, seeing, hearing etc. What caught me was that he claimed to not be remembering the time and place but being there at that second. Anyway it was cool. For me, I find music and smells do the trick and many times create powerful emotions, good and bad. Especially so when I hear the likes of Louis Armstrong, Johnny Cash or smell second-hand smoke blended with an elixir of B.O. and Aqua Velva.

I'm going back in time to when I was a scrawny kid dreaming of someday getting away from that nightmare of week-long drinking binges, sleepless nights, fights at school (with kids and teachers) and the nightly Kraft Dinner and cut up hotdogs mixed with ketchup…Mmmm! I really just wanted to be a kid like the ones I saw on TV at the time. Danny Partridge from the Partridge family was the main one. He had a single mom too, just like me, except they played in a band and his mom didn't get sloppy drunk on a regular basis. I was sick of babysitting my mom half the time. My sisters were always out, so somebody had to do stuff like shut off the stove when the food was emitting black smoke or turn off the stereo as it skipped on a record for hours as everyone dozed in drunken stupors. My brother didn't appear to give a rat's ass; this was his idea of opportunity, and wherever there was confusion, it was a veil for just that - opportunity. He was on it like white on rice. Think about it: a house full of drunk adults, booze galore, money in their pockets as they lay passed out on some hand-me-down threadbare couch. The house thick with the smell of stale beer, spilled wine aging nicely in the inch-long forest green shag rug. Can you say "party"?

Don't get me wrong, I was, after al,l just a kid, so the variety was intoxicating for sure. My mom's new friends and endless procession of "uncles" were sometimes cool. They would occasionally try to get to my mom by chit-chatting with me about school, girls, fights and movies, and they always seemed to get around to asking about money. Especially when we had the house. This was the retirement package/lottery ticket that had eluded them during their youth; if they could only get rid of those fucking kids. Eventually, one who was known as "The Cowboy" found the right combination to pull that off. I would sometimes think, if he was just a bit smarter than my dog's food dish, he probably would have patented it and called it "the velvet-covered-brick technique for weak women" or perhaps "pimps…because bitches won't slap themselves," if he was so inclined. As for my sisters, they looked at most, if not all, of them, as pathetic examples of what "men" were. They tolerated the situation and got out as soon as they could, but really I think they felt empathy for my mom and believed she deserved a date or two, even if they were losers. Looking back, I would agree. My brother, on the other hand treated them with unbridled disdain and open mockery. I guess this limited the quality of "suitors" and would have scared off the decent ones.

I used to watch my mother smile and fuss over them, fixing drink after drink. As the night wore on, their well-mannered façade dropped like a toilet seat, their voices growing loud and crude; Jekylls and Hydes the lot of them. Like money, alcohol seems to exaggerate character. The good get gooder and the bad, badder. I wondered why my mother wasted her time with these losers, who would laugh and talk about war, religion and politics with the depth of a soap dish.

Big plans were going to happen, according to them, as they slurred out leftover dreams from a long-forgotten past that had expired like sour milk. Thick clouds of smoke hovering above the living room and like cancer drifting up the stairs towards my bedroom. The smell of stale beer and country music keeping me up on many a school night.

I always knew when my mom was getting tipsy; she would start to use my name a lot and her English accent would get stronger. She was generally a happy drunk and would never say anything inappropriate unless she was provoked. Then she'd come back with a cutting line in her defense.

Somehow she would say something to the "uncles" that would piss them off. That probably wasn't too hard to do, as these alcoholics had some fairly short fuses. They would complain about work (if they had jobs) or lack of money - that was a major recurring theme in all conversations I can remember. Yet, somehow there was always enough for cigarettes and Dial-A-Bottle. Their spice in the morning? Hard booze or beer over corn flakes for breakfast.

Even back then, I knew this wasn't normal, and I think my mom was embarrassed by me seeing her in a total "soup sandwich" situation. That didn't stop her though. She was lonely and she was raised in an era when men were supposed to take care of their wives and children. That's what her dad did. So she wasn't equipped to deal with this fast-changing reality where men bailed, leaving the women in charge of working, raising kids and keeping the house together.

The best way to describe how I felt during these events is like picturing a bad hangover in the hot sun, no water or aspirin, and having insomnia at the same time. Exhausting is how it looked, and very messy. I tried to clean up and keep things under control, but it was hard for a nine- year-old to know how to make things better.

One of my mom's favorite drinking pals at the time was "Uncle Arnie" (my brother called him Arnold Ziffel, after the pig from Green Acres). I didn't see why he was any more special than the rest, but he seemed to make my mom laugh and liked to take her out and have fun.

Arnie had a buddy who drove a perpetually dirty Ford Country Squire station wagon that towed an 18-foot piece-of-crap of a boat. One morning, after a 24-hour drinking binge (I have no idea how they stayed up that long), Arnie had the brilliant, drunken idea of taking my mom and me fishing.

I was up early, watching TV and eating my puffed wheat. I was ready to settle in for my Saturday morning routine of cartoon watching, followed by a trip to the candy store for candies and a cream soda. A boat trip wasn't on my agenda, but apparently I didn't have much choice. Don't ask me where they got the energy, but I guess they were fueled by the exciting idea of a day out on the water.

According to Arnie, the best boat launching area was at Horseshoe Bay – about an hour's drive on the winding coastal highway. Before I knew it, I was sitting in the front seat, squished and sweating between my mom and the fat, B.O.- stinking pig-man. The dashboard was covered in all kinds of shit: cups, maps, gloves, half-eaten food - you name it. Now I was starting to feel hungover.

Everyone was wasted except me, which was a good thing, as it turned out. Arnie went flying up Taylor Way, taking the corner to the upper levels highway at breakneck speed. The early morning mist hovered over the road, preventing any clear visibility. But it was so early that there were hardly any cars on the road. I wouldn't have minded running into a cop round about then. We swerved between the lines, and each time we got close to the edge I had glimpses of the sheer drop of the cliffs below. I had to keep grabbing the wheel and pulling it in the opposite direction he was going, as he yammered on and laughed. "What a cute kid you got there…ha ha ha!" Yeah, hilarious.

Somehow we made it to the boat-launching spot without pulling a Thelma and Louise. We launched the boat and away we went, full-speed ahead. Lots of laughing, more booze and no kind of plan for safety.

"Where's the life jackets?" I innocently asked.

"There should be one under the seat!" he said, as we zoomed away, and I was hurled to the back of the boat, the wind burning my eyes and freezing my t-shirt-and- shorts-clad body. Fun stuff.

Did I say they had enough booze? Apparently not, as it wasn't long before they decided a pit stop was needed at Reed Point Marina, on the way to Squamish.

"You should slow down a bit," I told him as we hurtled full speed towards the crowd on the pier.

"Listen, kid," he yelled through the wind, "I've been boating since before you were a gleam in your beautiful mother's eyes."

He throttled back and the boat slowed down. Whoosh it went, and then, just as we were about 20 feet away, he shut it off, or so he thought - what he really did was push it to full throttle. The boat jerked up and whizzed into the crowd of people, going halfway up onto the dock. We were all thrown to the back, and almost tipped overboard. Everyone was screaming and ran away; I thought I heard some people laughing like they were at a theme park.

One quick-thinking guy grabbed the front rope and stopped the boat from flipping sideways and either landing on top of us or tossing us into the frigid sea. Arnie tried his hardest to get up, but his beer gut was making it difficult. I was the first one safely on the dock, and my mom and Arnie looked at the crowd as if to say, "What the hell is everyone one looking at?" After a few moments of contemplating the severely-dented boat, Arnie and my mother sauntered up to the restaurant, laughing and stumbling.

They ordered lunch and joked about their wild adventure. I ate while they downed about five drinks each without touching their food. They ordered more beers to go. I wasn't looking forward to the journey back.

"Maybe we should wait a bit," I suggested a few times before we boarded.

"Nonsense, it'll be dark soon," slurred Captain Arnie.

It was a toss-up for me. Drive back with Crew Drunkie-Drawers while it was still light out, and maybe take the wheel again and steer us away from a ghastly death, or wait until it was pitch black and I couldn't see a damn thing. Looked like I didn't have much choice. Off we went again into the choppy sea, swerving this way and that, my lunch almost a plastering itself across the side of the boat. I have no idea how we got home, but apparently we did. As they told it, a great time was had by all.

I guess that's provided you were blind drunk and relying on a ten-year-old to navigate.

Chapter 9

Playground Politics

"Our deepest fear is not that we are inadequate. Our deepest fear is that we are powerful beyond measure. It is our light, not our darkness, that most frightens us. We ask ourselves, 'Who am I to be brilliant, gorgeous, talented, and fabulous?' Actually, who are you not to be? You are a child of God. Your playing small does not serve the world. There is nothing enlightened about shrinking so that other people won't feel insecure around you. [That is insincerity to them and you.] We are all meant to shine, as children do. We are born to make manifest that glory of God that is with us. It's not just in some of us; it's in everyone. And as we let our own light shine, we unconsciously give other people permission to do the same. As we are liberated from our own fear, our presence automatically liberates others. This is our duty." - Nelson Mandela.

"Be bold and courageous! After all, that is the only way the world has ever moved forward. Nothing slow about it. As Nassim Nicholas Taleb wrote in the book 'The Black Swan, ''Evolution doesn't crawl. It jumps.'" – JLH

Staying in school during that time was a challenge for me, or should I say I was a challenge for my teachers, who had no idea how to control my wild behaviour. By the time I was in grade two, I'd already been kicked out of three schools for a variety of reasons, but mostly for fighting. I'm not sure I cared that much about being kicked out, but I did care about the subsequent beatings I was in for when I got home.

I started Brock Elementary in grade three, and within a short time I proved to be too much for the principal, who, on a weekly basis, let the specially-made thick leather strap fly over my miniature hands; the smack echoed halfway down the hall.

"This is going to hurt me more than it hurts you," he'd say.

I didn't know why he'd say that, since I was the one who couldn't hold a pencil for two days afterwards, which got me in more trouble for not doing my work, and more trips to the office for the strap, and on and on it went.

I expect my mom must have thought she'd discovered gold when the invention of Ritalin came along. Mother's little helper drug. It was probably recommended by a teacher or some other mom that I try out this experimental new drug that was supposed to help calm down hyperactive kids. (Today it's handed out like candy by parents who have their priorities ass-backwards. Back then it was a miracle cure – or so people thought.)

It came in a liquid form: a thick, coppery substance that had a bitter, sweet taste that almost made me gag. My mom called it "calm-down medicine." Well, it made me calm all right; in fact, I was pretty much comatose. The other kids didn't know about it really, although I wouldn't have kept it a secret. The Mental Brothers started taking it shortly after me, since I was the test case for our area.

I can remember switching from super-hyper in class, kind of an ADHD poster child, to Rip Van Winkle. At first the principal and teachers thought it was a wonder drug, a cure for those impossible-to-manage children like me. Then I think they realized that maybe it wasn't having quite the effect they were looking for. The teacher would be shaking me, trying to wake me up in the middle of class, while I'd be drooling all over my desk. We cut the dosage in half, but that didn't help either; at least not enough to slow me down or still put me out. So, after a few months, my mom stopped feeding me the copper junk, and my wild antics started up again.

It was around this time I started my love affair with martial arts after seeing movies like Fists of Fury with Bruce Lee and Billy Jack with Tom Laughlin. I figured I didn't have much of an advantage with my size, but I if could learn to fight like Bruce Lee, I'd have an edge and start winning more fights than losing. I was no different than the other boys in the Projects who needed a stronger male influence, someone to could look up to. So began my mentorship by movies.

With no money to go, I'd take the hour-long bus ride into town by myself and sneak into the dark theatres by any means possible. There, in addition to Bruce and Billy, I would find the role models I was looking for: real men like Sean Connery, Clint Eastwood and Steve McQueen. I could easily get lost for two hours and imagine myself in their world, living a life of danger and excitement and heroic endings.

For as long as I can remember, I'd enjoyed performing; not that there were many opportunities in my younger, underprivileged school years. But one event stands out pretty clearly in my mind, which I suppose could have put me off for good. It was in grade three and Brock Elementary was putting on a concert. I was chosen to play a part by my teacher, a plump librarian type who always wore Quaker-like dresses and thick glasses attached to a long chain. I was excited at the prospect of playing a lead role, as maybe a pirate, or an evil baddie. I agreed before I even knew what part I'd be playing. The teacher showed up the next day and started dishing out the roles and costumes. I was, to say the least, confused when she handed me a pink body suit, which, as can be imagined, got some chuckles from the girls and sneers from the boys: "What's this?" I said, starting to panic. Her answer? She gave me a giant pink bunny head, with large floppy ears. That makes it all okay. I thought, Whoa! this isn't what I signed up for.

Yes…I wanted to be on stage, and be one of my heroes of the day: Sean Connery, Steve McQueen, Charles Bronson, James Coburn or Lee Marvin and knew how exciting it would be, but I still had to be cool. But a bunny costume? Did James Coburn start off in a bunny costume? I don't think so. I tried bargaining with her. I'd do the role, even sing the song and do a small jig, but I would not wear some stupid bunny costume. She seemed to find this amusing, which infuriated me in front of the other kids, and she still insisted I would wear the full costume to play this part. It was apparently going to be good for me and help in building character.

There was no getting out of it. The day of the performance arrived, and I cried and freaked out all the way from the changing room to backstage. I would have bolted if it wasn't for the teacher with her grip tightly clasped to my puny arm, pulling and dragging me the whole way. She shoved me onstage.

I looked out at the jeering faces. A few people snickered. The music started, and I took a big gulp and began my song: "The little bunny's ears go flop, flop, flop…the little bunny's feet go hop, hop, hop." I hopped across the stage and heard more snickering. I realized they weren't laughing with me, they were laughing at me, and that was all I needed to hear. I ran off stage in tears and tried to escape as fast as I could, but "Aunt Bea" was waiting in the wings. She grabbed me by the hair, gave me a few slaps round the head and topped it off with a stern lecture.

A few of my friends were in the audience, but they didn't back me up. I could see them from backstage, along with some teachers who were still laughing. Finally, the old bag let me go. I ran outside and sat on the bench to get away from everyone and try to regain my composure.

I sat there for a minute or two and thought about how I was going to live down this latest humiliating incident. Before I even had a chance to come up with a decent plan, aside from kicking some serious ass, I heard hollering and squealing as the rest of the school stampeded from the concert hall into the playground. I looked around frantically, but there was no escape. The school bully spotted me right away (how could he miss me in my pink costume?) and he and his two toadies sauntered over to me with evil grins on their ugly faces.

They started hopping around.

"The little bunny's ears go flop, flop, flop..." they all sang.

A crowd started forming around me in a semi-circle, and they all laughed. I felt my face flush as bright as my costume. I stood up and charged at the bully, ready to kill. He was going to pay for the entire school's mockery.

He was a skinny kid, about two inches taller than me with black curly hair and could probably easily win the fight, but I didn't care. I gave him a good hard kick to the balls. I figured that would be enough to shut him up, and I started to walk away. Unfortunately, that was just enough - enough to get him angry.

He sprang up and ran at me throwing punches, and we wrestled to the ground, with him on top of me, punching my face. I covered up, but that had little effect, so I reached up and grabbed his hair and jerked him over to the side until I was on top of him and started whaling on his face. I heard a whistle go off, and the playground monitor jumped in and ripped us apart. The whole thing lasted about a minute, but it felt like an hour. For some reason I was the one who got the blame (that was nothing new), as she yanked me by the arm and marched me off to the principal's office.

"I was defending myself!" I yelled. "Why aren't you taking him in?"

"That's for the principal to decide," she said.

I sat outside the office and listened to the monitor tell her version of the story to the secretary, casting me as the villain. We waited for the principal to come back from lunch. My bunny costume was torn and muddy, and blood was starting to dry on my nose. My stomach grumbled. I didn't even get lunch that day, and I was thinking how totally unfair it was.

When the principal arrived, I started to give my side of the story, but it was no use. He knew who I was and he'd already made his decision before I even opened my mouth. Again, another case of a troublemaker from the Projects who deserved exactly he got. He slowly walked round to the other side of his desk and opened the drawer. I knew what was coming. I guess he figured the strap would be the most effective reminder that fighting is not allowed at school.

"This is going to hurt me more than it's going to hurt you, boy," he said.

Where did I heard that before? Oh yeah, the other ten times or more I'd received this antiquated form of punishment, i.e., torture. He dished out blow after blow without any remorse. When it was finally over, he ordered me back to class.

I walked out of his office, my hands throbbing and raw. The rage was now double than it was at the beginning of this day of humiliation. I didn't try to hide my tears as I walked down the halls. I saw a few worried looks from a couple of teachers, but no one stopped to see if the poor kid in the shredded bunny costume was okay.

I thought about the unfinished business with the bullies, and made a plan to get it taken care of. The Mental Brothers backed me up this time, and our little crew waited after school for those who were involved in "The Bunny Laughing Conspiracy." We caught one of the followers as he was trying to duck out the back of the school. The three of us jumped on him and pummeled him till he was screaming and covered in blood, and I started to feel slightly better.

But I knew it wouldn't be too long before I was back in the principal's office again and I'd be saying goodbye to yet another school. Knowing I had a crush on a girl called Cindy, my boys dared me to make a move.

"Come here, Cindy," I said. "I want to tell you something".

She leaned in and I gave her a long kiss on her puffy lips. That one was too much for the principal. He kicked me out. Apparently, at that school, fighting wasn't as bad as kissing a girl.

The next school was Brock Annex, which was another section of Brock Elementary. I minded my own business and didn't look for any trouble, and for a few months it didn't find me. But at every school there's a bully who needs to prove he's top dog. I seemed to be a shit-magnet, so it was inevitable that some kind of showdown was in our future.

He was a red-haired, freckled kid and his name was Scott. A real prep type with his Tad and Biff sweaters. Probably on a first name basis with Thurston Howell III. I don't know what initially got me on his bad list. Maybe it was because I lived in the Projects, where most kids weren't allowed to ever set foot, so he figured I was an easy target. We started getting into scuffles on and off, and I wasn't winning many. Once was on a field trip, when a girl called Leisha took a sudden liking to me.

We were walking along when she grabbed me and pulled me into the bushes, twenty feet from the teachers. She told me to kiss her and feel her up. I wasn't about to refuse, and in fact afterwards decided I'd like to make this a regular thing. But Scott wasn't too happy. He saw us come out, all disheveled. Apparently I'd been messing around with his girlfriend.

I said something like, "Well, she never mentioned it to me," which led to some swearing and sweater pulling, but nothing more because the teachers were close by.

He was bigger than me, which was the norm, so I had to work up a plan of sorts if I wanted to put an end to these incidents. I decided to simply ambush him. I hadn't done anything like this before, but it worked out so well that I used it many times after, usually on my own against the bully (who is only really tough in the team setting).

One day the opportunity to try out this new strategy came when he got the better of me in a verbal jousting match, right in front of a group of girls. After his last winning remark, he turned away laughing, and walked into the library section, which was just a series of unsecured shelves in one corner.

I saw red, and not just the colour of his hair. I watched him choose a book and sit with his back to the shelf. My mind raced through several options of revenge that would cause the most pain and humiliation for him. I noticed how precarious the bookshelves looked. With a surge of adrenaline, I walked over to where he was sitting and pushed one of the heavy book-laden shelves on top of him.

"Screw you, carrot top!" I yelled.

I would have jumped up and down on the bookshelf too if I had the time, but no such luck. My euphoria lasted for about three seconds as I watched Scott get crushed and heard him shriek. The thrill was amazing. Just like going down that first big hill on a roller coaster; fast and hard; a huge rush as you head in the direction that seems clear. It was addictive, like any other extreme sport, and I was hungry for more.

A couple of girls were screaming. Scott's face was barely visible from under the pile of books, but I saw blood streaming from his nose. (Later I found out I had broken his arm and he had some facial damage and a slight concussion. This was totally satisfying for me.)

As for the teacher that came upon the scene at that moment, it was a nightmare for her. I mean, what's the first thing you do when you swat a wasp's nest? Run! And she should have too. But unfortunately for her she didn't. She grabbed my ear and started twisting it, which was a good call for her I guess, since my ears were big and they offered a nice target. But she didn't know about my secret weapon: new platform boots! Huge soles for maximum impact to the unsuspecting, beehive-hairdo teacher.

Pow! The first kick, she let go and grabbed her shin, crying. The second kick dropped her to the carpet, her hair came undone, Buddy Holly glasses flew off, mascara trickled in black streaks down her face. She lay there crying in a heap of melted emotion. I stood triumphantly over her, proud of my domain of destruction and ready for whoever was next. The other kids stood round and stared at me in horror as if I were some wild, caged tiger let loose. A couple of girls screamed and called for the teachers. Other kids ran, terrified, from the room. Another teacher came running to Miss "Beehive's" aid, and shortly thereafter, the principal, Mr. Three-piece-brown-suit-and-brown-shoes, poked his head round the corner to see if everything was all right. His look of horror quickly turned to anger when he saw it was that Hodgson kid, again! I had no real exit strategy set up. He marched me down the hall, twisting my ear. His face was red.

"What is wrong with you?" he said. "I've never seen this kind of behaviour. There's no place in the school system for you. What are we going to do with you? One thing is for sure, you are going to get ten on each hand this time!" which I got. Then he called my mother. She wasn't home, so they told me to go home and not come back until they talked to her.

When my mom found out what happened, she gave me the belt. Obviously I was not allowed to go back to that school again. It was near the end of the year, about three weeks before summer break, so I had some sitters and went to a neighbour's house for the rest of the time.

I had no idea why I acted like that, nor did my mom have any idea of how to control the situation. Between having to deal with my brother and me, it's no wonder she started drinking so much. Looking back, it's not something I'm proud of.

The new school I was attending was pretty fun. I was popular for a change and started meeting the odd girl that was not that odd, a good challenge to have as it turned out especially at that particular time in my hormonal roller coaster ride. I was also in a situation where studying was possible and I could concentrate to some degree. I do have a short attention span, even to this day,, but I was passing most subjects, and it like the feeling everyone gets on those rare sunny days in Vancouver (Canada's Hawaii). Things were looking up. I actually felt a bit good about my too-skinny body and thought maybe, just maybe this was the one: a school where I fit in and did not have a home life of chaos. But it was not to be. After being there about four months, it became the same old, same old. Daily interactions (fights) with jocks and getting the thick, well- used dark brown leather strap across my hands or butt once a week or so.

One Halloween I was walking around with a pocket full of firecrackers in my too-tight button-up GWG jeans, and as luck would have it, the hot cherry-red tip of the punk (incense stick) we used to light the firecrackers brushed against my light purple turtleneck sweater and beat all the odds by dropping into my bulging right side pocket. Bang! They started going off one at a time, then in multiple mini-explosions. I screamed bloody murder that could be heard for blocks around. Try as I might, I could not get the buttons of those jeans undone. As for my pals helping me? They ran away, of course. I can say that the smell of burning flesh is like frying a rancid steak. Especially when you mix in some sulphur and gunpowder.

I got a third-degree burn on my right leg about the size of a side plate that today looks like an explosion or water colour in the rain. I've been stabbed a couple of times and had my head split open more than once, but other than going through the windshield of my brother's black 1964 Ford Falcon (he ran a stop sign), I can say this was the most painful thing I have physically felt to date. Oh yeah, there was this little bonus: after about two months a nice thick solid scab had formed over the pepperoni-pizza-looking burn (with extra cheese and the smell of anchovies...Mmmm good!), this grade seven bully (bullies have been around since humans started walking upright and they are not going to disappear any time soon - unless they get neutered that is - and by the way, girls are drawn to bullies, a biological thing for breeding with the Alpha male I would suspect), picked a fight with me during recesses and like most times I didn't back down. It was a my-little-mouth-writing-cheques-my-body-couldn't-cash kind of scenario. Live and Learn as they say, but some of us don't seem to learn as fast as others.

I wasn't up for it really, but of course, as I said, my mouth was, so he kicked me in the leg, ripping the entire scab clean off. I almost fainted from the shock, and I swear I saw a flash of light. Blood ran down my leg, turning my dirty white socks into dirty red ones. I started to cry and dropped to my knees. He and the other boys laughed (bullies always travel with a pack) as they ran away. Unfortunately for him I got it together just long enough to focus on an egg-sized rock lying near my left hand. I picked it up and through watering eyes let it fly. Bam! The trajectory was perfect. It hit him in the back of the head, splitting it open and sending him sliding face-down onto the gravel playground. Now he was crying too. The other kids screamed for a teacher to come help. Of course the ex-wrestler (jock) gym teacher, just happening to catch my amazing rock throw action but missing the bullying part, came charging across the gravel field like a mad bull towards me; not pausing as he grabbed me by the back of the neck, his powerful fingers digging into my skin. Off I went in giant steps as he pushed me towards the principal's office. I was still heaving a bit and trying to tell my story, that I was stopping the kid from being mean to others and he kicked me on my burn, which was by now this huge bleeding mess that looked fake. Didn't matter. I had done so many other things that I was guilty for sure. I got the strap and was sent home. I told my mom what happened and she was mortified and, to her credit, she went to the school. Not sure what happened, but she tried.

A few months later, I was walking down the hall when out of nowhere appeared my partners in crime, the Mental Brothers. Unbeknownst to me, they had moved just a few blocks away and had enrolled in the same school. It was a fine recipe for trouble and I had an appetite. In no time at all, we were getting into fights, breaking into lockers, going through the purses and coats of every teacher and skipping school. And yeah, getting the strap every other day. This couldn't last long and didn't. I was asked to leave and not come back, the bros lasted a bit longer but couldn't conform to the new rules laid out for as a condition of their being allowed to stay. It goes without saying that my grades were now in the Cs and Ds.

Eventually the school had had enough and kicked me out.

Chapter 10

Tough Lessons for a Young Entrepreneur

"Kids should have two bikes; one to ride and one to rent."

– Jim Rohn

My dad's visits were pretty sporadic, but I was always excited to see him when he did show up. You never knew what kind of gifts he'd bring, or what kind of car he'd be driving.

On one occasion, he showed up unexpectedly with five brand new TVs. They had apparently fallen off the back of a truck, and gee, weren't we lucky that all five of them didn't get broken? I didn't ask any questions, just thought it was super cool. We went from having one small black- and-white to a house full of TVs; one in every room. They came in a bunch of sizes, and since he showed up at dinner time, we were all there to help unload them.

My mom stood on the porch, taking in the scene. I could see she wasn't too impressed, but that didn't stop her from helping with the lifting. My favourite TV had a six-inch translucent glowing trim around the outside, which I thought was neat, until my sister threw a slipper at me and missed, but cracked the trim. It still looked cool, but it never worked the same.

The reception on the TVs was poor, but they all had their own set of rabbit ears, so you could get three or four channels. I can remember trying to watch Jane Fonda and Lee Marvin in Cat Ballou. I had to keep going from TV to TV to get the best reception, calling my mom each time to fix the rabbit ears.

Other times we were excited to jump in my dad's Caddy and go cruising around town. I liked to make sure all the neighbourhood kids could see me. Dad would sometimes take us out shopping, which was a big treat. My clothes were outdated most of the time and I was accused of wearing flood pants, but they were clean and I never noticed or cared.

One of the big highlights of those shopping days is when my dad took me and my siblings on a shopping spree at Woodward's. He must have thought it was a big mistake with all of us running around with shopping carts. The main purchases for me were zip-up platform boots and a Rat Patrol hat with the sides folded down. Not the most practical outfit for every day wear, but my crew was pretty impressed when I showed up in these fancy duds.

Just before Christmas 1969, he showed up again, driving his Caddy, and walked in carrying a briefcase full of jewellery boxes. I thought this was total pirate booty and must be worth gazillions of dollars. I emptied the boxes onto the living room floor and spread them out, examining all the sparkling stones and shiny pearls. I figured my father much be rich by now if he could afford to buy all this loot. My brain started working overtime on what I could do with them. Most of it, if not all, was for women, so there was no use in me hanging onto it. And it seemed way too obvious to wrap it up and give it to my sisters and mom for Christmas.

It didn't take long before I had the brilliant idea of selling it to some rich people and using the money to buy Christmas presents for my family. Seemed like a simple enough plan. In my eight-year-old mind, I saw the operation going smoothly, and ending with me walking home with pocket loads of cash.

The next day I dressed in my most presentable jeans, sweater and boots, and trudged through the snow for about a mile to the West Side. I walked up the first long driveway to a huge house with white pillars and a fancy carved wood door, rang the doorbell, pressed my hair down and waited. The door opened and a fat old lady wearing pearls and a silk blouse looked down her nose at me.

"Yes?" she said.

I launched into my well-rehearsed sales pitch, confident I was offering a deal that anyone in their right mind would find irresistible. But before I'd even finished, she slammed the door in my face. Hmm, that didn't quite go as I imagined. But I wasn't about to get discouraged this early in the game.

I walked across the manicured lawn of the neighbouring house and tried again. This time a younger elegant-looking lady answered with a smile. But after giving me a quick once-over and hearing my opening lines, she said, "Not interested," and slammed the door.

Maybe this wasn't going to be as easy as I thought. I tried the next house, and this time a couple of nice old grey-haired folks welcomed me into their stunning foyer. I looked around and tried to act as though this opulence didn't impress me. They led me into their white-carpeted living room and sat me down on the plush blue velvet couch.

"Now tell us more about these lovely jewels," said the old lady.

I saw her give a subtle nod to her husband and he excused himself and left the room. Again, I launched into my sales pitch. She listened to me intently, smiled and nodded, seeming very interested.

"Well, after all that selling, you must be very hungry. Why don't I get you a snack?" she said.

She left the room and came back in a few moments later with a tray full of cookies and a big glass of milk. We sat there chatting away with me feeling very civilized and thinking this isn't so hard after all. I could easily get used to living in a mansion like this. Maybe they'll find me cute and want to adopt me.

A few minutes later, the old guy came back in with a fake smile and joined in the conversation. Then I heard the doorbell ring. The old guy jumped up and opened the door. I heard some mumbling and looked up just as two police officers walked through the doors. What the hell were they doing here?

"This him?" one of them asked. They eyed me up and down suspiciously. The old guy nodded. The other cop approached me.

"These folks tell me you were trying to sell them jewellery. Where did you get those, kid?"

These guys looked nothing like the cops I'd seen on TV. About fifty times nerdier. Very polite and no foul language. But their look said I was guilty and there wasn't much I could do to change their minds.

I knew I wasn't doing anything wrong, but I was starting to feel like a criminal by the way they were eyeing me up.

"My dad gave them to me," I said.

"Uh-huh. Where do you live, son?"

I told them. They looked at each other.

"Okay, you're going to have to come with us," they said. "Put your hands behind your back"

What the hell is going on? "Why? I didn't do anything wrong!" I protested.

One of the cops handcuffed me and nudged me towards the door.

I glared at the grey-hairs who looked down at me with concern.

"What the hell did you call the cops for?" I yelled at the old lady. What a bunch of liars I thought. I hated them.

The cops dragged me outside and guided me into the back of the pungent-smelling squad car, the blue vinyl seats worn with distant memories of every poor slob finding out that crime just doesn't pay. I had no idea what was going to happen so I sat quietly and watched the forest green lamp posts stream by through the scarred plexiglass divider, wondering what was next…and thinking so much for a kid trying to make a bit of money to surprise his family (as dysfunctional as it was) with a few Christmas presents. Note to self: beware of the grey-heads, especially those white people that have brown skin from expensive vacations and teeth as white as tigers. They are Trixie.

Chapter 11

First Time in Jail

"Forgiveness is always free…trust is always earned."

- JJLH

I expected the cops would just drive me home and my mom would clear this up in an instant. Didn't happen. Instead, they started driving in the wrong direction from my house and I had this sinking feeling in my PB&J-empty stomach.

"Where are you taking me?" I asked.

"Just gotta check something out … and do some paper work," was the off-handed reply, as if I was twenty-five years old. Ten minutes later we arrived at the Oakridge police station.

The old Oakridge station, I knew well, as it was right behind the Oakridge mall, my hunting grounds for all sorts of goodies; yet I had never been invited inside before. They pulled me inside. It was the middle of the day, so there was very little going on there. Just the black phones occasionally ringing, fat cops scattered about the vanilla-painted cinder block walls and a long-haired freaky hippie, with his ripped jeans, moccasins and tassel vest being paraded in handcuffs through a steel door. I suspected he was in for some major crime like smoking a joint or getting caught urinating in public. Dirty Hippies. That's what the cops would have thought, I am sure. I also half thought I would run into my brother since he spent most of his time in police custody even then. He would for sure explain the whole thing to the pigs; after all, he was my big brother and was supposed to watch my back.

One of the huge twentieth-century centurions ushered me to a table off to the side of the entrance where he told me to empty my pockets, which I did without question. Then he searched me, just in case I was packing a blade or possibly some chewing gum which I could stuff into my mouth and choke myself with during unforeseen bouts of remorse for my crimes. The contents of my lint-filled Kmart blue jeans were two really round excellent throwing rocks in my front left pocket (nothing ever went in the right after the fun and games of 40 firecrackers going off, leaving their third-degree-burn legacy), my shiny, white Jack Rabbit special Hot Wheels car with the twin blue stripes (one of my favourites), all of which were unceremoniously taken away. That included my briefcase, full of what the cops thought was the catch of the day and certainly pirate loot. After this invasion of my personal space, (put your arms in front of you, clasp your hands and that's the distance), they finally told me to sit on this hard, ass-worn, wooden chair and to not move until I was told to.

About this point I was starting to feel scared and the lines from The Wizard of Oz started creeping through my dense brain: you're not in Kansas anymore, Jake. I got it, this wasn't like the movies and I wondered if they were going to throw me in a cell and who else would be in there with me. Some big, fat, sweaty, balding, child-molesting Bubba perhaps. This could go awry (as if it hadn't already) very quickly with me being a surrogate stuffed toy (with benefits) for some Charles Manson psycho. Great, a tattoo on my butt saying, Property of Bubba. That would have ended badly for him, as I waited, not unlike the tiger who only looks like he's resting 23 hours a day, but no. He waits. How that could have played out, who knows? But one day the opportunity would present itself and I would take advantage of by perhaps covering him in my Blue Blanky, not before dousing him and it in lighter fluid of course; the ultimate hot dream - can you smell bacon? Never happened, thank the big man upstairs, although I could see a cell with its stainless steel toilet and, of course, no seat cover. I pondered how easy it would be to fall in and how dirty it might be, which would be impossible to tell with the dull green cinderblock cell walls littered with names and symbols carved into the paint, by who-knows-who as they take all your cool sharp stuff away. On top of the 10-by-10 room was what looked like a 40-watt bulb encased in a dirty

Lexan cover situated in the middle of the 10-foot ceiling. The thought crossed my mind; why cover the light, who can jump up 10 feet and what would they do when they got ahold of it? My bro told me sometime later that it was covered so no one would jump up there, rip off the metal around the Lexan (while holding themselves by one finger), unscrew the bulb and either stick their finger in the socket or take the bulb with them on the way down, break it, then use it to cut their wrists or quickly fashion some primitive weapon using stuffing from the mattress, woven into string then tied to a collection of plastic utensils collected over a series of days with the crappy meals. Well anyway, the cops got me a sandwich, ham and processed cheese, as I recall, on pasty Wonder Bread (my favourite), and a paper cup of milk. All good.

One of the cops came back and asked me what my phone number was so they could call my parents. I told them I lived with my mom only and that my dad lived in Chinatown (too much info I know, but I liked Chinatown for some reason) so he would not be answering. Funny thing is, as I write this I still remember that phone number. They came back a few moments later and told me no one was answering the phone, no surprise. She was either working at her chambermaid job or having a few cocktails with her NBFs discussing how the men in their lives were losers and the kids were animals. Not sure she would have said that even if she was gin drunk. Well, hours went by and I was getting antsy, my mind working overtime on multiple scenarios: What if no one answers? Maybe I'll have to miss school…that would be cool…or they would drive me to school in the cop car, and then come and pick me up every day until they talked to my mom. Hmm, this could be fun, but I don't want to sleep with Bubba in a cell, so maybe they'd let me sleep at home and then come and get me in the morning and lock me back up; feed me first, then drive me to school. Could happen. Finally, when it was starting to get dark, a different cop came over to me, I guess the other guys got tired or went for donuts, and said, "We spoke to your older sister, so you can go home." I looked up at him with my best deer- in-the-headlights look and said, "Thank you," yet thinking now I know why my bro and his gang hate these dudes.

I was led back into a police car, no small talk or, "Hey we're sorry about the mistake." Nada. Just a rather fast drive back to East Van, where there was really little attention paid by most of the neighbours as this was a regular occurrence at the Hodgson estate. The big copper with his cliché puffy red moustache opened the back door and ushered me out (In case you didn't know, you can't open those things from the inside; fire hazard for sure, but who cares, you're in the back because you are deemed guilty until proven otherwise. Right? Not.). I got out and he lightly held the back of my spindly neck with his baseball-mitt hands. Before we got to the battleship-grey painted stairs of our house, my mom burst open the screen door, wearing her floral patterned housecoat, her jet black hair a wild mess like she had been wrestling. A half-done Black Cat No. 7 smoke in her ruby-red lipstick painted mouth.

"What did you do this time?" were the first somewhat slurred words out of her mouth. Not the reaction I was hoping for.

The cop in my defense blurted out, "Hold on there. He apparently hasn't done anything wrong, according to your daughter who answered our call earlier."

My mom said, "What daughter?"

The cop was stumped at that one. He regained his composure and said, "Well, how many do you have?"

She said, "Three in total, but only one is at home".

To this, John Law said, "The one who answered the phone, called herself Pam."

My mom said, "Oh yeah, she was home earlier."

The cop surveyed the situation for a beat or two thinking something to the effect, this figures, wild kid, East Van, wild family, textbook case. Opened and Closed: Hyenas raising Hyenas on the East Van Serengeti. The circle of (bad) life is well at hand. All is as it should be. The have-nots are back with their kind and the haves can sleep well another night as we, the twentieth-century centurions stand watch; standing in the gap and validating the taxpayers' (we were tax-takers) investment. As you all know, crime will always be on the rise, regardless of the stats. I went up the stairs, tail between my legs, and feeling like the loser I was, my mom saying go to your room. I will deal with you later. After some mumbled chatter I heard the door slam.

Then the expected "Jake, come here" from my mom.

I knew I was in for it. My mom looked at me with eyes of disappointment and flashes of light- filled daggers. I know her greatest fear was that I would follow in my brother's tainted footsteps. She was of course right, and I did. Don't mess with mama bear's intuition. As I lay on my small cot waiting in anticipation for yet another well-deserved beating (which never came, I guess my mom got the picture: I was just trying to be an entrepreneur) with the extension cord, broom handle or dreaded Slipper of Vengeance, I couldn't help but think about how those rich folks set me up. It sucked! And I was a mad as a storekeeper when I just grabbed ten bucks out of his till. The grey-heads would pay I mumbled under my breath, offering up milk and cookies to me was the equivalent of asking a crackhead if they wanted some free rock. Yeah, that nice retired couple were going to get a second visit from the kid from the Projects, that was for certain.

How it rolled out was as expected; a few days later, me and the rat pack paid dropped by. That's all. It was about eight at night and snow was falling in those magical giant flakes that stick to your clothing and eyelashes. Perfect I thought, as I love Christmas. It was the time for giving, and they needed a retribution gift.

Our meeting place was always at one of the several steel-and-cement-reinforced incinerators; for those who didn't have the luck of growing up in the Projects, these things were basically an outdoor garbage fireplace of sorts, with a huge metal and concrete lid that had to have a weighted counter-levered handle so it could be opened. These fairly common things to the Projects across North America, were about five feet high (not including the cement step up to it) with a three-by-three-foot opening (you can work out the metric conversion), to drop garbage in, and coming off the back of each of them was an 80-foot high chimney that was supposed to carry those pollutants away from the hundreds of families living below their toxic cloud. You could throw most anything in them but there was, as I recall, a red and white official-looking steel sign that said 'no aerosol cans'. The word: "no" to me back then meant "maybe" or "go for it." Not sure what the concern was, but I'm sure it wasn't environmental in nature. A lot of fun for the local natives, especially when you would get a roaring fire in their belly then help their digestion along by tossing in a few cans of hairspray. Can you say BOOM? The 60-pound lid would spring open with this tremendous bang then crash shut, and we would scatter like cockroaches when you surprise them in the middle of the night by turning on the kitchen light in search of that life-sustaining drink. We high-fived for a few seconds, then focused on the task at hand. I know it seems stupid to tell a bunch of forgotten boys about your troubles and plan of how to get retribution, but regardless it makes one feel good to think others care, even at ten years old (can you hear the tinny violin?). One of them brought the group pillow case with pre-selected throwing rocks. We parlayed for a couple of moments, making sure everyone was in agreement with my reasoning behind giving Mr. and Mrs. Grey-Head some payback. They were, and we headed southwest to the land of Milk & Money. Fortunately for them, it only included a reluctant keying of the driver's side of their late model burgundy Cadillac with the optional soft-top, chrome spoked rims and matching coloured spare tire rear bumper setup. For an old tanned couple with unnaturally white teeth, they sure had a pimped-out Caddy slumbering in its way-too-clean carport, dreaming of being driven to its limit. Not too many years later I would have been happy to make that car's dream come true by stealing it, but not tonight. Our crescendo of retribution was aerodynamically selected stones from our fave pound on little mountain being hurled at their living room window. I heard the loud smash and saw two figures jump up and scream.

"Merry Christmas!" I shouted, and we all ran off into the night, laughing.

I retraced my steps to figure out where I'd gone wrong in my childish business plan: knock on doors; sell jewellery; get money; buy Christmas presents. Seemed simple enough.

I was a bit jaded after that and began to really dislike and mistrust rich people. I understood that some people had better stuff than me and I figured it was my right to take what I wanted. But from then on, I decided it would be smarter either just to steal what I wanted directly, or to steal the money and then just buy it.

Chapter 12

Trying on Religion…Catholic School

"Don't you just love getting advice from peopleborn on third base and act like they hit a triple, when in reality they had the advantage of family money, being born at the right time…made money on property as demographics/immigration changed or did it the old way and married into money." -JLH

After my first stint in jail, my mom had had enough. She must have thought she'd have to take a more drastic approach with me if I was ever going to learn how to behave. So she decided to send me to Catholic school.

St. Andrew"s Catholic School was on 45th Street, a few blocks east of Main Street. It was very strict, and run, obviously, by nuns. For the first time in my life I had to wear a uniform, which I hated. Grey pants, white shirt, a tie and a green V-neck sweater.

The first order of the day was prayers, followed by lots of teaching about the "Good Book." No men were there for some reason. The nuns, bless their hearts, were determined to Stop Satan from trying to get in to this cute little boy's body. But as the poem goes, "There is a Satan, there is no doubt, but is he trying to get in me or trying to get out?" I suspect they weren't sure.

They didn't believe in the experimental teaching system called ITA (Initial Teaching Alphabet) that had helped me learn more easily at my last school, which I had been kicked out of for pushing a book shelf on a kid and kicking a teacher more times than was necessary. So even though I was in grade three, they decided I should be held back a year, just to see how I'd do. Then if I could show them I should be in grade four, they'd be happy to move me up (or kick my little white ass all the way down the hall and back to the stinking Projects, where my kind belonged). Apparently my mother didn't have the ability to dispute it and I do not blame her whatsoever.

Mother Superior and I had many run-ins. She was in her fifties, had grey hair and wore wire-rimmed glasses and the black and white robes of her order. She always looked constipated and mad. In a word, scary. She was the one who gave out most of the whippings. The rest of the teachers seemed to be burned out. Who knows? Maybe they'd had one too many hell-children sent to them

The first incident happened when I was in the church. As per tradition, I was supposed to put a donation in the candle box so I could light a candle. I dug deep into my pocket, but all I could find was a quarter. Now, I didn't mind making a donation, but I wasn't going to put a whole quarter in. I could use some of that change for candy. So I figured, why not see if I can get some change? I pried open the box and started looking around for a nickel and dime as change. I actually had no intention of stealing for some reason, but as fate would have it I suddenly heard a booming voice say, "Hey! What do you think you're doing?"

I guessed right away it wasn't God talking to me. I doubted He'd be that angry over a mere 15 cents. I looked up and there was Mother Superior, striding towards me, her black robe swishing and her thick black hard-sole shoes clicking on the terracotta stone floor. I pulled my hand out and started to explain. I knew how it must have looked. But there was no way she was going to believe my story. She grabbed me by the ear and yanked me on my tippy-toes all the way to her office. With a smile, she got out the strap and let it wallop over my tender hands, over and over again.

"You will burn in hell for stealing" she told me. I don't recall worrying to much about that at the time, as my hands had all my attention.

The next major event took place out in the playground. It began innocently enough with a game of tetherball. For those who don't know, tetherball is a game played with a volleyball tied to a rope that is attached to a tall metal pole. It's a fast and wild game that has plenty of action for the players and spectators. Now, if you lose, that's just the way it goes. But if all the other kids are watching an important grudge match between two Samurai of the tetherball dojo, well that's another story.

This game was full of drama; we were neck and neck right till the end when I scored the winning point. To my surprise, the crowd cheered for me. My opponent wasn't too happy about this. His name was Bruce; he was a blond kid who was pretty popular and not used to being defeated by some scrawny kid from the Projects. Instead of being a good loser, he figured he'd get his own back by trying to make me look stupid.

He shouted out to the crowd "Jake's being held back a grade because he's a retard and takes medication for it every day"

That may or may not have been true at the time, but since everyone started laughing, I did what any self-respecting kid would do: I let the tetherball fly, smashing him in the side of the head, and then ran at him full-force, unleashing the power of my almighty mushroom ring into his face. The mushroom ring (stolen from Woodward's), was truly awesome, with psychedelic colours and huge mushroom-shaped top with paisley print; fantastic for enhancing the power of my bony little fist. Pow! Smash! Down he went, holding his bloody nose and cut lip.

The pride I felt was overwhelming and my body was raging with adrenaline. The other kids had formed a circle around us and were screaming the usual "Fight, fight, fight!" But once again, my glory was short lived; one of the nuns came running over and stood between us. Naturally I was blamed again and received several lashings from the Strap of Purity. I think Mother Superior was starting to lose faith that she could drive Satan from my body.

In most schools I'd attended, substitute or student teachers didn't stand much of a chance of keeping the class under control, and this included St. Andrew's. We had a student teacher there who was no more than a teenager and had probably just graduated from school, I suspect. One day, she caught me chewing gum and ordered me to the front of the class. I guess she wanted to make an example of me. Little did she know she'd picked the wrong kid to mess with.

She told me to stand in front of the class with my gum on my nose. I guess her method of punishment was humiliation, but I wasn't going to play that game. Instead of acting ashamed, I laughed. This infuriated her. She yelled at me to go and stand in the corner and I refused. She shoved me by the head so hard my face smashed into the wall. I think she pushed me a bit harder than she intended to, but it was too late. I snapped.

"Fuck off!" I yelled at her, my face red.

She grabbed the yardstick and whacked me across the back. She lifted her hand to hit me again, but I was faster than her; I yanked it from her hand and started beating her with full force over her whole body until it broke in my hands. She fell to the ground and crouched into a ball, her hands over her head, a sobbing heap. The class of thirty grade three kids was screaming. I ran from the classroom and looked for a place to hide.

Someone went and told the Sisters. This got them to mobilize the minions fast, to track down the non-believer hell-child. A group of grade seven boys found me on someone's porch about a block away from the school. Some keener tracker, their general of sorts, a grade twelve kid with a hunting knife, grabbed me. He wasn't going to take no for an answer (the knife at my throat was the first clue). I had no choice but to go along with him like a lamb to the slaughter.

He walked me back with the knife still at my throat, displaying me like he'd found the winning ticket to Willie Wonka's Chocolate Factory, putting his weapon away as we entered the school grounds. A crowd followed. The school was abuzz. Naturally I was scared, but I was also mad at what turned out to be more humiliating than the gum incident that had triggered this whole chaos.

The knife-wielding boy dragged me into Mother Superior's office. A group of boys stood outside the door watching and calling me names under their breath (they didn't want to swear - oh no - but pull a knife on a nine-year-old, that's perfectly okay). I sat down and didn't say a word. The nuns sent the boys back to class and came back in, looking at me with disgust.

"You sit here until we decide what to do with you" one of them said, and they left the room, closing the door to behind them.

Now I was thinking I was born at night, but not last night. If they thought it was okay to send out a hit squad to capture me, what would they come up with as punishment after a bit of planning? I wasn't about to wait to find out.

As soon as that door latch clicked, I casually got up and walked out of the office like it was all a big mistake. Once I was in the hall, I started running, and this time didn't stop until I was back in the safety of my old neighbourhood.

Chapter 13

Taking the Kid Out of the Hood or Taking the Hood Out of the Kid?

"Getting on the back of the tiger is far easier than getting off." - JLH

A few months after I returned home from Catholic school, we received the "good" news that my grandfather, on my father's side, Jake L. Hodgson, had died at the ripe age of 96. Funny, I was not that excited about it. I was curious about him after hearing the tales of his family's great wealth and, of late, owning steel mills in Wales and Europe. I imagined he was really rich, living on an estate and regularly played polo with the Royals, who confided in him on matters of state; plus Mi6 needed his help on directing the actions of the Double 00s. I also knew he had never cared to meet me or my siblings. That bothered me deep down, but no one ever spoke about him until I found that old newspaper clipping about him being the oldest ice skater in Canada.

I had always wanted to meet him some day though and find out where we came from and how I could get rich too. But I learned early on that rich people were different. He and my two uncles were snobs, and from what I heard, the uncles didn't want us getting ideas we could change our station in life (by sponging off them).

So considering I never actually met him, the news of his death didn't make a huge impact in my world, but that changed a few months later when news came, via my dad's brothers contacting a lawyer (following the notification to the proper authorities that he had a wife and children on welfare he wasn't supporting, aside from the occasional ride in a candy-apple-red Pontiac with a white convertible top, or a string of

Cadillacs, fake jewels and used TVs). There were five of us in my little Lemony Snicket family and, as it turned out, I also had two half-sisters. One lived in Alberta and surprise, surprise, the other lived with me but my mom never mentioned that my oldest sister had a cowboy as her biological father, (that was, until fate had him move into an illegal basement suite across the street from us). The lawyer contacted my mom, saying my dad was to receive an inheritance of $100,000. Price of an average wedding or nice car today but a big chunk of cheddar in 1970. (Not sure what the motives were at the time; that story comes later, but it was cool they did it. Yes they were and are wealthy gents, who, like most of the wealthy, live contrary to the popular beliefs of the soap-opera-watching, Netflix-bingeing masses like me.) How so? Well according to the book The Millionaire Mind, a study of the habits of 700-plus millionaires, and a few of my observations, the following are some of the traits they have:

- They only spend the dividends of the dividends from investments.

- They do not send their kids to private schools. They move to the best neighbourhoods and send their kids to local public schools.

- Approximately $50,000 is the average amount they spend on a car (with all vehicles totaling about one percent of their net worth, according to one of my wealthy mentors).

- Approximately $4,000 is the average amount they spend on a watch.

- They never feel they have enough money.

- They are self-employed.

- They make most of their money from rising real estate prices; especially in Vancouver where the average cost of a home/apartment in 2016 was $1.2 million (and the average annual income was $35,000.)

I guess I see them like the farmer in the valley that doesn't want all the land, just what's next to his. A human condition, I suppose, or, as First Nations people would say, a sickness. This "family money" still did not come easy, nothing worthwhile ever does, so my mom had to fight hard to get it, and that included some help from an awesome organization called Legal Services Society, basically lawyers who want to help people who are broke to fight those who aren't broke, for little pay. Probably the only lawyers God loves.

My mom won and she bought a house as soon as she could, paying a huge $27,000 for a four-bedroom house in the far East Side. In today's dollars that property would be $1.2 million, so it was a big whack of cash.

I think all of us believed life would get better from then on – and to a certain degree it did. We had moved away from the row house. Our new home was a Vancouver Special on a normal street in a working-class neighbourhood, with grass (no broken beer bottles to step on) and a clean sidewalk. We had a wood-burning fireplace, an apple tree in the back yard, and a back deck with a view of downtown Vancouver and the mountains.

I was excited about the idea of getting my own room; posters on the walls that I liked, and my own transistor radio on the station I wanted, LG73. I even had a fresh start at a different school, Grenfell Elementary, for grade six. A chance to be different and hopefully get settled and make some cool friends.

There were lots of normal kids and families on our block and surrounding streets; you know, the ones that had two parents (female and male), went to school, had bikes that weren't stolen. That's where I was introduced to the great Canadian kid's pastime, street hockey. I was never really good, but I made up for it with aggression and enthusiasm. It was a lot of fun until something made me mad and I beat up some kids from the other team, or even the kids on my own team for that matter. Pretty much anyone who made eye contact. Although I was small, they learned not to mess with me. Eventually it led to them playing games without telling me, so feeling alienated and humiliated, I did things like smash their street hockey nets into pieces and take their orange or red hard plastic street hockey balls. Yes, I had issues.

Halloween, though, was lots of fun and the kids in the new neighbourhood got so excited that they kind of forgot about the past, as kids do. We would talk and plan out our costumes, thinking about all the houses we had to go to; all the kids dressed up in the safe, parent-patrolled streets, well, most Halloweens anyway. One time, I managed to get candy that was laced with LSD, had me swinging with Spidey and flying with Superman for several days and gave me flashbacks for about ten or fifteen years after. Can't say it was intended for me but considering what a little shit I was, plus my brother's antics, it is possible.

Like I said, the idea of getting away from the bad influences of the Projects was a great concept in theory, but in reality, we'd only changed the stadium not the players. It took about six months before things began to unravel. My brother started bringing gang trouble to our quiet street. We were "entertained" by drive-by shootings (a new term for Vancouver at the time, I suspect) every other week. It got so bad, the insurance company refused to pay for any additional floor-to-ceiling windows and my mom stopped calling the police.

How bad was it? For a few months we had a male UBC student boarding with us. Can't recall his name but he was a cool, six-foot-three guy working his way through medical school, who narrowly escaped a bullet in the forehead while sitting with my mom and two of my sisters eating a rare dinner in the dining room instead of the kitchen. The bullet flew through the living room window, smashing it completely, and landed in the wall just above his head.

He moved out the next morning.

Chapter 14

Department Store Sleepover

"Popular=Normal=Average…I was never popular. "Odd" or "danced to the beat of a different drummer" were more the terms I would use to describe myself. All I can say to that is thank you, God; so far behind the curve, I ended up being the leader and trend setter as the PNAs,, a.k.a. Lemmings, circled back as they do." - JLH

After a while I started settling into my new environment. I even had a couple of kids to hang around with (not the ones I'd beaten up during the street hockey games). To me, they were a bit strange in that they were well grounded or something; I didn't relate. I guess to them I would have seemed the opposite – maybe that was the attraction. Whether or not the parents knew their kids were hanging around with me is another story.

One sunny Saturday afternoon, a couple of the two-parent kids and I went to the local mom-and-pop cinema, as in owned by a family that played real movies, not pornos (I think the movie was The Majestic with Jim Carey) and saw the highly anticipated Disney classic Island at the Top of the World, a movie about an expedition to the Arctic to find a missing child, where a bunch of Vikings are discovered. All of us thought the movie was really cool and we left the theatre, thinking we were Vikings and looking for adventure of our own.

We started walking towards home, when suddenly, right there in front of me, appeared Mr. Entertainment himself: Dale, my best buddy from the Projects, who I hadn't seen for two years. It took less than five minutes of high-fiving, hugs and "I can't believe it…what have you have been up to?" "I missed you man"; "Do you remember when…yeah!" "The good old days!" before we locked in on a plan.

"Hey, let's head up to Oakridge like the old days and hang out," I said, totally stiffing my other friends and forgetting about the fact I was actually grounded and suppose to go the five blocks home after the movie. So much for that thought - it lasted about as long as the last grilled cheese sandwich fresh from the pan in a government-run group home.

Not much jingle in our jeans, so we did what any street-wise kid would do. Hop on the back of a bus. How does that work you ask? Well, you simply stand at a bus stop that has other people waiting and, as they board the bus, you fade into the background and casually step up to the back seat of choice for those who have no money to ride inside. That is, you hang on tight to the cable boxes on the back of the trolley bus. Simple? Yes. But don't slip or you will end up under the car right behind you, usually honking its horn or yelling some inaudible advice (to you or the driver) that, even if I could hear it, I would have brushed off as the rantings of a cop-wannabe. What could be better than the wind in your hair, the feeling of freedom and the rush of speed? Yay! Our version of a sports car or motorbike. Just like old times, two pals hanging out and, as John Kay of Steppenwolf sang in the legendary Born to be Wild … Lookin' for adventure…and whatever comes our way. I could relate, and so could my older mentors of the day who live their version with the added emphasis of FTW.

When we got to the mall, we ran around and scoped out where all the store dicks were (some we knew, some we didn't) and picked up a few snacks and beverages from the food floor, clothing from another store, two down-filled sleeping bags from a camper we'd broken into on the parking lot and, most importantly, a nice selection of Hot Wheels. Good times! We planned to stay in the department store for at least the night but if all went well we could maybe stay the whole weekend, like (for those who can't relate) going to the cottage for the weekend.

Well time flies when you having fun, so it got late, the store announced it was closing in fifteen minutes and we figured there was no turning back; the English saying "in for a penny, in for a pound" seemed appropriate. We had no thought about the future or the fact that our families might be wondering what happened to us, going to a Saturday matinee movie several blocks from home and then, poof! Gone. Not making it home for mac and cheese with some cut up hot dogs and a topping of ketchup? That was not normal for me.

The patrons filed out like domesticated sheep but we had found a great hiding spot in the luggage department. We had been stashing our loot there during the day (including sleeping bags, pillows and a cornucopia of delectable snacks) so, come closing time, we were ready for bed. To be sure, we had not seen any after-hours guards before, as we had never been in the store after-hours before. As the saying goes, we didn't know what we didn't know, which equals pure unadulterated ignorance. As I see it, being stupid and ignorant are completely different things; one is just dumb, as in being born at the shallow end of the IQ pool; the other, lack of experience, or as one of my mentors John C. Maxwell would say, lack of evaluated experience. So that really didn't cross our pea-sized brains and soap-dish intellect and, as sure as a bear poops in the woods, we didn't consider the possibility of guard dogs. I mean … really? Dogs to protect dry goods, toys and appliances? WTF? Remember this is in the '70s.

At first we stayed pretty quiet, whispering in the dark and excitedly eyeing up our spoils with our new Eveready flashlights. Life just doesn't get any better than this; two pals having a sleepover with a spice of danger. I could see the crimson red glow of the EXIT sign off in the distance and it made me feel secure for some reason. The only sounds other than our breathing at times was the far-off banging of the pipes as they changed shape after the air-conditioning units shut off, and of course the janitors with their floor-waxing machine humming away to perfection; the chubby cleaners' keys jingling like sleigh bells at Christmas. Other than that, it was as quiet as church on Halloween.

Sleep was out of the question as per any sleepover, never mind our rather unusual digs. The massive sugar high from our candy stash didn't help the matter much, I suspect. So we talked a lot and goofed around and then decided it was time to find somewhere that didn't have coffee- drinking guards and hungry German Shepherds sneaking up on you in the middle of a dream involving some actress who thought you were so cute. Could happen. It was almost midnight when we made our move; never once thinking to grab a few watches or some jewelry. No. Candy, Hot Wheels good! Expensive stuff bad. Kids. What can I say?

We gathered up all the loot and put it in the sleeping bags thinking we were being quite like Ninjas, but I'm sure we were probably being more like noisy rats scratching away in the attic on a cold winter's night. But we made it out looking like two dwarfs stealing Santa's Christmas sacks. We headed north-east across the massive parking lot, keeping to the shadows the best we could, weaving our way among the fifty-foot lamp posts' light circles. If you think about it, two short people with giant bags over their shoulders trudging across a mall parking lot in the middle of the night would draw attention, I would suspect. But we made it to our goal, like determined climbers reaching the base camp on Everest; our camp though was the big ornamental bushes at edge of the parking lot the corner of 41st and Oak. Without missing a beat, we plunged headfirst into the pitch-black sanctuary, our sacks getting stuck behind us. It didn't take us long to get our new home set up, and once again we tried to settle into a good night's sleep. That didn't happen, as you may have suspected, so after a few hours of real or imagined spiders, bugs and bark mulch in our hair, faces and sleeping bags, we decided it was time for a swim. After all we were on vacation. Our lowbrow version of Club Med.

As the mall was about ten blocks from our old stomping grounds, the Projects, we knew from past reconnaissance of the alleyways in this affluent West Side neighbourhood that one of the larger apartment buildings nearby had a nice blue pool that was heated and needed some attention. So we headed in its direction, avoiding being seen by cars and buses as much as possible, which wasn't hard as it was like 3:30 a.m. and literally only a block away. Up the dark alley we went until we came upon the familiar turquoise brick wall surrounding our after-hours spa. Up we went, which was a bit tricky but team work makes the dream work, don't you know? So we were up and over in about five seconds. Steam was visible in the full moon's light; this was going to be awesome. No time to think about swimming trunks, we just did some good old-fashioned skinny-dipping; making plenty of noise with our cannonball jumps off the diving board, whooping and hollering until - you guessed it - someone yelled from above, "Hey, you kids get out of that pool! We called the cops."

The magic word…Cops! Our skinny white asses were out of there as fast as you could say white on rice, big daddy! Like smoke from a pipe, we had grabbed our stuff and scrambled over the wall, leaving only our wet footprints glowing in the moonlight. Off we ran into the cool summer night's air, back in a flash to our hedge-covered lair. We arrived, wet and shivering, like bugs to a flame; we were looking for heat but hadn't really thought about the drying-off part. No worries though, it was starting to get light so we would obviously get warm soon; but in the meantime we tried to catch some shut-eye, which was okay until the birds started chirping on the bushes, inches from our heads. They didn't seem to realize humans were napping in their living spaces, or didn't care. We cared and were up so I guess we weren't real woodsmen after all.

At around 6:30 a.m., cold, hungry, tired and no longer feeling we were Vikings or belonged in the legendary circle of the three "I's"…you know, the young man's plague, or from a military HR perspective "prime recruiting beef," inner-city males that feel they are Immune, Immortal, and Invincible. Anyway, we decided to head to the bus stop we had stood at some many times before and try and get home. They say there is no right or wrong, just good intentions, so my intentions were to have some fun and go home and face the consequences of my actions; but life has its own plans, as you know. We hadn't been standing at the deserted Sunday morning bus stop for more than five minutes when I noticed a burgundy car go past us. No big deal; it just happens to be one of my favourite colours, that's all.

What struck me as odd was when it came by for the third time, slowing a bit more as it did. Hmmm, I started thinking, it was odd as the sedan pulled up in front of us and this pot-bellied thirty-something-year-old guy with a greasy comb-over, sport coat and non-matching checkered shirt with the collar on the outside, exposing his turkey-like jowls and flushed red face confidently yells out to me, "Jake Hodgson! Are you Jake Hodgson? I was about five feet from the car, so this jolted me as I knew instinctively this was not right. "Get in the car right now!" He commanded, "I'm a policeman and your mom sent me to find you! She's worried sick."

Hmmm. Say what you want, but this was a plausible statement. No questions. Could be one of those undercover cops like on Mod Squad but a fat ugly version, I thought, but the thing was, my mom didn't know many guys that had cars. They were mostly bus people. Yet his tone was convincing, like a father figure; for those of you who grew up with one, that is, you may have fallen for it at that age and who knows what road that would have taken you on? Sure as shit wouldn't have been a trip down the coast to Disneyland; no, probably a shallow grave after being raped and tortured for a week or two. Even for Dale and me, who were street-smart for sure, this caught us off guard; plus being tired, cold and hungry didn't help as the prospect of a quick ride how seemed attractive. So I what did I do? I walked towards the car door obediently, as a good boy should, Dale hanging back for some reason, yet, I thought why not at least get close enough to look in the car, what could that hurt? Still a small voice in my rather empty head whispered don't question authority. You're in trouble and better just face the music now and get in the Fat Policeman's unmarked car. After all, he was an adult who knew my mom. Then by some miracle (of course not divine intervention, no way, life is just luck and happenstance, right? Just like the Universe or a garden that is not looked after, it only grows an abundance of beautiful flowers, fruits and vegetables to nourish your soul and body. Right? Not a never-ending attack of thorns and weeds. It just happens like the Big Bang theory. And here we are. Well, whatever helps you sleep on airplanes is your deal. I like to believe that it is far more than that luck). I digress. Just as I was contemplating opening the door and getting in the nice warm vehicle, visualizing being home and eating a warm bowl of oatmeal with a scoop of strawberry jam mixed in as fruit or maybe brown sugar and a few raisins, (after a beating, no doubt), then bam, as the legendary chef Emeril Lagasse would say, two things caught my attention: one, there was no police radio in this unmarked squad car, (no cell phones back then), and two, I happened to glance down at the dirty pavement after I broke eye contact with the pedophile hunter of lost boys, and I noticed on the inside of those black and red-trimmed rubber boots I hated wearing, almost as much as I hated soggy wet feet (I must admit rolling the rim down from my skinny white calves to my bony whiter ankles just made it easier to move my bulking 47 pounds of sheer intensity) was my name JAKE HODGSON in big, black letters, right side up to me, but upside down from a passerby's point of view. At that second I had a flash of brilliance that probably saved my life, that being, maybe it took this soul vampire three times to drive by to figure that out.

What did I do then, you ask? Well, I slowly walked to the window as his lips were still trying to spin his web of ice cream-flavoured lies, with the purpose of getting me in that car for his demented version of the ultimate joy ride, which I am certain included duct tape, a musky sock in my mouth and a bucketful of petroleum jelly to say the least. I took a deep breath as I faked a sheepish smile while reaching for the door handle; his eyes widening with excitement while an ever-so-slight grin escaped his chubby cheeks as he licked his lips, his anticipation bursting out like the drool from a salivating dog anticipating the sweet taste of fresh meat. At that second I managed to extract an Oscar-winning "greenie" spit ball, sucking it from the innermost cavities of my skull and (while smiling like Opie from Mayberry, RFD) let it fly, nailing the unsuspecting psycho in his crimson pock-marked face. To say he was surprised would be an understatement of Biblical proportions; his dreams of trying to satisfy that insatiable appetite dashed forever by a solid horker delivered by a street kid who should have been far too dumb to work out the situation, especially at seven in the morning.

Dale and I both turned and ran, laughing hysterically, dropping half the loot we had taken with us from our home in the bushes as we made our escape. The car screeched away, probably going to swing around and catch us on the other side of the mall parking lot, but not to be. I knew that trick, so we doubled back to the bus stop and just as we were thinking we were in the clear, up pulls, of all things a real cop car. I guess it must have looked a bit suspicious, a couple of kids running at full speed at 7 a.m.. Well, I imagine the psycho was either watching us from a distance or cruising by nonchalantly hoping we didn't say anything to the cops, as if they would have believed us anyway. The cops switched on their flashing lights and both got out of the black and white and simply asked us what we were doing (not buying the story of out for a walk) and proceeded to tell us they were going to give us a ride home. I of course said something like "thanks but the bus will be along soon," To which one of them replied that the bus didn't run for another couple of hours on Sunday mornings. It was 1972, after all, and I really don't think we had much choice in the matter. They talked into the radio while we sat in the back of the car. Our pockets and hands were still full of metallic coloured Hot Wheels and our other goodies.

I heard the crackling voice on the radio come back with "Two missing boys … you've got them? Are they Jake and Dale?" They asked us what our names were and I was thankfully not quick enough to lie. Not that they would let us go. It was only then it dawned on me that I was way up Shit Creek without a paddle or life jacket, those familiar butterflies all flying this way and that in my empty tummy. The car sped off to the East Side with us in the back looking like a couple of puppies in the back of the dog catcher's van heading to the pound. They dropped Dale off first.

"You wait in the car," the big fellow told me.

I think they were amused to a certain degree, or possibly relieved, because the truth be told many kids, far too many, don't make their way back home. From my encounters it is luck all right, as in opportunity, meeting one of the devil henchmen at work on the highways and side streets and alleys in search of the ultimate prize - an innocent soul. I'm sure the evil one hands out bonuses or extra poison rations for those deeds of sorrow.

The back door of the sweat-smelling squad car opened unceremoniously and Dale was ushered out, big hand on the back of his neck. A quick glance into his grey eyes told me he had his own share of lead butterflies. That was the last time I saw him.

It took them about ten minutes of discussion standing on the poorly-constructed, paint-chipped stairs of his rental house. His mom and what I assumed was her new boyfriend seemed to be arguing with the two young centurions, for what reason I had no clue. I mean it could have easily been as harsh as "Why did you bring him here?" even though the body language of the "man of the house" portrayed I am a take-charge kind of guy, damn it! This greatly-filtered long distant view of mine quickly became reality as I watched him unceremoniously grab my BFF by the ear and jerk his ass up and over the small step into their dumpy abode. The cops seemed startled by this, and even at my age I could tell they were disgusted by their encounter with his so-called guardians. They turned from the house and descended the stairs without any further comments to the rather puzzled-looking couple. Silence for the first few moments as we sped away from the uncomfortable scene. Then after they called in on the radio they began to analyze the situation that had just unfolded. Not their concern any more, but I somehow found it comforting that it seemed to bother them nonetheless. The forest green lamp posts flashed by as I stared out the side window contemplating my own fate.

As they searched the street numbers for my address I noticed the curtains move on the big front window. Someone must have called ahead. Oh shite! Panic setting making me go stiff like rigor mortis, my heart rate jumping to rabbit speeds, as I began to unload the pockets of my too-tight Wrangler jeans stuffed with Hot Wheels, change from the dozen cars we had broken into, and candy, and I stuffed what I could into the food-crusted crevices of the dirty blue plastic back seat of the cop car. I felt sick as the car slowed to a stop in front of my house and the boys slid out of the front seat of the cruiser and opened my door from the outside; as there are not handles in the back for those of you who have not had the privilege of being chauffeured by the taxpayers' pit bulls. I stalled for a beat or two before putting my still wet, no-name runners on the curb, sheepishly getting out, my eyes focused on the ground, not daring to make contact with the cops or whoever may be waiting at the top of our stairs. I was just about at the sidewalk when one of the boys in his dark blues said, "Hey kid, you forgot your stuff." I had a major butt pucker experience that probably made me constipated for a week.

"Oh yeah...umm, thanks...yeah, I forgot". I lied as my weak little mind scrambled to figure out how I was going to explain the toys, candy bars, and things, to my mom. There was slim-to-none chance she would believe "but I found the stuff'! The big cop scooped most of it into his huge paws, cupping it like water as we headed for the house.

Sometimes when I look back and think of it, it reminds me of Pinocchio who didn't heed the advice of his new father, Geppetto, who told him "Come straight home after school." He ended up on the Island for Bad Boys and I was definitely sailing in the direction. That island is just a metaphor for where the missing kids go. I have often thought that if I had one super power or magical gift it would be to find all the lost children. Corny, I know, but I've had that thought for decades.

"Is this your son?" the cops said to my mom, who was looking down at me with a combination of shock, disgust and relief.

"Yes," she said as she turned to me, her eyes burning a hole through the back of my head. "Where have you been? We've been worried sick!"

Before I could answer or spin a feeble lie, one of the cops spilled the beans and told her the scenario of where they'd picked us up. My mom for a change was speechless and had nothing to say but "thank you." I can't remember what happened after that, but it probably involved a smack or three, then off to my room. But I do recall a comforting thought that she (and my sisters, who had apparently been out checking garbage bins for me), seemed relieved that I was safe. Then again, I could have blocked out what really happened, I can't say for sure.

I was definitely grounded, of course.

"Poor man's golf: pitch &putt and driving range; Poor man's vacation: movies and the gym. Poor is always money related, as only money buys time" – JLH

Chapter 15

Flirting with Pyromania and Serving Up Some Payback

"When you need a moment of insight, make time to waste time." - JLH

A few weeks before summer holidays, the Mental Brothers got kicked out of school, so we ended up getting into separate schools, but breaking up the team was not going to go unanswered. So what to do? As it happened, one hot afternoon we were taking one of those long kid walks in the summer when the days lasted forever, and we ended up wandering near the school. At that moment, I had an epiphany. "Hey," I said, as we stopped across the street from the school, "I think we should burn down the school. What do you think?" As if we did any thinking at any time.

They said, "Hell, yeah!"

So off we went. scurrying up the side of one of the school buildings and onto the roof. I found a pile of garbage cans and lined them up near a drainpipe, which made the climbing easy. I went first of course; they were reluctant participants, I would say. Once on top, I yelled, "Let's go before someone sees us!" Point: we were on the corner of two busy roads and across the street from a few stores, so, yeah, we were seen.

While waiting for the bros to get up the drainpipe, I walked around on the loose gravel thinking about what I could do to get this baby burning. To my delight I saw a box full of old newspapers through a small window above the classroom door. Hmm, I wonder if I could get through that window. Only one way to find out. Without any real thought of getting hurt; (still the age of the three I's...Immune, Immortal and Invincible), I leapt to the small roof, which was about six feet lower than where I was standing and four feet away. After surveying the situation, I decided going in was not necessary for what I had in mind. So I just kicked in one of the white wood framed windows with my fake brown leather three-inch platform boots and dropped a lit wooden match onto the bone-dry paper.

At about that time, Eddy, the older of the bros popped his head over the ledge and innocently inquired, "What are you doing?"

I replied, "Burning down the school. You?"

He took a long drag on his Player's Navy Cut cigarette and said, "Just hangin' out, man."

About that time Shazam! Another perfectly conceived plan, I thought as the box burst into flames.

"Holy shit!" exclaimed Eddy.

As the blaze flowed across the walls of the school like spilled milk on the counter, that was our cue to get the hell off that roof as fast as we could and across the school yard. Cars were already starting to slow down as the black smoke billowed into the pale blue sky.

At about that second, realizing we were totally in the open and in the light of day, racing across the busy street away from the burning school, cars screeching to miss us, we just might get in trouble for this. Hello! Light bulb going on! All of a sudden I stopped running, putting my arms out to the sides, stopping the bros from bursting by me.

"Walk!" I shouted.

We were being total "heat bags." Better late than never as I always say. We then kind of sauntered for the next block, hearts racing like caged cats for the first time. Here is the key error in my so-called plan. I said

"Let's act normal and go into the Chinese store," which was across from the school; perfect line of sight I was to find out later. We walked into the store, bought one can of White Rock Soda (cheapest brand at the time) and a small bag of chips, all the while glancing at our ever-growing masterpiece. The wrinkly tanned store owner and his wife also kept looking at the now-bright-yellow-and-red flames jumping to the sky and then at us, then at the flames, then us and excitedly said things in Cantonese that I could not understand. Well, not literally, but body language said it all. They saw us coming off that roof.

That's when I said to the boys, "Let's blow this popsicle stand."

A day later and a dollar short as the saying goes, since the son of the owners just happened to go the school, of course, and he, of course, recognized us.

As we headed to the door, the black-haired Hong Kong Bruce Lee wannabe squeaked out something to his parents in Chinese.

The dad blurted out in Chinglish, "Why you do dat? You bad guys!"

I turned and gave him my best tough kid smile but inside I thought, we are screwed.

By the time we left the jam-packed little store, the smoke was really billowing high into the sky; cars were pulling over to watch my handiwork but I thought it best to exit stage left. We did the old walk-slowly-until-around-the-corner routine, then bolted down the side street as fast as we could, laughing, swearing and high-fiving all the way. With the sound of distant fire engines rolling through the hot summer air, we headed to my house, which was about eight blocks away. But like most budding pyros we had to see our the results of our efforts (the reason that cops take photos of the crowds during fires or riots; the culprits often try to blend in with the gawkers, excited and proud as they behold their works of art; and the new world of facial recognition software, I imagine, makes their work that much more effective). Look at those flames, I thought, as we walked quickly, catching glimpses of those beautiful yellowy-orange spires between the suburban houses with their neatly trimmed lawns, leaping like basketball players into the warm summer sky. "Wow!" I said aloud. "This is cool," while secretly feeling this was way bigger than I expected and would undoubtedly have some kind of payback. I really didn't want it to get out of hand but, in for a penny, in for a pound, and there's no taking back the sound of a ringing bell.

I had to get a better view.

"Guys, follow me!" I said to the brothers as I saw a ladder in an open garage.

In a flash we three caballeros grabbed the long cool aluminum ladder, that turned out to be surprisingly heavy. With some trouble we got it leaning against a house, which of course we never considered may just have occupants at home - details, details. It took two of us to pull the rope, slowly moving the upper part of the extendable ladder towards the white-painted rain gutter. This took a surprisingly amount of coordination; for those who have not done this, you need to pull the rope while simultaneously pulling the heavy ladder away from the cedar siding. Now the tricky part comes as you get to the overhang of the roof. This takes a pull, plus a big push away from the house; sounds easy, but when the ladder is 20 feet high and weighs more than you and your pal, it gets dicey. Pushing too far from the house can send the potentially body-crunching metal frame crashing backwards to the ground. So one more big pull while making all kinds of noise and a strategic push away from the house and "Voila!" we had our access to the penthouse.

The view was spectacular. The flames were clearly visible, and so were the firefighters in full gear, swinging axes to release more of the trapped flames, which were more than happy to be free. The sweet smell of burning cedar floated on the air and reached our little noses five blocks away. More and more people could be seen gathering on the street below the school, the yellow coats of the firefighters darting in and out of the burning building. We hung onto the crest of the steep roof, mesmerized by our masterpiece and the amount of action it had created, occasionally glancing at each other and grinning like Cheshire cats. We watched them battle, kid-made warlike mini-generals moving the troops from afar. It was twisted but somehow empowering for us who had no power. I can see how things like this could be addictive because they impact the world immediately, feeding the human condition and the thirst to be known as an individual or better yet a celebrity; after all, deep down inside we instinctively know we all should be celebs driving Bentleys. Yes!

Anyway, it ended when the roof caved in, leaving only the walls of the building standing. We kept watching for a while but soon got bored and slow-slithered our way down the steep pitch of the black shingled roof sticky hot from the summer sun. We were uncharacteristically quiet when we left the yard, fading into the unpaved alley of the East Side. A sinking feeling began jabbing the walls of my stomach like bad seafood as I made my way down the bank of the abandoned railway track. I knew we were definitely up Shit Creek with neither paddle nor life jacket.

I went around to the back of our house thinking this would make a difference, then up to the back porch. The door was unlocked as my mom was home and one of my sisters. She was in the kitchen doing dishes and said something like, "You're home early," since I was usually gone from sunup to sundown in the summer. I replied, "Yeah, I'm not feeling good" and slowly walked to my little room. Sitting on the side of my bed surrounded by a half a dozen felt embossed black light posters stolen from the store in Gastown, it occurred to me that the Chinese store kid could have known us. My heart rate probably jumped about twenty beats per minute at the thought of that. This began a back-and-forth walk to the big front room window, peeking through the curtains, expecting the worst. It took about an hour before I saw the black and white cop car slowly cruising down my street. I could have choked on my heart as it leapt up my throat. I was instantly praying God, don't let them stop…God, keep them going…God, I will be a good boy, I promise, just let me off this time. To my relief, the squad car ever-so-slowly floated by my house, the two cops inside looking left and right. I thought for sure the driver could see me through the crack in the curtain, so I dropped to the floor almost pulling the curtain rod off the wall. I lay there for what seemed like an hour but it was more like ten seconds until I thought I should take a look and also spotted my mom glancing at me from the kitchen door. I pretended to be playing around and hiding in the curtains. She returned to her work and I peeked up over the white window sill expecting to see the back end of the cop car disappearing around the corner. But it was not to be. To my horror the cops were talking to a few of the kids on the block; I could not hear what they were saying but I could see the fat kid, Kenny, nodding his head up and down then pointing directly at my house. Bam! I was busted.

From there on in it was one of those so called out-of-body experiences as I saw the giant black- suited cops get out of the car. The kids stepping back, now all pointing at my abode, me still staring wide-eyed in disbelief through the curtain. Then in my pea-sized brain I thought I had caught a break because it looked like my giving treats to the fat kid's German Shepherd that was named Sailor could pay off as he started barking and showing his rotting teeth to the two cops. But no, Kenny scolded him and he obediently lay back down on the pavement. Wimp! He must have given him more snacks than I did. A split second after that I saw Kenny's fat right arm and one of his pudgy fingers pointing at my house. Crap! I was in it deep.

Looking back, I wonder how I ever made it past puberty with no male parental guidance and only sporadic direction from my mom, although she did try her best. Compound that with my intellect, the equivalent to a soap dish, and some inherent ability to be some kind of a shit-magnet.

As it turned out the Chinese store kid did know me and had his parents call the police about five minutes after we left. Well, I can say one thing: I never spent a dime at that store again, that's for damn sure.

It took all of about sixty seconds for the cops to park and start banging on our screen door. By this time, I was in my bedroom pretending to play my big fire yellow and red electric bass guitar, (I saved the $25 to buy it by many means, not all legal, from a pawn shop in Gastown, it took me about another six months to get a small amplifier—that's when I realized it didn't work). I was enjoying the calm before the storm as it were. I could hear my mom walk to the hollow white door of my bedroom, pause for a second as some muffled conversation initiated between her and what I supposed was the cops. A last-minute call from the Governor for a kid feeling like he was on death row perhaps? But no, the door burst open with my mom's bright blue eyes flashing like fire in the dim light of my Robin's egg blue ten-by-ten north-facing bedroom.

"Jake!" she yelled, "What did you do?"

I instantly rolled in to my most innocent and incredulous look, like what are you saying...I am the baby of the family just sitting here trying to teach myself the opening theme song to my favourite police TV show "Barney Miller"? But that ship had sailed a long time ago.

My mom had sucked up a lot of my wayward behaviour, and she was gagging on it about now. Not missing a beat, I, of course, pushed it like any wild animal does when it comes to some form of survival instinct. I must admit she hesitated, thinking something like "No, not my son…he would never burn down a school." Well, that bubble burst as she snapped out of her momentary lapse of reason.

Then with the speed of a mamma grizzly attacking an unsuspecting hiker who unwittingly got between her and her cub, she jerked me to my feet by my thick curly locks, my pride and joy bass sliding off my spindly knees hitting the wood floor with a solid thud.

I was airborne for a split second and then came unceremoniously sliding across the one-inch forest green pile shag carpet, scrambling to keep my so called cool as I rolled up into the corner of our blue crushed velour couch. That was a shock, but not as much as looking up and being face to face with two angry-looking public servants who carried guns. There was a moment of uncomfortable silence, as to be expected while my mom and the cops just glared at me. Then one of what we then called pigs, spoke.

"We have a witness that says you and your two friends set the school on fire about two hours ago. It will be best for you if you just admit it and tell us what happened."

Still in shock, I, of course, started lying as fast (Mom always said "Jake, you lie like a sidewalk.") as I could, coming up with stories of not being near the school, being by myself, whatever. But lies are like webs and you got to keep track of all those friggin' thin threads. And I was not that smart and must admit, I have the utmost respect for spiders. Well, as I was like ten or eleven years old, it's not surprising I slipped up on a few of the small details which, of course, turned into bigger and bigger gaps in my story, and at some point I could no longer defend anything as the noose of my lies was strangling me. The inevitable conclusion to this was simple: I caved in to the sheer weight of my unsubstantiated bullshit, and before you could say "Bob's your uncle" (all of about three minutes I would reckon), I was sobbing like a baby and confessing my sins.

"Yes I set the fire! They deserved it…they bullied me every day because I was the new kid."

I told them that this grade seven kid kicked me on my burn for trying to defend another kid who was being picked on. I almost got my ear ripped off by the PE teacher as he dragged me to the principal's office. I told them the truth but the principal didn't care … they gave me the strap as blood from my salad-plate-sized, pizza-looking, gangrene-smelling burn rolled down my right leg and soaked into my clean but threadbare socks.

"I told my mom!" I exclaimed. "She knows about that. I'm not lying" I sobbed as I stared into my mom's eyes, not wanting to look at the police for fear they would not believe me.

Well, that didn't work as they coldly said, "We don't care about that. That's not why we're here."

About this time, I started to see red as I realized I was done and there was no putting the smoke back into the camp fire. Once again this was one of those moments when you look back and say "Yeah, I was part of the lucky sperm club" because at that age I was what they called below the age of reasoning in North America. If I happened to be caught doing this in, say, India or China? Well, you can guess how that would have turned out.

Fact be known, I truly hated that school and I saw black when I thought about it. I didn't feel an ounce of remorse over trying to burn it to the ground. I would have roasted marshmallows, made s'mores and invited my friends and family if I could have. My only regret was getting caught. And as I was only in grade five, I rightly thought there was little chance of getting arrested and dragged in front of my peers by my curly dark brown hair down the chipped battleship-grey steps out on to the matching pavement and into the back of the every idling ready-for-action black-and-white. I must admit I did suspect the two Young Turks would have loved to given me a few slaps for my lack of instant remorse and, failing that, possibly a few shots to the head with their nicely polished teak billy clubs. And of course, if I had been somewhere in South America for instance, they may have been secretly hoping I'd make a grab for one of their cool blue black .38s snapped snugly in their shiny black leather holsters. Of course at 47 pounds soaking wet I probably couldn't even hold it with two hands; no immediate threat there.

Instead, I got the civilized version of a beating, a stern talking-to. Don't get me wrong, the two cops took turns yelling and standing up, then pacing across the shag carpet and making sure they could be clearly seen by the twenty-some kids and neighbours clustered around the cop car in front of our house. Not sure, but I think at times my mom was a bit scared by them as they stooped down to drive key points of the lecture home, inches from my pale white summer-freckled face. As all things do, this too came to an end and they reluctantly headed for the door saying things like "this is only the beginning ... we will be back ... you are in deep, son" and so on.

As the door closed I had a split second of reprieve before it got real ugly. No sooner had that door lock clicked off, when my mom's shoe came off and she leaped at me like a puma lunging for an unsuspecting hiker. I gotta admit I was fast, but not that fast, my vision of escaping out the back door or better yet grabbing the ever-comforting, warm and friendly Hudson's Bay blanket off the couch, wrapping it around me and diving through the five-foot-square window to the left of the door. Makes sense as it would save time; cutting an artery never crossed my gnat-sized brain (Child Soldier), those plans evaporated as fast as they materialized as my rather spry mom caught me by those same said curly locks and basically body-slammed me into that thankfully cushy shag rug. You know, it's no wonder me and most MMA fighters are bald. The long hair or stud looking pony tail dudes look good for the women but get their asses kicked in the ring, and they wouldn't have done too well on the carpet with my mom that day either. Well fortunately for me she was skinny but had poor cardio, so after about ninety seconds of beating me she was done and gasping for a cigarette. I was not so tough after all, and welts were everywhere I couldn't cover and what I covered got more welts. I was crying like the child I was. 'Spare the Rod, Spoil the Child' the Bible says. This I can say with confidence; if I had been disciplined by a male I would have gotten the message a lot sooner.

This brings me to a true story from an African animal reserve that had some young elephants creating havoc with the game wardens and the tourists. The fact that even young elephants are rather large means scolding them is generally not a good idea long-term. This, of course, is a problem compounded when they are wild elephants not accustomed to being told where and where not to go. The solution was rather old school. Someone decided what was needed was to bringing in the male bull elephant. The young studs immediately stopped their aggressive behaviour and that was the end of it.

This tale is not meant to take anything away from the single moms, like the one that raised me, and who probably are raising half the world's future leaders, but the male impact on the family unit is not just that of fiction. It is the difference-maker when applied properly. Like a canoe, if you're only rowing on one side, the boat eventually will go in circles, regardless of the current.

> "When trust goes down, speed goes down and costs go up". This is equally true in your personal life as it is in your corporate one. - Stephen M Covey & JLH

Chapter 16

Double Bounced

The next school I attended was Norquay Elementary. I'm certain they wouldn't have let me in if they had first found out about the other school; they did receive my records not too long after, but it was too late by then for the principal to do much. It was the law that I could attend any school in my so-called catchment district, but that didn't stop him from requesting a parent-teacher conference three weeks after the new school year began in September. As we walked the ten blocks to the school on that crisp autumn morning, I couldn't help but wonder what the reason was for the meeting. For crying out loud, I had just started there and hadn't even gotten into a fight with a kid or teacher as of yet. Well, my day started off pretty much as usual, some puffed wheat with powdered milk, (that's powdered milk mixed with water in a jug), a piece of white toast (Wonder Bread of course!) and a bit of strawberry jam. My mom and sisters were all busy fighting over the one bathroom, so they paid little attention to me, and my brother was either sleeping in his room in the basement, not at home, or in jail. So I was left to my thoughts, which generally didn't go beyond what was on TV that night. Then, out of nowhere, my mom walked into the yellow-painted kitchen wearing her red woolen coat, which was clean but out of date, her slightly tattered handbag over her arm. I instantly knew by her posture, the flash of her eyes and her tone of voice that she was stressed. Still I'm thinking, What? Why is she so pissed? Well, the answer is obvious now, but at the time I couldn't figure it out, but I should have clued into at least the fact that she had to either miss or go in late to work at her chambermaid job at that motel about three miles away. But no, I was just upset at the injustice of it all.

So I guess me and the school were both screwed from the get-go. Anyway, Norquay was just a few blocks further than the other, but in a different direction and with several hundred more kids. That fact was compounded by the building itself, made of queen-sized red bricks and shiny white framed big wooden windows, casting a majestic shadow over the pre-World War Two house from its perch on a small hill.

The Norquay School experiment too did not last long, as soon as the usual new-school kid grace period, of about two to three weeks, wore off. Then there were the questions like, "Is it true you burnt down your last school"? And, "I heard your brother went here but was kicked out for punching a teacher." I must admit having some questions asked is in itself cool as you feel kind of special because your so-called peers are interested in who you are and where you came from. That is not the case for most who ask the questions I confess; they just want info so they can use it as currency and barter against you to improve their own status. It is that simple and one of those universal truths based on, amongst other things, the need to propagate the species. I get that this notion does not appear to fit well with the technology era, but it is true nonetheless and based on science. The common term (a and current media focus prompted by several high-profile suicides and murders), is nothing more than bullying. And I for one can say it won't be stopping any time soon. It will take some years of evolution yet that can possibly be shortened by a phantom second, but in all reality evolution does not easily succumb to the media, or what I like to call medialution (as in, just because you run some news on a subject for a day, week or month, it really has minimal impact on genetics. For those of you who feel different, I would suggest you do your homework.) Saying it's not right has limited impact in the short term. Think of it this way: if you deny gravity exists and jump off a building, that does not change the impact. Point: I've been telling my dog almost every day to stop dropping in the middle of the kitchen and licking his genitalia. I get that he needs to be really clean or, more likely, he just likes it, but guess what? He still does it and is shocked every time I call him on it. Yes, I get the fact that his intellect is that of a young child but after nine years I'm thinking along the lines of DNA blueprinting.

Moving on: my next educational stop was Carlton Elementary. One of the cool things about this school was the trampolines they had in the stand-alone building that housed the nicely lacquered cedar floor gymnasium. This was rolling into my last year in elementary school, called grade seven. So of course I was the new kid at the school but was also now one of the big fish in the small pond. About once per week we had a chance to jump on the trampolines, but for the most part their orange rubber skins, pulled tight by that baby blue steel frame, just taunted us, or me anyway. So eventually I had to take things into my own hands because once a week wasn't enough to quench my thirst to bounce. So what's a poor boy to do with all that pent-up energy and desire? (I had a medical condition for sure, one of the Ds or simply a case of too much sugar no doubt) Well, how about skipping out of class early and slipping into the big gymnasium one Friday afternoon of a long weekend? That could work. Yes! I stood motionless behind one of the thick folded teenty-five-foot crimson red Afghani cotton stage curtains for ninety minutes as the school cleared and janitor did his quick mopping of the badly scratched wooden floor. By the time I heard the sound of the big steel doors and clacking of the lock protecting the trampolines, curtains and stacks of cheap wooden chairs like they were precious pieces of art, I was sweating like a baby pig heading for the butchers. I cautiously peered out from the musty-smelling drapes into the cavernous pitch-black room. No sound and no sight. I could actually not see my own hand in front of my pale freckled face. As I listened for the old Asian cleaning guy, who was probably onto my scheme and at that very second was possibly crouching, like some toothless tiger with one more kill in his heart or a rogue Ninja blanketed in the convenient veil of darkness, waiting for his chance to get me with a throwing star or poison dart. But no, it was just me scared shitless of the dark with my heart beating so loud I wouldn't have heard a rabid pit bull barreling towards me dragging its dog house and ten-foot stainless steel chain behind it, salivating at the thought of ripping out my tender white throat with a single bite of its vice-grip- like jaws. I guess it goes without saying my plan was slightly ill-conceived and never included him shutting off the big hanging lights in the windowless brick building, which was really more like a bunker than a gym for children to frolic carefree in the afternoon sun. I moved ever so slowly with an immediate appreciation for Helen Keller as I brailed my way to where I envisioned the door was, ever aware of the fact I was perched on a five-foot stage. I felt my way to the stairs stage left in about five minutes and then slid along the wall. By this time my eyes had begun to adjust to what was not as dark as I originally thought. Finally feeling the cool brass of the panic bar on the exit door, I knew I was free and pushed it open. The sun burst in, splitting the dark into a million little pieces, and I was blind for a second as my two partners in crime (and about a dozen other girls and boys who had caught wind of the plan), stormed through the opening. All was as it should be for early adolescents looking for some innocent fun at what was tantamount to getting free tickets to the circus with unlimited rides and cotton candy. We all had a great time basically doing nothing except jumping for hours, laughing most of the time on the giant orange twelve-by-twelve polypropylene trampoline.

All and all it was a safe thing to do, regardless of the no-adult-supervision aspect, but as fate would have it, all good things seem to come to an end. One of the boys who I didn't know got what is called "double bounced." What this means to trampolining is what a supercharger means to a car: instant power. This kid was ejected not straight up, as is the so-called plan (people do this on purpose and one of my pals thought it was good timing), but no, he shot up and off like a rocket fifteen feet into the hot gym air, landing on his back and producing a loud smack as his hurtling body hit a few rows of the stacked wooden and steel lacquered chairs. You could have heard a mouse fart from two blocks away as he travelled in what looked like slow motion to all that were there. We even held our breath for a split second but then broke out in hysterical laughter, so hard that three of us actually collapsed and rolled on the floor, tears bubbling down our skinning cheeks with smiles so large they could crack a pair of glasses. Living in the moment with zero loyalty or concern for those outside our circle of trust, we gave no thought to the possibility that he might have broken his back or neck or, worse, that he was dead. He didn't move for a few twilight zone moments, but then he began to talk, mumbling some almost inaudible gibberish to the effect of, "What happened?" Because we were still laughing, we did not reply; the memory of his face as he went soaring skyward was clouding our vision. and I kept thinking That just happened. You couldn't have made that up in a million years. Fortunately for his sake, not all the kids were as detached as me and the bros were, and a couple of the girls scurried off the trampoline to help him off the chairs. His fun was over for the night and probably for the entire long weekend by the looks of it. Such is the fate of a daring young navigator in the Sandwich Islands, but not us. We were just getting warmed up and in our prime, and we quickly forgot about him and the others that left with him before the steel doors hit their asses; collateral damage, isn't that what they call it? No big deal, just a flesh wound or as my late brother .W.A.W. would say, Score Me A Tear, as by this time I had already been stabbed, bitten by German Shepherds and Dobermans, arrested many times and had third-degree burns as badges of honour, so he wasn't going to get much sympathy from me.

It got a bit late and the others, all of whom were Norman-Rockwell-type two-parent kids (with the mom probably staying at home all day to take care of the house chores, feed the kids and do all that other stuff women used to be able to do when North American men could actually produce enough money to support that type of lifestyle) had to leave for a sit-down family dinner. That was all fiction for me and my kind. The Mental Brothers stayed for a while longer, as I did, then they left heading to their so-called homes (I guess home was where they lay their heads) to get some food and sleep. I watched them go, but stayed for a bit longer, surveying my accomplishment. But I, too, needed to go home so I rolled off the big orange fun pad and onto the shiny wooden stage, my three-inch-soled zip-up dark purple leather platform boots making a solid clump as they hit. As my plan was to make this party central and to barter anything for people who may want to come in, I carefully slipped a folded match book cover between the latch and door so to the casual observer it looked like it was locked. The eight-block walk home was good to cool off, yet I did wonder what non-Norman-Rockwell event would unfold when I got there. Doing the so-called homework was always a crap shoot, never knowing where the dice would land. That was the story for all of my school years and I for one have the utmost respect for any kids who make something of themselves (not just as a celebrity or an athlete) when they are competing with peers who have a distinct advantage - at least in the early years that is. Those kids who make it out of the gravitational pull of their marginalized predetermined low expectations of any worthwhile future have a major advantage in the later years. Unlike the others, these kids have had to sing for their supper and are always hungry.

The next day was Saturday. I did my usual ritual of getting up at about 7:30 to prepare for the 8 a.m. start of Saturday morning cartoons. This included, but was not restricted to, turning up the forced-air heating, then positioning myself over the vent in the front room with an old baby blue velour type robe of my mom's, creating a bubble-like enclave of warmth, with of course my big black and white cat, Miss Kitty, tucked securely under my wing. This lasted about ten minutes, as the heat kicked in fast and the cat didn't really like being squished. The next procedure was putting the TV on the right channel for the first of my shows. In general, the rest of the family was sound asleep, but on occasion there would be some leftover friends of my brother's passed out on the couch. This was not good. I had a routine and, in retrospect, I was (or still am), suffering from some form of compulsive disorder. How bad could it get? Well, one morning my bro had two buddies passed out, one on the big couch, the other on my favourite chair, an heirloom, so to speak, handed down from my mom's parents. It was a big faded burgundy-coloured corduroy high back chair, what today people would call a chair and a half. That I could actually deal with as I made my standard Saturday morning fare of PB&J toast with a nice big bowl of puffed wheat drenched in expertly-balanced powdered milk. The challenge was the pale red-headed kid in jeans, black t-shirt and Wallabees passed out in my big chair, no doubt suffering from a wicked hangover or still bumping along high from sniffing a plastic baggy squirted with model-making glue or a nail-polish remover called Polly. If he had been high on weed or heroin, he would probably not have woken up, and if he did he would not have been so friggin' angry. It was clear from the first syllables out of his rotten-toothed foul-smelling mouth that he did not appreciate, had forgotten (like the story of Peter Pan), or had never experienced the euphoria for a kid of the Saturday morning ritual known across North America as, Saturday Morning Cartoons. The punk sat straight up and yelled, "'What the fuck is goin' on?" to the sound of Rocket Robin Hood's opening theme song, which had startled him from some non-obtainable dream of riches, bitches and fame.

I guess he thought he was at home, so the unfamiliar surroundings added to his stress and confusion, transforming him from Sleeping Ugly to The Incredible Hulk in a split second. It took about another second for the dude on the couch to wake up and two seconds later for my bother to come bolting up the basement stairs from his lair, apparently concerned for the safety of his family. In hindsight, this was refreshing; he was a rogue pit bull at the best of times. As for me, sitting in my pajamas with my toast and cereal, blue robe wrapped around me for warmth and protection, I was shocked at first, but seeing my brother's face in the hallway door frame gave me a boost of super kid power. I knew that as much of a screw-up he was a dog that does not shit in its own bed, he would still protect me if push came to shove. So as my bro's buddy edged toward me, yelling obscenities and feeling confident enough to plant his skinny butt in one of the forest green crushed velvet love seats near the fireplace about three feet behind me, I calmly slid back from my breakfast of champions, making sure not to spill my cereal or cup of Earl Grey tea. I stood up to my full height of four-foot-two and looked directly into his bloodshot eyes. His mouth was still flapping, but I could not hear what he was saying, and with a slightly demonic grin forming on my cute little freckled face, I robotically turned to my left and picked up a Presto fire log, stood about a two feet in front of him holding the five-inch by 18-inch compressed wood-chip log in both hands, and studied him for a second, realizing he had no idea what was about to happen.

He was still chirping at me while my brother and his other buddy watched with mild amusement through bloodshot eyes. "What are you going to do with that you little puke?" he smirked.

No sooner had the words left his mouth than I let the sturdy three-pound cylindrical projectile fly, hitting him square on the bridge of his sizeable nose. Smack! The log broke in half on impact, the event somehow unfolding in slow motion before my baby-blue eyes. As expected, this shut him up, but the stillness lasted only a few seconds while I bathed in the glory of my handiwork. Then, once he caught his breath, out came a banshee-like scream, ripping a hole in the tranquility of my Saturday morning routine.

My brother and his pal (great case study for the saying: with friends like this who needs enemies?) immediately broke out in hysterical laughter, both rolling to the carpet. This coincided with my mom and three sisters all bursting into the dimly-lit front room, a brilliant sliver of golden sun revealing the bedlam of the situation: all three teenagers on the carpet, two laughing and one not so much. And me standing there in my Mighty Mouse pajamas, looking as innocent as Opie from Mayberry RFD. I had broken the kid's nose, which was now spewing blood down his dirty black t-shirt, face cupped in his hands while he screamed like a scalded baby. It didn't take much time before the red stuff made its great escape from the fleshy human prison it called home, squeezing its way through tightly-clenched fingers as gravity pulled it to a new home called un-vacuumed shag rug. My mom came rushing to the aid of mouthy boy, tea towel in hand to catch the blood. So much for Saturday morning cartoons. No remorse, only contempt, for the cartoon stealer. Like an unrented hotel room, this morning's cartoons could never be replaced. So of course he deserved to have his nose broken. My mom, on the other hand, was not so calm.

She yelled at me, "Jake! What did you do?"

I, of course, said in my baby voice, "Nothing, mommy. He tried to punch me, so I threw the log thing at him."

My victim immediately started yelling between his sobs of pain, "You effin liar, I never did anything. I'm going to kill you!"

My mom kneeling in her pink flannel night gown looked up at me, and I could tell she believed him over me. But there was no proof, and my brother and his pal were still laughing, not giving a shit what happened to this guy. My three sisters were just standing there in disbelief at the ongoing crap me and my brother brought to the house. They didn't stay long once there was no real emergency as they saw it, but that didn't stop them from making comments such as "You little bastard," or "You little prick. You'll pay for this." I just looked at them with my best version of what I like to call the big-eyed-kitten look, all the while wondering if my cereal was soggy and my tea was still hot and if I could possibly catch the last half of Land Before Time. Great show about a family whose rubber raft goes over a huge waterfall and they land in the time of the dinosaurs   Could happen. Don't kid yourself. Well, as you might have guessed, I didn't get to have my breakfast or watch cartoons, as my mom was really pissed at me for some reason. In my mind that was totally unreasonable - just because the entire household got woken up to a nightmare of my making. Totally unfair I thought. That guy deserved it and anyway, who was he? No one I had ever seen before and certainly not a close friend of my brother's. So what was the big deal? I was sent me to my room as I pleaded, "Can I at least take my breakfast with me?"

The answer was a resounding, "Get to your room before I pull out the wooden spoon!"

That got me moving as my boney backside had broken enough of them and I had many a time prayed for all wood to die off on the planet. Then again, she would have just used the extension cord, slipper or clog as she had in the past. There was just no getting away from her administering one of Newton's most popular laws, every action has an equal but opposite reaction. Back-talking just had no return on investment from what I could work out; my older siblings had ruined that for me long ago. And at this stage of her life there was no way my mom was going to let her youngest offspring get mouthy without some quick consequences.

Off to my room I went, hoping that didn't last too long as me and the boys had a full day of hanging out at the gym to look forward to, and, if we were lucky, some girls might come by for some jumping fun as well. I got back into bed and soon fell back to sleep, and the house soon went quiet after my brother and his pals left and my sisters and mom returned to their rooms, trying to forget about what had happened. It took me until around one in the afternoon to convince my mom to let me go out and play, but eventually she relented and I was off like a shot heading back to the school for some exercise, but not before meeting up with the boys and swinging by the Chinese store to steal some candy and a pop or three. With our pockets full, we cruised up to the school auditorium and the big metal doors. As planned, it was not locked and in we went. We bounced and wrestled and basically had some harmless fun for a change, after all we were only around twelve years old, so playing around was just about as good as it got. Some other kids showed up after a couple of hours, and lo and behold it included two of the prettier girls from the school. We were rock stars for a short time, everyone having a good time, coming and going as they pleased. One of the girls even went to the local hangout called Substop and brought subs, chips and pop. Living large, and the party was never going to end. Well, I guess some of the neighbours who weren't invited got a bit suspicious about the comings and goings from the side door of the school gym. I guess I wasn't living up to my self-proclaimed reputation of being of spy-calibre.

At about 3:00 p.m., me and the two brothers decided to call it quits; the other kids had left hours ago so, no big deal, we would just come back the next day. As I pushed the cool-feeling heavy steel bar that opened the gym doors, sunlight temporarily blinding me on that crisp Canadian afternoon, I heard a dog bark and a deep voice say, "Here they are.". It was the pigs with one of their famous pig hounds, a nasty German Shepherd. Well, as the last syllable fell to the cold hard cement, the Mental Brothers melted back inside the gym, the big metal door slamming behind them, leaving me to my own devices. I was caught like a deer in the headlights of an unemployed Prince George hunter. In other words, I was DOA by my own design and once again the slippery bros eluded the noose.

In a flash they were out the other side of the building and across the gravel field before the words "There's two more back inside!" fell from the cop's donut-crusted lips. The leaves were orange and yellow as fall had begun to take its grip in the Northern Hemisphere, a mild wind tossed the fallen leaves around playfully. In a perfect world I would have been feeling exhilarated after a long day of honest play. But it was not to be; that bubble of imagination was popped after a few paces out that fun house door and the savage barking of a German Shepherd lunging at me as if I was a murderer, not a kid who stayed behind in the gym so he could jump on the trampoline. I guess that circles back to my current understanding of how lucky I was to be born poor in a rich country based on Christian values. Contrast that to a poor country running its system on non-Christian values; you connect the dots.

At that moment in my brief history of screwing up it didn't really matter. I was the first one out that door and that was that. You would think I'd know better hanging out with the Mental Brothers; we had a history and, as fun as they were, they just didn't watch my six as they say; they watched their own, which is what brothers should do, so no bad feelings.

Before you could say my oldest daughters coined phrase 'Son of a Monkey Spank' one of the Young Turks grabbed hold of me by my GWG jean jacket, saying something like, "Where do you think you're going?" I blurted out some crap about the door being open and we were just jumping on the trampoline. True as it was, he still escorted me briskly to the back seat of his cop car. Even though I was 12 years old, it was already a too familiar scene; blue plastic bench seat, no carpet, the smell of puke, urine and Lysol mixing together like some troll's aftershave; scratched Plexiglas partition between the back and front, and of course no door or window handles. Yeah, I was FUBAR kid-style. Well, after about twenty minutes waiting in the back of the car, the two police officers came to the car with one opening the door. All a big mistake, I was hoping they would say…you can go, son. Our apologies didn't happen. Instead they said, "Tell us the names of your friends who got away." I suppose if they offered to just let me go for ratting them out I might have given it a second thought, but they didn't. Instead they did the hard-ass cop routine which, to be honest, scared me, but that was about it.

After asking for my address, they drove me home. When we pulled up to the house, there was a slight glitch in the plan; instead of letting me out, they told me to stay in the car and they would be right back. That shook me, as it was different than other times I'd had cop chauffeurs drive me home. I had a butt pucker moment for sure.

I watched from the back seat as the two cops walked up the path to our two-story grey stucco house, one of them talking into his walkie-talkie; probably using the remainder of their brain power to work out the logistics of where the next donut break should be, I thought jokingly. My smile dropped to the sticky floor of the cop car when the dull aluminum screen door swung open and my mother, the warden, stepped onto the small cement porch wearing a bright flowered patterned dress from Woodward's, a look of bewilderment on her face, her eyes burning a hole through my empty skull. I was definitely in Shit City without a "Get Out of Jail Free" card, that was for sure. I'm still no lip reader but I can read body language, which is proven to be something like sixty percent of communication among humans. They talked to my mom for about fifteen minutes. Then, finally, they started walking back to the car; I was wondering what my mom was going to do as she watched me from top of the stairs. How bad could it be I thought? I was only jumping a friggin' trampoline…no harm no foul, right? As the boys approached the car, something really odd happened; they didn't open the door and let me out. Instead they got back in the car and started the engine. My heart began racing. Then the unimaginable: my mom turned on the heels of her pink fuzzy slippers and disappeared into the house, the sound of the hollow wooden front door slamming behind her. WTF? I began to panic "What the hell is going on?" I yelled in my best big boy voice, which probably sounded like a ten-year-old girl whining about her missing Barbie.

Without any emotion the robots replied, "You're going to be taking another ride with us. Your mom doesn't want you, so we're taking you to the Juvenile Detention hall."

"Why?" I whined as I my emotions went into overdrive, crocodile tears bursting from my eyes like someone turned on a faucet. "I was only jumping on the trampolines. I didn't break anything or steal anything, I promise. Just let me go home." This was as sincere as I had ever been.

"Not going to happen, kid", said the cop driving. "What you did do is what's called a B&E or breaking and entering. That's against the law. Normally we would not be doing this, but since your mom said you can't come home, we have no choice but to take you to Juvie."

That option hadn't occurred to me. I had heard of it, of course; it was basically kid jail. About that time there was a huge lump in my throat, my heart was racing like a cut cat, my mind flooded instantly with images of what Juvie would be, based on the many stories my brother, who had been there many times, had told me. I felt sick and subconsciously reached for the nonexistent back-seat-of-a-cop-car door handle. The drive from then on was dead silent and seemed like a dream that went on forever, like falling and never hitting the bottom; that was until we turned into a park-like setting with this incredible view of the bluish green North Shore mountains, rising majestically out of the inlet. It would have made for a great photo to send someone with a caption like, "Hey, wish you were here," but this was no resort I was going to, that was for sure. This was more like checking into Motel Hell with Freddy Krueger as the manager. It was one of those classic "You're not in Kansas anymore, Jake" moments. I was sick to my stomach, scared shitless, and filled with dread. The words of so many teachers and cops rang in my ears: "One day you'll get a rude awakening."

Apparently this was my first wakeup call.

> "Leaders cannot be created in a classroom. Those who are have a dubious distinction with no followers, so in essence they are just taking a walk." - JLH

Chapter 17

Sleepless in Vancouver

The Juvenile Detention Centre was a gothic grey stone edifice built around the turn of the twentieth century as a place for orphans and wayward youth; it basically looked like a combination of a church, prison and miniature Harry Potter's Hogwarts school, minus the cute little owls and magic tricks. The police car slowly made its way around the sweeping circular driveway, stopping under the giant stone-pillared carport. The passenger cop got out and opened the back door and immediately said, "Don't run." In retrospect, that was exactly what I should have done, except that I was in shock over the situation unraveling in front of my bloodshot eyes. There was no way that chubbabubba could have caught me. Then again, I did meet a kid years later who got shot in the ass (yes, he showed me the scar), by a cop when he bolted from the bus taking him and thirty others to a prisoners to Oakalla, which I would years later get to visit as a visitor for my brother and then as an inmate. But who knew? Then again, I was just a kid and we weren't in Rio or Bagdad. This was Canada; clean water, fresh air, no garbage on the streets, no homeless people (too cold), home of "please" and "thank you" and, let's not forget. Canadian bacon. (I guess American or Chinese bacon is just not cool enough to advertise.) The cop kept his fat fingers snugly on my right shoulder, so there was not much chance of making a break for it.

We approached the big staircase, which to my very short legs felt like it was twenty feet wide and ten steps, but in reality it was just tall steps. I kept thinking I'm going to wake up from this; this is just a bad dream. This is not happening to me! But like the movies where the expendable character is just about to be hit by a train or attacked by a psycho killer with an axe, closing your eyes doesn't seem to stop the dying.

The giant oak doors, like something out of Lord of the Rings, seemed to swing effortlessly under the power of my captors, leading me into a classic marble-and-oak-trimmed administration area. One of the cops nodded to me as if to say sit over there. I understood and obediently walked to a long dark wooden bench, its seats worn five shades lighter by generations of butts before mine. I guess the upside was that I wasn't in nickel-plated handcuffs. No one spoke to me for some time but I could see the lips moving and the eyes glancing towards me as they talked amongst themselves. I did catch one of the cops saying something to the effect of "his mom wouldn't allow him back in the house."

A woman peeked around one of the big cop's shoulders; she looked down as if I was a bad dog who had just shit on her ornate Persian carpet or ripped up her favourite Bugs Bunny slippers, extra-large and sweaty. I didn't know if I was going to be there for an hour or for a week. This was my first intro to a scared-straight reality show of my own producing, and I was scared. Can you say guppy in a barracuda tank?

Juvie was geared towards young offenders for the most part, but back then they virtually never raised kids to adult court, so we were all equals: lions and lambs, or, in today's vernacular, kittens and pit bulls lying down together, as it were. That included a multitude of teens that, for example, accidentally killed their step-father, raped the girl next door, or set fire to someone they disliked, along with those who jumped on trampolines. That isn't to say that your roommate would necessarily be the psycho kid who would jab a pencil in your throat while you slept, but then again, you never knew.

Check-in was simple; the cops officially said good-bye to me. Actually it was more to the effect of "good luck, kid" as I was escorted by one of the guards from the admin area through some ominous-looking oak doors with big brass locks and handles. Stepping over the threshold was an epiphany that said, "Welcome to the big house, Jake. Have a wonderful time." Twenty feet later I was in a Spartan-type room with a steel table, white linoleum floor and three wooden chairs. This guy in his early thirties with a blue and grey uniform asked me to sit down, which I did without hesitation. He then pulled one of the three simple plastic Bic pens from his shirt pocket and began writing something on a paper snugly attached to a clip board and began to ask me some basic questions about health and history; the one that stuck in my mind though, was 'Do you know why you are here'? To this, I paused for a second, thinking in a flash that maybe this was that mistake I'd been praying for since getting arrested earlier that day.

But alas, I said "Yes, I got caught breaking into my school gym."

He looked at me for a second with a slight glimmer of empathy, then wrote something on the page. I was thinking that it would be handy to be able to read upside down, but I did not have the skill and still don't. The next step in the induction process was not surprising; we finished up in the intake room and headed further into the bowels of the castle, passing through another set of locked doors, but these ones were metal and far more intimidating. Through them we went into a large hallway with pale blue walls and battleship-grey cement floors. About ten paces past the doors was a small serving-type window on the left, except there were no burgers, fries or ice cold bottles of Coke at this window, it was for clothing. I was asked what size pants I wore, to which I said I had no idea. This quickly led to being asked what size shirt I wore. Again...no idea was my response. "How about runners?" the guy asked. I blurted out size five, proudly. Sixty seconds later he unceremoniously dropped a neatly folded bundle of clothing on the chin-high counter. It consisted of forest green pants with an elastic waistband, a matching green button-up heavily starched collared shirt, along with a pair of dark blue gym shorts, a grey t-shirt, two pairs of grey wool socks, a pair of white briefs and worn pair of black and white Converse canvas high tops. That was that. I was good to go apparently. My handler then led me down the hall and through another set of doors, his ring of keys echoing down the cement hall way with its many hotel rooms. The place was dead silent, which made me more freaked-out than I had been already. It was early afternoon, so, as it turned out, the other tenants were doing chores or some type of recreation. Yet, at a few of the windows there were faces peering out at me and my NBF.

We stopped abruptly in front of one of the metal doors; the guard quickly unlocking it with the precision of a sushi chef while saying, "You'll be in here," like he was showing me to my table. The room was about twelve feet by twelve, as I recall, with two sets of bunk beds and a window, but no sink or toilet. I stepped inside with the key master saying that everyone would be back in their rooms by 4 p.m. to get ready for dinner at 5 p.m. just before he pushed the door shut, locking it as quickly as he had opened it. There seemed to be only one bunk, a bottom one, that was not already taken, based on some personal effects placed neatly on the tightly-folded grey wool blankets. I sat down and pondered my predicament, feeling very small and alone, shocked by the reality that my mom did not want me and that my actions had consequences that were not part of any Brady Bunch or Partridge Family episode that I had ever seen. I cried for a solid hour, saying over and over, "I was just jumping on a trampoline…I didn't do anything wrong!" I ignored the fact that I had technically broken into the gym. "We didn't break anything. I just stayed when it closed." A grey area in my books. Well, that snot-nosed-kid mantra came to a screeching halt with the sound of that door lock turning. I instinctively knew there was no empathy for crybabies in this twilight zone daycare for wayward youths and future lost boys. The door swung open with a creaking sound that sent chills up my spine like fingernails on an old fashioned chalkboard. In came three boys, two of whom were aboriginal and about four inches taller than me and just a lot bigger; the other was an Italian kid who was basically short and stubby with a solid unibrow and an infectious smile. He said "Hi," while the other dudes looked at me with contempt. I was thinking And I have to sleep in here? These guys are going to choke me out with my own underwear then stuff those runners down my throat and tell the guard I committed suicide. Nightmare! I, of course, tried to be tough, giving them a nod and my best tiger stare. Whatever! I was twelve and had no real grasp of the situation I was in, but then again I did have some God-given intellect and some years of street smarts, not that they didn't. Didn't take more than a few minutes for one of the chugs, as we used to call them, to ask me what I was in for. I should have made up some graphic tale of robbery, blood and hand-to-hand combat with a Doberman, but instead I said, "B&E." That was somewhat respectable, I guess because they dropped the issue and like identical twins turned to the comic books tucked under the musty smelling, sweat-and-tear-soaked, pancake-flat, black-and-white-striped pillows that had but a distant memory of being fluffy and full of warm loving goose feathers.

Uncomfortable silence fell on my new home as we all did what we could to keep occupied until the dinner buzzer. That seemed like hours, but in all reality it was about thirty minutes or so. The door unlocked and out I went to meet the natives. I only moved about three steps before my solid little Italian stallion roomie grabbed my arm and whispered, "Stand against the wall until everyone is out, then we walk together to the dining hall". "Oh," I said, surprised the kid talked to me.

Everyone came out, and we walked about a hundred feet then turned left down the hall for another hundred or so then through a pair of green metal fire doors and into what basically looked like any cafeteria from one of the dozen-plus schools I attended, with the big foldable picnic-table-looking things with steel frames and faux wood tops. It was the usual: slide your tray along the counter and get whatever was on the night's menu, then sit wherever you wanted. But as expected everyone broke off into little packs; I assume it was with those from their rooms, as in who else would they know? Right? Well, as it turned out, those who had been there a while (it was up to a year, I believe, before being raised to adult court), or who had made a fast name by beating someone up or being in for an act of violence, a badge of honour in low places for sure, had a following of minions. A quick scan of the hall and some risky glances into a few eyes said most had been here for at least a few weeks. I was keenly aware that my awkward moves and hesitant steps telegraphed weakness to these baby tigers, just as it would in any jungle. I tried to blend in as fast as I could with my tray of salty Beef Stroganoff, mushy overcooked vegetables, rock-hard bun and tapioca pudding. As expected, it didn't matter how small I tried to make myself, all new kids on the block needed to be tested, and that took all of about forty-five seconds. How is that, you ask? Simple. As I headed to a table in the far corner, a black-haired kid smacked my tray out of my hand and quickly turned to his pals like nothing happened. Well, I was in the spotlight whether I liked it or not, and as I was one of the smallest boys and wasn't lucky enough to be one of those brightly-coloured frogs with the poisonous skin which all predators knew to stay clear of, in this jungle I would have to come up with my own version of don't mess with me or end up as some bigger animal's poop droppings faster than I could spit.

So what to do? Well, everything kind of went into slow motion, but what I recall was simply grabbing the kid by his greasy locks on both sides of his temples and jerking him backwards off his warm, comfy bench. I was as shocked as he and his buddies were by my reflex, and as I only had a plan A, a distant plan B being, I hoped, (not a good plan, as Napoleon said, "Hope is not a strategy") that the guards would save my ass before he and his pals stomped me into hamburger as everyone calmly finished their tapioca. And yes, it was over as fast as it started along with a lot of screaming, swearing and kicking, food and drink going airborne and not making me very popular, that is for sure. Fifteen seconds or so into the scene had three guards on us, and I can say I lost some locks of my own to one of the women guards and gained a few fingernail cuts to the scalp. Up and out we went through those same doors, like pit bulls caught at a cat show. Downside had many levels, two being that he was in the room next to mine, and I was hungry.

One interesting thing is that it was just like meeting someone for the first time and having the inevitable question come up in the first ninety seconds: "So what do you do?" (Doctor, lawyer, talent scout for Playboy, etc.), the boys in Juvie did something similar, but it was more like "What are you in for?" and "How long did you get?"

If were are lucky enough to be in for a violent crime, it automatically upped your status and set you apart from the thieves, arsonists and so forth; thankfully there weren't many underage pedophiles or skinners (rapists), but if there were they would either have been separated somehow or they would never have admitted to being charged with those crimes, that is for damn sure. But as my first few hours clearly demonstrated, getting pegged as a small fry sucked, and making fast friends that were either bad-asses or just big was as good a strategy as any. Regardless, everyone gets tested at some point. I mean, if you draw a line in any sand, someone is bound to cross it. Funny thing is, when I managed to get some escape velocity in my early twenties and join the job world, that testing was still there, same fleas, different dog, made up of a paper-thin veil called corporate ethics, or should I say situational corporate ethics? Just another jungle, in reality, separated by about two seconds in the evolutionary clock with a foliage of steel, cement, glass and electronics; predators on two legs called Managers, VPs and Presidents. So the "I just want to do my time and don't want any trouble" that is shown in the movies, resulting in the poor sap getting beaten or worse, pretty much sums it up. It's always trouble, all the time. The boat that brought your last load of crap just left port because another is just about to dock and unload its cargo.

As it turned out, the kids ranged in age from twelve to eighteen (at 19 you went to adult court and jail, lucky you), and I was by far the smallest of the twelves and the perfect storm of a big mouth, no size to back it up, and no place to run kept me in check. Not smart - just self-preservation at work.

There was no real rehabilitation program in place other than mandatory attendance at school. If you didn't like that or felt that the classroom rules didn't apply to you, then the guards magically showed up and you were escorted unceremoniously to your room and were not allowed back until you showed you deserved it. Didn't take long for anyone running that game to understand that lockdown was far worse than the classroom. If you still didn't make it, you were on permanent cleaning duty that meant floors, bathrooms, lunchroom, and gym. The big institutional kitchen was separate and had its own crew. I'll talk more about that later. To sum it up, this was basically a North American zoo for adolescent animals. Like all zoos, it was a place to keep the wild things contained so the bottom of the food chain and keepers of the keys could sleep at night without the fear of us prowling through their dreams.

As for the types of kids, as you would expect, they were all tough. In fact, some were pretty much psychotic, with no remorse about beating the crap out of anyone who might look at them sideways. And also, as expected, there were always a few ready to fight the new kids, and I was no exception.

One of the laws of that little jungle was to never let anyone see you cry; that was just asking for it. But under the blanket of darkness called "lights-out," one could hear the muffled sobs of those who couldn't keep it in as they cried themselves to sleep, and, yes, I was one of them. I was lonely, and I'm sure the other boys felt the same way. Those first few nights were rough and left an indelible impression on my soul and mind as I sat on the big stone window ledge for hours staring out at cool white moon slightly obscured by the paint-chipped heavy-gauged wire mesh. Even then I thought it odd that my roommates slumbered as if at home in their beds, or maybe they had just been here longer than me and somehow got used to it. Dead silence to the point I could hear my heart beating so loud I thought it would wake someone up. The church-like quiet only occasionally broken by the sound of the old cast iron hot water pipes used to heat the castle, and the clinking of keys as a guard made his rounds.

I kept wondering how I managed to get myself in such a place, and why I couldn't seem to control my actions. As I sat there feeling sorry for myself, fat tears running down my cheeks, I realized I was, for one of the first times, scared and homesick.

They sentenced me to six weeks, which is nothing to an adult who has done time. For one who hasn't, it would be as shocking as having a hairdryer dropped into their bathtub. I was twelve years old, and when I think of my daughters at that age, I can hardly believe what kind of kid I was then. Six weeks in confinement to a kid works like dog years: an hour is a day and a day a week and a week a month. Get the picture?

I hated my mom for not taking me out of the cop car and have never completely forgiven her, but, as it is with moms, you still love them. She did what she thought was best for me and the family at the time. I see that now, but then it was one of those nightmares you just can't seem to wake up from. I kept re-living the moment when the cops went up to the door and talked to her, then the unbelievable few seconds, almost in slow motion, where they both got back into the car and drove away with me still in it. I know now that she was simply practicing some tough love, but it didn't work, and that lesson was indelibly etched on my subconscious.

Mornings came real early, like 6 a.m., except Sundays, the Lord's Day; we got to sleep until 7:30. That was a treat for sure, but it was busy work from the get-go each morning with a long list of chores to do before breakfast, then school for four hours or Sunday school on Sunday, with mandatory daily physical activity, which lasted two hours and consisted of dodgeball (that is, some kid whipping a rubber ball at you and you're out if he hits you…last kid standing is the winner…being the smallest is not an advantage in case you were wondering); or basketball (full contact style, don't you know?); and boxing (I avoided that one too); laps around the cement-floored gym (not a nice wooden floor; remember this was more like an old castle and the gym was an afterthought). I mean do kids need exercise? No, damn it! This not a health club, it's a jail for wayward youths who have had a bit too much of the spare-the-rod parenting style so much more popular in the twentieth century than the previous one. No, the deal at that place was more like lock 'em up and let them out to eat and possibly go to the bathroom if needed. Well, in all reality, the objective was to make sure everyone was tired come lights-out. And it worked for the most part. That doesn't mean there wasn't some shit that happened between roomies. They were not chosen for compatibility from what I remember; they were sent wherever the spare bed was. I was lucky and didn't have much of a challenge with the kids that rotated through.

I tried to make friends with as many big guys as possible, for protection. Just think of the sucker fish that spends its life attached to a shark, or the clown fish hanging out in the poisonous tentacles of the sea anemone. If you're twelve and only eighty pounds, you do whatever you can to work things in your favour.

Cigarettes have been one of the main currencies in jails for decades. At that time, if you were over sixteen you were allowed to smoke. I never did, but I collected as many as I could so I could use them to buy friends, candy, comics or whatever.

I don't believe the term politically correct existed at the time, or if it did, the guards didn't care. Getting a few slaps by one of them, or having some enforcer type kid work you over to get in good with one of the guards was not that uncommon even in Juvie.

There was one Scottish teacher, ex-military I believe, who had a thick neck to go with his thick accent, and this was coupled with a short temper and a swift-moving wooden yardstick (metre stick to young Canadians), that he carried around the big library-looking room with its fourteen-foot ceilings and four giant stone arched windows. He seemed to be waiting for any excuse to let it fly, landing with a loud crack on an unsuspecting student that appeared to be lacking interest in that particular subject or maybe just not understanding his Scottish accent. It really didn't matter; the whack was the same for either, and lipping him off got you an automatic time-out, which meant locked up until dinner.

Out of all the mandatory chores, the number one draft pick (for those who could make a choice, that is) was working in the kitchen. So how did I get into the land of milk and honey? Well I'm not sure, but it probably had something to do with me being by far the smallest kid in the joint, yet packing a Jack Russell-like attitude, I would like to say pit bull, but, truth be told, I was just too scrawny. My so-called street cred as they say, had been tested enough, I guess, with multiple altercations within the first ten days, most of which I lost, but I guess they liked the entertainment and the fact I would need to be unconscious to stop fighting. The kitchen had a lot of perks to it and of those, the number one was being close to the source of all power: food. So getting to snack a bit during the day was a big bonus, no question, but the fun didn't end there as the chef and his help played music and the guards seemed to leave the kitchen to its own devices. Interestingly enough, the only people working in the inner sanctum of the juvenile correctional facility that weren't correctional officers (the teacher was definitely a cop of some sort) were the chef and his fulltime understudy. He was not stereotypical for a chef of the day, I might add, as in he wasn't a big fat guy. Of course, today all the Iron Chefs are iron men studs who look like they never eat their own cooking. He was a rather cool cat, dressed in the shining white armour of a traditional French chef, minus the tall hat. If that was not enough, he was also tall and slender, with long fuzzy sandy blonde hair and a nicely trimmed goatee, accented by the occasional glint of a gold tooth that flashed when he laughed, which was often. So needless to say, he was a spark of freedom in a cloud of repression.

His helper, on the other hand, could have been an ex-con, but that impression was based solely on his appearance, which included an earring, (that is, one in the correct ear of the day; the other ear meant you were gay, in case you never heard that urban myth), and he had lots of tattoos. By today's standard of course, he could very well have been a primary school principal at a prestigious private school who only smoked marijuana for his glaucoma. Did I mention that they would often take a break by the big steel back doors, which just happened to always be opened because the chef wanted fresh air? It took me all of one "It's your turn to empty the garbage" commands to identify an easy escape route, and I seriously considered it. It was as simple as going down five stairs, walking twenty feet, then quickly scampering to the top of one of the big garbage bins. Throw a blanket over the razor wire and, poof, a short blast down to the waterfront, and you could make your way under the docks for as far as possible, and you were free - or something like that. The caveat there was that the chef or helper would stand at the door and watch you dump the garbage. Of course, they would have a smoke or quick toke of weed. And yes, I had a few puffs on occasion; I mean, I had to fit in and all.

The truth was that the kitchen was an exit to freedom from my point of view. The only fly in that ointment, I realized, was that I had nowhere to go. My mother didn't want me, and going to my dad's in Chinatown could have been a short term option, but then what? No going home, and I was only twelve and subconsciously knew I couldn't survive on the streets for very long. So much for the great escape plan for me. So it was to be plan B: wait it out. My mom would come get me soon. Or would she? Well, as I waited, there were fights over just about anything. I mean food, gym, toothpaste, TV shows, ping-pong, basketball, magazines, and of course the never-ending shuffle for status. It was basically a case of dogs marking their so-called territory and establishing their place in the pack hierarchy.

As I have explained already, I was the new pup in the kennel, so I had no status whatsoever. That meant either backing up to security, which is similar to cutting back expenses ongoing, thinking that will get you financial security. Not going to happen unless you are all good with eventually living in a cardboard box as the cost of living overtakes your fiscal responsibility efforts. "No security, only opportunity," General MacArthur once said - probably during his campaign to nuke Russia after dropping the A-bombs on Hiroshima and Nagasaki. As you may expect, there was nowhere to hide from the bullies. The biggest altercation I had in my short tenure actually happened in the kitchen with a chubby Italian kid with thick curly black hair and matching eye brows. I would guess he was a year older than me, an inch taller and at least twenty pounds heavier. We had started in the kitchen around the same time, although I think he was there a day or two earlier, and that was the seed of the altercation. The cook looked at both of us and said that he wanted a big pile of potatoes peeled and cut and he didn't care who did it just as long as it was done by the time he got back from picking up some supplies. Well, me and the Italian stallion blurted out "Sure, I'll do it." He paused for a split second thinking that he should maybe pick one but didn't; he smirked and said, "Just get it done." He whipped off his food-splattered white apron as he spun around tossing it nonchalantly, and cruised out of the cavernous institutional kitchen as if he was leaving a club. Time stopped. This was obviously a chance for a so-called promotion because one of the older inmates who had been a helper had been released from the institution without any warning to the chef (and why would they?). All of us collectively came to the same conclusion: that would sure beat shit out of cleaning dishes and scrubbing grimy once-light- green tile that was now infused with years of scum, making it almost impossible to clean. And, yes, that was probably the task at hand: just keep us busy and get us tired. So that was the gig to get - cook's helper - since he didn't have to do any chores outside of prepping breakfast, lunch and dinner. He didn't even have to empty the garbage. This was big time. Lots of snacks and most of all, it didn't feel like you were in jail, but more like you were a busboy or chef's helper in a restaurant. Now that was status. As he didn't care who did it, I thought why not me?

Unfortunately, the chubby kid thought the same thing. Even though I weighed nothing compared to him, I didn't think twice about voicing my opinion and had quite a convincing tone and glare when I was mad or embarrassed. Before I could say a word, my competitor said casually, as if I was some private school kid who ends up in a public school lunch room in a poor part of the city, "I'm doing this, so fuck off and do something else!" I admit my pulse jumped about twenty beats a minute as the adrenaline surged through my body, prepping me for a fight-or-flight scenario. This one was fight because we were locked in the kitchen, so flight was not on the menu; and besides, who did he think he was?

My mouth kicked into gear before I could catch it. "Why don't you fuck off, fat boy?" I snarled back. This instantly caught the attention of the other guys in the kitchen, with one of them saying, "Go watch the door for the bulls. This should be good."

No sooner had his words fallen to the greasy floor, then bam! Pudgy Boy punched me in the stomach with his fat left arm. The impact of his 20-plus-pound-heavier frame knocked the wind out of me and had me gasping for air. I bent over and staggered backwards, colliding hard with the long stainless steel counter covered with pots and pans of every size imaginable. So what did I do while he sucker-punched me? I simply seized the thick metal handle of the closest pot and, without pausing, smashed him across the face with it. This spun him in a complete three sixty, his hair seeming to lag behind him by about a second as he spun. He shrieked with shock like a schoolgirl, and the other boys shrieked with excitement, loving the unexpected move by this skinny little punk. I, of course, hoped that was the end, but to my surprise he put his head down and ran at me like some kind of mad midget bull. The fat little bastard was holding the side of his face while driving me backwards against the cool steel table for what felt like an hour, but it was more like five seconds, while he tried to recover from the impact of my little equalizer.

I panicked because I still couldn't breathe, my white-knuckled fist still clutching the pot for dear life as another surge of adrenaline jerked me to action. I was not sure what his plan was; maybe he thought he could drive me into the big bottom shelf then start kicking me in the face; that's what I would have done. I didn't know and wasn't going to wait to find out, so I started pounding his chubby-bubby back with the edge of the pot; this got his attention, but he wouldn't let go, so I kept at it, this time on the back of his neck, probably three or four times until he started backing away holding his neck. He was he hurt for sure? I mean, I would have been. For God sakes this kid has got to be hurt, I was thinking. The other kids were whooping and yelling by this time. "Get him, man!" yelled some skinny pimple-faced kid with the remnants of a black eye. "Fucking kill him, dude!" said a scruffy blonde kid, then adding, as if there was some jail justice being administered by a court of my peers, "He deserves it!"

I think most of them were voting for me since I was smaller, and I guess everyone loves the underdog. Then again, there is a reason that saying, no honour amongst thieves, has been around for last few hundred years or more. I was a kid and had no interest in killing anyone or even fighting for that matter, especially since I knew at a cellular level that I'd been lucky so far and I wasn't about to push it; so best look for an exit strategy quickly before Porky gets his second wind. I bolted for the big kitchen door but, of course it was locked. I mean, hey, we were criminals who deserved to die in a grease fire, or in my case, get beaten to death by Mighty Mouse in front of a handful of wannabe cooks. Without any delay, I started kicking and pounding on the door which immediately pissed everyone off since they would all get in shit if the bulls came. But that was my plan: get rescued by one of the guards. Embarrassing, yes, but whoever said survival had to look cool was probably basing it on their experience with bad service in a five-star restaurant. It took about two seconds for one of the kitchen crew to lift me off my feet and start carrying me back to the ring. By this time the Italian kid had gotten his act together to some degree and I was dropped right in front of him, with the boys making a circle around us. For our own safety no doubt. This included all the kitchen utensils being out of reach. Oh shit. They wanted me to what? Fight fair?

"When you're out-weighed or outnumbered," as the famous Ron Sitrop, my Kiokishinki Karate instructor, told me years later, "you have to use an equalizer: a brick, a garbage can lid, a knife, a bat, whatever. Position the guy with his back to the stairs and push him down them. Remember, it's better to be judged by twelve than carried by six."

I tried to run between them to anywhere, but it was useless because I couldn't break through. A split second later, my opponent grabbed a handful of my hair and jerked me off my feet. I slammed hard onto the cement floor with him trying to startle me simultaneously. I yelled out something stupid - "I'm sorry!" - like that was going to totally calm him down.

"Yeah, you're going to be sorry you, little fucker," he said, out of breath.

But before he could get his fatness nicely settled on top of me so he could take his time pounding my face and head into the floor, I squirmed down and out between his legs, leaving him wondering where I went. He quickly got up and spun to face me, that boy loving every second of it, and me sweating bullets trying to figure out how to get the hell out of there.

'No way out, go further in," say the military strategists. So I kicked him as hard as I could in the balls with the lower part of my shin. Bang! He dropped to his knees, his face in contortions like a woman giving birth. It was over - for now at least. The motley crew of kitchen helper yelped with excitement just as we heard the keys clacking at the door and could see one of the crew-cut guards peering through the small window, oblivious to the two-round rumble in the kitchen. He knew something was up.

"What the hell is going on in here?" he barked like a junkyard dog. He couldn't see the fat kid from the door because he was shielded by the big counter. We all seemed to gel with looks of total innocence on our faces, instinctively forming a kind of human wall so the kid could get up and regain his composure. He did a pretty good job too, pretending to organize the mess of pots and pans I had created.

We all rattled off "nothing," like we had been rehearsing the lines for a school play. "We were just fooling around," said the oldest boy. He let a slight grin escape, showing a front tooth missing and the rest in need of some power brushing and the installation of a set of braces. Never going to happen for that guy.

"You're a fucking liar!! The guard shot back. "There's no fooling around in the kitchen. Where the hell is the chef?" he barked.

"He's gone on a supply run, sir," said a kid with red hair, genuinely nervous.

"Who's in charge then?" he demanded.

"Chef usually lets me watch over the kitchen when he leaves, sir," said the toothless boy.

"Is that right? Well you don't seem to be doing a piss-poor job now, based on the noise I heard from down the hall." he said, his ears getting very red.

"We were just playing around a bit. No big deal, sir." I said, trying to sound like an innocent little blue- eyed, freckle- faced kid. Which I was, of course.

"Fine. Just don't let me see this happening again. And I'm going to talk to the cook about this. You shit disturbers should not be left alone." On that note, he spun his short stocky frame on the heels of his impeccably polished black boots and stormed out of the kitchen.

We all stood still for a beat or two while one of the other boys peered out the small dirty window to make sure he was gone. When the kid gave the all-clear our focus turned back to the situation at hand.

Thankfully one of the biggest kids said, "You both drop it. Get back to work, and stop fucking around. If I get canned because of you-two's shit, I will personally beat you both unconscious."

Gulp!

On that note, bruised and battered, me and my frenemy exchanged glances and turned and went about our business as if nothing had happened. The cook showed up about two hours later, and he was mad as a hornet. It took all of 60 seconds for the I will beat you unconscious kid to rat us both out. Nice. The cook banned us from kitchen duty, as we clearly were troublemakers. I was all good with that; I didn't want to be locked in that kitchen fighting ring with that kid again. We had a few scuffles and pushing matches after that, but for the most part, he kept his distance. I guess I had made my point. Plus, some of the other teens heard about it and thought I was a "tough little fucker," so luckily for me I was somewhat, I guess, hands-off, which meant fewer hassles from the other kids. That certainly made my life a bit easier, but let's not kid ourselves; it wasn't a home of any sorts. Maybe Harry Potter liked Hogwarts and I might have to if I was doing magic, but this castle-looking place sucked, as it was supposed to.

Sundays, on the other hand, were meant to feel like old home week. You see, most of the eighty-plus residents were in for set times ranging from weeks to months but some were sent to Juvie because the authorities didn't know what to do with them because they were minors (under eighteen in Canada) when they committed their dirty deeds. So this meant they could be held there for something like a year and, if that was the case, they most likely going to be bumped up to adult court. Then, if found guilty, it was off to the Big House to play with the Big Boys - adventure, excitement, meet all kinds of new men friends. Sounds great!

But that was all forgotten on Sundays; we were all just boys looking for some family ties. Sunday after lunch was visiting day. You would usually know ahead of time if someone was coming to visit, but sometimes they showed up unexpectedly, and when they did, it was like a mini-Christmas. Everyone was excited, and rightfully so, as this was the link to the world we knew. It was held in the lunchroom and was basically an open-air affair with no rules like sit across the table from visitors, no touching visitors, all packages need to be left with guards before coming into the hall. Stuff that real jail has and, in most, there is glass between you and your guests. So some, if not most, of the boys, would get care packages, which they were allowed to keep. They would get checked after the visitors all left the hall but as long as they only had things like chocolate bars, pop, comic books writing stuff, it was all good. Unfortunately, my mom never came. I waited each week, certain she would be waiting in the lunch hall, but it didn't happen. I was one of a handful that didn't get visitors after about four weeks. I recall one kid's parents brought me something as well. I guess the kid, who I can't remember, was a friend of mine at some level, and he must have told his parents I had no visitors or care packages. I suppose you could say I had some pals in there, but what exactly does that mean in kid-prison? In the many maximum security prisons, your friends only come in two categories: one would help you move, the other would help you move a dead body. We were more like a pack of rats scurrying round Hogwarts than actual friends. Then it happened; my mini-Christmas and my favourite aunt showed up. She lived not far from the place, so it was easy for her to walk there as she, like my mom, didn't drive. It was great to see her and my care package, including my Oh Henry! bar (that was her nickname for me). She is still my favourite aunt

Later on, I asked my mother why she never came to see me, and although I can't recall her exact words, I know it was along the lines of "Been there, done that, got the blood-stained t-shirt from your brother." She was basically tired and hardened after years of dealing with the daily canoe full of shit he brought home, like a gift of sticks for the fireplace. Plus, I guess with her new best friends, she was too busy to take the bus out to see me on a Sunday, or her drivers were just too hungover, or more like still piss drunk and needing a few shots on the cornflakes to start the day. Breakfast of Champions, don't you know?

Six-weeks later it was time to go home and I can say that I lost some of what was left of my boyish charm. The events of that day are kind of surreal; definitely not how I anticipated my grand departure would go. I had been dreaming of this sunny day where I would come out of the gates and my mother would be there waiting for me. She would be standing there like Julie Andrews in The Sound of Music, with this forgiving smile. I would go running into her arms and she would hug me tight, like she did long ago. I could see it so clearly…and hear "The Hills Are Alive with the Sound of Music." But it was not to be.

Regardless, I was still happy for about thirty seconds. Like I said, six weeks for a kid is a long friggin' time. Then I saw her. The over-educated, under-ambitious social worker, a star no doubt down at the local child services office; in her late twenties; cheap pantsuit from Zellers, I would suspect; black hair parted in the middle; black-looking eyes nicely framed by matching glasses. Probably spends her disposable income on trips to a Fashion Week spin-off in Waco, Texas. Yet there she was, waiting to pick me up. About a split second after she said, "Hi," and put out her hand as if we were doing some kind of business deal, I glanced to the left and right, thinking I should do a Speedy Gonzales on her and boogie out of this scene. But just as quickly, I came to the conclusion I had nowhere to boogie too. And as stupid as I was, being a street kid was not on the agenda that day. So she had a new plan and it didn't involve me going home, at least not for a while. I decided that part of my childhood was over forever. The bubble had burst, so no dream, just the continuation of the nightmare, you know like when you wake from a scary dream, heart rate hitting one sixty, and you realize you're still in another one. That gets the sweat rolling. I was about to add another chapter to my life story and it would involve a whole new business called "group homes;" like a dog kennel really. Yeah, that is not too far from the truth. Get paid to shelter at-risk youths and make extra money by keeping food, clothing and entertainment costs to a bare minimum.

"Where's my mom?" I asked, sincerely. She stared at me for a second, no words leaving her pursed lips. I then asked, nervously, "Are you driving me home? Is… is that why you're here?"

"I don't know where your mom is at this moment," she said in a nice-but-firm voice. "We need to get going," she said, ushering me into the passenger side of her no-frills white Dodge Dart. I got in and she closed the door, but not before I noticed my small ivory suitcase and another bag I recognized from home sitting in the back seat.

No sooner had she put the key in the ignition than I asked her again, "Are you driving me home?" She seemed flustered by my question, as she gripped the hard light blue steering wheel as tight as she could. Without giving her time to reply, I then blurted out. "Where did you get my suitcase from?" I knew in the pit of my stomach the answer was not going to be what I wanted to hear.

"Well," she said, pausing for what seemed like an hour, "we're not going to your house."

"What do you mean where not going to my house?" I said my voice cracking into some high-pitched tone, the beginning of puberty no doubt. "What's going on? Where are you taking me? There must be a mistake. I want to call my mom! I want to call her right NOW!" I said frantically.

"Yes" she said calmly. "No problem, you can phone her when we get to where we're going." By this time, my breathing was fast and uncontrolled, I was about to lose it and my driver knew it. She started diving noticeably faster, running a yellow light enroute to God-knows-where, and even He wasn't telling. I'm sure this was the end of a very long day for her and the last thing she wanted to do was transport a little kid who was scared and, considering where she just picked me up from, capable of who knows what? I suspect she would have offered me a puppy at that moment just to buy time and to elevate whatever guilt she was carrying from her motherly instincts (not sure she had any) or her own childhood. I didn't know what was going on, and by this time I was crying like the little kid I was.

"I want to go home. I won't be bad any more. You can tell my mom. Please tell her. Please take me home."

I was going to a new home, and one that would give me the first of many rude awakenings to come. But the thing that I couldn't shake was the thought that my mom would never do this to me so there must be some mistake, and someone would work this out very soon. But for now, it felt as if someone had stabbed me in my little evil heart while I was held down and force-fed a cocktail of fear and loneliness, shaken perfectly to produce a deep scar and a lingering flavour of bittersweet hate towards my mom and authority at large.

Looking back, the words to the song Hotel California would have fit nicely: "You can check out anytime you like, but you can never leave." The Perry Home had no locked doors, so I could leave any time I wanted, but I just had nowhere to go.

"Imagine dropping this tiny pebble into a pond... The ripple effect will carry over a great distance! This moment with you... The ripple has started!" - Dragon, The Bruce Lee Story

Chapter 18

There's No Place Like Home... Unless It's a Warehouse for Wayward Youths

"It's not that complicated...all men need a dragon to slay and a maiden to rescue...the challenges start when the maiden no longer wants to be rescued and the dragons are long dead and forgotten by all except the men." – JLH

-To make money from the masses in the twenty-first century, engage in a career of distraction as they yearn for all things leisure. JHL

The owners of the business known as the Perry House, Bud and Kay, met me at the door with big smiles. She had a grey short beehive hair-do, snowbird tan, big teeth and gold-rimmed glasses with a chain around her neck so she wouldn't drop them. Bud looked like a combination of a U.S. Marine and golf pro: buzz-cut hair, well-tanned, gold necklace, golf shirt and an expensive- looking watch. They looked like they were in it for the money; that's all I can say.

As we walked towards the back door across the immaculately manicured lawn with flowers and shrubs looking like something from Better Homes and Gardens, the brilliant white farmhouse- looking door swung open. "Welcome to Mayberry RFD," I thought she said, or maybe it was "Welcome to Fantasy Island." Whatever. I was at this moment having an out-of-body experience. So it all sounded like blah, blah, blah ... nothing seemed real. I smiled mechanically and stuck out my hand to meet theirs as I was guided into the house.

"I'll show you your room," said the smiling Kay. I glanced back at the lady who drove me there and she was talking quietly with Bud, my little suitcase and the other bag sitting at their feet. No question, the place was nice: big commercial-type gas stove with a flat grill for cooking bacon or pancakes, rich wood floors and a huge farmhouse-style picnic table in the middle. We walked down a hallway, turned right and then went up two flights of stairs. There were two fairly spacious rooms for the tenants, who were all out at that moment, I suspected at school, but as it turned out, I was one of two going to school. The other boys opted to drop school, so they all worked.

"You're in here. You get the top bunk," she said rather coldly.

She said some other stuff, but I didn't hear anything else. I just climbed up the wood frame bunk and lay on the bed. As she turned to go, she said, "Dinner is at 5:15 on school days and six o'clock on weekends."

What that meant was "don't miss a meal because there are no snacks. That costs money, don't you know?" Three squares a day was the deal at the Perry home, and as Kay did all the bulk institutional cost-effective cooking and was a smoker, the food was either tasteless or super salty; let's just say it sucked but filled the empty belly. As for my driver/social worker, she took off never to be seen again. And her promise of the phone call to my mom? Well, that turned into a not-today-maybe-tomorrow kind of deal that lasted about a week.

When I did speak to my mom, in between my sobbing and telling her I was sorry and wanted to come home, she told me that I had to stay there for a little bit, and then I could come home. No definition of what that "bit" was. I guess it was until I had learned some life lesson. If there is a bright side I could see at the time, it was that I was glad to be anywhere other than Juvie, or what I would now call Hogwarts School for the Mischievously Gifted.

The difference between a group home and Juvie is simple: one is a house, the other is a jail. I suppose things were better in some ways; I could walk to school, the mattress was thicker, there was carpet on the floors, and I didn't have to view the outside world through dirty wire-covered windows. But other than that, it was the classic, different dog, same fleas, me and the bullies ,who now not only were in the playground but in the next bunk below me.

The house sat on top of a hill in the north-east side of town, which must have been a blue-collar residential area in the not-too-distant past.

Few shops in walking distance, but easy access for those who did not rely on public transportation. No doubt this house once belonged to the boss of some company with its five thousand- square-foot mansion look, situated on a quarter-acre corner lot. The majestic-looking building just didn't fit in to that lower middleclass demographic. Point in fact, we were not allowed to ever use the front entrance. I guess every company has to have its rules, or anarchy might gain a foothold. The neighbours, I would bet, never guessed that it was a group home (often referred to as a kennel for lost boys) and I would also wager Kay and Bud never broadcast that to anyone, especially their pals in Palm Springs. They were just hard-working people, somewhat independently wealthy, with lots of relatives coming and going. Let me make this clear: they were not bad people, but it was strictly business, and a damned good one by all appearances. I think Bud may have had a part-time job outside of the kennel business, but I can't be sure. I suppose if his son, Ernie, ever reads this he will certainly straighten that out. It was hard to know, as they kept their personal life strictly separate from the business life, which is smart, but it did keep us guessing since the garage held few top of the line Cadillacs, a new Cougar XR7 for their son and his new motorcycle. I would say the limiting factor to some additional wealth for them was they were restricted to six wards at a time, which must have pissed them off, as twelve would have made good business sense, economies of scale and all that rot.

After meeting Kay and seeing the fine performance she gave, I'm sure the social worker must have figured I'd be embraced in a warm and loving environment and basically well looked after. But the façade dropped pretty quickly after the door clicked shut and I was instructed in the rules of the house. It didn't take long for me to understand this wasn't going to be some easygoing, big happy family situation.

Not surprisingly, everyone had chores and she expected things to be done right. This, of course, did give us a small allowance, well at least mine was small, but there was no cash if the job was not done to her standards, which were, of course, super high. Being the newcomer and the smallest/youngest, I got stuck with toilet cleaning duty most of the times. This didn't go over too well with me, and I made my feelings clear but did the job anyway. One thing for sure, she did not like my attitude and I did not like her Wednesday meatloaf. (I still can't eat that shit because of her.) "You're not leaving the table until you finish everything on your plate," she'd say to us (usually me). "I'm not having you boys scavenging around the kitchen for food in the middle of the night."

Coincidentally, and a shock to all, upon meeting their son Ernie, it turned out he had been one of my many Big Brothers in the past who started out with good intentions then dropped me because I was way too much work. Not that I could blame him. I personally, at that age, would never have put that much time into a kid like me. He did try, and I now appreciate how hard it was for him, a rich kid, to relate to me, yet here I was in his house. This became immediately awkward as he did not talk to me, even though we had been out to movies and on his motorbike many times in the past.

As for the other residents, I didn't know exactly why they were there, but I suspect it was everything from drugs and other crimes to being victims of sexual abuse. I am and have always been a quick study and one who could make fast friends in most situations, and I thought this should have been business as usual. But as adolescents go, they, like me, were unpredictable, so it proved to be a challenge. For starters there was this sixteen-or seventeen-year-old (just on the border of going to adult court) kid from Italian/Mexican/Brazilian-looking origin. No idea of his nationality, but he had been there for at least a year and for some reason (could have been my blue blankie, my mom's old velour robe ... yes, I must have had some insecurity issues at the time, which is understandable to some, but not to my fellow lost boys) he hated me from the get-go. I tried to act tough, as any sign of weakness was exploited to its maximum potential for fun or profit (it didn't matter) so they would constantly steal it or rip it away from me, and if they couldn't get it, I got a few punches (no marks on the face) to the stomach for non-compliance.

I'd only been there a few weeks, safe to say I didn't know the pack hierarchy, so I defaulted to my usual Jack Russell stance: trying to lead big dogs with my small bark and big mouth. If you were wondering how that worked out for me, if it is not apparent, not good. A sixty pound body handicapped with a two hundred pound mouth can be a bit of a problem in schoolyard, Projects and streets. You learn to either fight hard or run fast. I did a little of both.

I was on my own again with no allies as the new kid; the other boys in Perry House were teamed up and I was the newest and youngest animal, so none took kindly to me being dropped into their cage.

The big house had many rules, and one was that when not in our rooms or eating dinner at the farmhouse-style kitchen table, we were to stay downstairs in the den. Not a bad room actually with its pool table, dart board, some old sturdy couches and a chair or two. I rarely played pool as the older boys dominated it, but that didn't bother me anyway because my favourite part of the den was the TV/Hi Fi, which means a TV in a large and ornate wooden cabinet with a 33/45/78-RPM record player and radio built in. The walls were light oak paneling floor to ceiling, and on them hung a few velvet Mexican-style paintings, from one of Kay and Bud's many trips south of the border no doubt. The floor was standard seventies shag rug of burnt orange colour. As I mentioned, other than our bedrooms or outdoors, this was the only place we could hang out. It was always cool down there (and in the house in general), with a sweet musty smell, and even today when I catch that scent, it always reminds me of that place and time. Three narrow windows sat high on the below-ground room wall, giving off plenty of light, since the house sat on a small hill facing southwest.

I'm not sure what the formula was for feeding and heating a stable full of throw-away boys but they'd definitely figured it out. They could have opened a chain or better yet sold franchises of K&B homes for Boys. Could have had a catchy tag line like, "We make 'em, bake 'em" or, "We break 'em,;" or how about, "Lost boys get found and turned around?" There was a door to the big back yard (full of Kay's do-not-touch rosebushes and a no-play zone), carport and unpaved alleyway. The property was surrounded by a wall made up of large jagged rocks for supporting the small rise the house sat on, giving it that little extra air of pretentiousness. Like bamboo, I bent to the wind of change - and still do for the most part - adapting quickly to my new home. What was a bonus and got me excited was a great selection of records belonging to who knows, but I suspect the boys of the past or K&B's throw away collection. Regardless they were cool and most of them new to me. My favourites were Pink Floyd's, Dark Side of the Moon (which I still love), Deep Purple's, Made in Japan, Alice Cooper's Million Dollar Baby and the sound track to the best western of all time, The Good, the Bad and the Ugly; Clint is legend and a distant mentor of sorts.

I was usually the first one home from the elementary school a few blocks away called Chief Maquinna. What was a bit different was that (and I will get to this shortly) the Italian/Mexican... boy - more like man - paid a half-aboriginal kid named Vince to take my lunch and beat me up as often as he could. Now, it's not that I wasn't able to fight back, but sometimes it doesn't matter how hard you punch back, they punch harder. That's when you have to go to plan B: use brains over brawn, as the old saying goes. So what did I do? Well, during a particular good beating on his part, I decided to ask him why he hated me.

His reply was refreshing. "No reason. Sasquatch paid me to beat the shit out of you whenever I could."

"Oh," I said. "How about I pay you not to do that?"

Long story short, it was a win-win for all three of us. Bigfoot thought he was getting me punched out, Vince was getting paid by me and him, and I was not getting any hassle from soap-dish-intellect boy at the Perry Home for Wayward Boys. Funny thing is that it did not take long for me to win Vince over as friend of sorts. He even started inviting me to his house for lunch, but what he really wanted to do was play the guitar for me and, wait for it … sing. As I can remember he was talented and his rendition of the Rolling Stones' Angie, was super cool. Anyway, I still was the new kid (once again) trying to grasp the concepts of grade five while on the move. For those of you that went to one elementary school, don't worry about it, there's no way you can relate.   One day I was sitting there listening to beautiful harmonica tones from the theme song to The Good, the Bad and the Ugly when my one of my buddies, A Mr.-I-hate-you-and-I-am-in-super-good-labourer's-shape, topped off by a bad attitude, came home from his construction job and stomped down the stairs to the rec-room where I was sitting by myself.

Now at this point, I hadn't had much interaction with him other than a few casual, "Fuck off you little puke or I'll rip your throat out." That kind of thing. I can attest to the fact that he could probably have done it quite easily as his hands were like sandpaper-covered vice grips with the smell of weed and tobacco. How do I know that? Well, I had them around my throat about five minutes later. So there I was, eyes closed, vinyl spinning smoothly, wallowing in the moment of the classic opening tune to the movie when, like I said, in came Neanderthal Boy, (he should have had a comic strip named after him). He stomped down the wooden staircase, dragging his knuckles behind him, headed straight to the TV-Hi Fi, scraped the needle across the record and slammed the lid shut. Without acknowledging me in any way, he then turned and picked up the old=school remote and dropped into the couch, while at the same time turning on his favourite show (no doubt to increase his monkey intelligence), Get Smart. Dumfounded, I sat there for I don't know how long, my pulse rising, the blood rushing to my freckled face and turning my rather big ears crimson red. Forgetting my reality (small kid, big mouth, new group home, not like foster home, ignorant Sasquatch, you get the picture), I jumped up and spat out, "What the fuck do you think you're doing?" I marched over to the TV, slammed the button off and opened the record player lid with my back to my NBE (New Best Enemy), and proceeded to put back on the album. Note to self: in the presence of a hammer, try not to act like a nail.

Well the needle never made it to the record. Bam! Bigfoot was on me like a cheap suit, wrapping his jailhouse-tattooed left anaconda-sized arm around my chicken finger-sized neck. This lifted me four inches off the ground, the solid wood record player cover slamming down with a bang as he choked me so hard that I couldn't squeak out a "Help! I'm being choked out by a Neanderthal and can't break free." He effortlessly tossed me airborne backwards, clearing the big dark oak coffee table and slamming me hard into the couch backrest. No sooner had I bounced off it, he had straddled me, both of his stinky mitts around my throat shouting, "I'm going to choke the living shit out of you! Who the fuck do you think you are?" apparently too caught up in his emotions or pent up frustrations to consider that he could be heard by anyone upstairs (or a block away for that matter), trying to, accidently of course, kill me by suffocation or snapping my neck.

Then a reprieve from up above (I say divine intervention), the Queen of the House came slowly gliding down the steep stairs, just enough so she could peer round the crest of the ceiling, saying, "You boys keep the roughhousing down or no dinner." This instantly changed his 'Hmm, Me Hulk, I crush larynx of puny human … must pop head like grape. Hulk smash!" to the altar boy demeanor.

Oh, what's it like to be choked? Well, I'm not sure how to describe that feeling, but for those who fly on a regular basis you may be able to relate to that feeling of having a cold and stuffed- up nose as the pressure changes on descent and your head feels like it's going to explode from the inside; this of course affects your vision and can make your nose bleed, as mine was at the time. That could have been from his elbow, but who knows? One just loses track of those small details when you are having so much fun. In a flash my agile monkey boy nemesis had spun off me, but not before whispering, "You say a word, I'll kill you in your sleep." He then said politely, "It's not me, it's the new kid. He's keeps screwing around and won't be quiet so I can watch my show." He was well versed in handling the Kay and Bud show.

I didn't say anything, as I couldn't actually talk and was just pulling myself up after being buried deep into the corner of the massive couch. Kay, with her infinitely wise parental abilities, said, "Don't use that language" to my pal, who robotically replied, "I'm sorry, Kay. I'm just upset."

"Okay, you", pointing one of her well-tanned diamond-covered fingers at me, "to your room for the night. I'll call you for dinner." I looked into the eyes of the thick black-haired kid and I can assure you there was no one home, but he had me this time. There was a smirk on his face as I got up and slowly walked up the stairs, passing Kay as if she was not there. Tears welled up in my eyes as I headed to my bunk bed. My neck hurt and I could barely swallow, but I said nothing. Why bother? I just wondered what was going to be next from my in-house bully as I had broken one of the cardinal rules of dealing with all bullies: you either shut them down the first time or they just keep coming back like a cold sore. I was not sure what I would do about him, but for now I would make sure I didn't end up alone with him. That, of course, didn't work; especially as he bunked in the next room. It became an ongoing sequence of pulling all the blankets off my bed, or just coming into the room while everyone was asleep and thumping me in the upper thigh to give me what is affectionately known as a Charley horse, or else a simple but powerful punch to the stomach. At some point, I decided I didn't give a shit what he did if I said something, so this one time I screamed bloody murder and woke up the entire house. Marine Bud came flying up the stairs, lights on, all the boys awake, me crying while clutching my blue blankie, blubbering out, "He punched me! That bastard hit me."

By this time, he was back in his room and of course denied the whole thing. Bud didn't know what to do, so he said to me, "Stop your crying and go to bed, and you," he went back to the other room, "I will talk with you tomorrow."

That stopped the nighttime ambushes, but that was about it. He hated me even more. All I could do was, I guess, run away. But go where? My dad's room at the Ivanhoe Hotel in the poorest postal code area in all of Canada? That was too short of a plan, but I did end up there and in his Chinatown digs off and on over the years. Fortunately though, every cloud has a silver lining, and mine was a kid who moved in named Roy. He was close to my age and unusually outgoing and charismatic, with a thick head of curly red hair and huge white teeth. Although we were most likely only about a year apart in age, he was much bigger and stockier than me. The bully, of course, tried to get him to fight with me, which did happen once, but after about a month Roy decided he liked me and he stood up to the other kid and said he wouldn't beat me up. I liked him too, and we started to hang out after school and that was cool, but that sort of all came to an end after he invited me to his dad's apartment for a sleepover. You see, his dad thought that a fun and relaxing thing to do was to have naked, hot oil massages with his son and his sleepover buddies. Well, that just didn't seem to sit well with me as I stood there in a child- sized lavender-coloured silk robe with black trim and matching black belt. Ever since my first Bruce Lee movie, I had wanted to have a black belt, but this was not what I had in mind. He had told me to put the robe on (obviously he had done this before with other of Roy's playmates), but then I thought about my gang of movie mentors: Bruce Lee, Sean Connery, Steve McQueen, John Wayne and Clint Eastwood, and thought "What would they do? Let another man give them hot oil rubdown, naked at the age twelve?" Sorry, Rock Hudson was not in my gang. I don't think so. By the time his dad returned to his big bedroom with the king-sized bed with lots of extra pillows where I was supposed to be relaxing, he instead saw me dressed and making a beeline for the apartment door. All I said was, "I have to go. I won't tell anyone." I can still picture his dad in his crimson silk robe stammering out something like "We can play other games if you like. Please don't go," his eyes wide with concern and jaw dropped open, young Roy beside him in his matching red kimono, saying, "It's okay, we'll have fun, you should stay. We can make popcorn."

Didn't happen.

Roy and I never hung out after that, and he moved back to his dad's house about a month or so later. As for me, I kept my word and never mentioned the offer of the hot oil rubdown from his dad. A point in fact, this was the third of five situations I put myself into where I could or should have been sexually abused or worse … ending up as one of those haunting photos on some envelope with the words "Last seen…"

Chapter 19

Enter the Cowboy

"The basic difference between an ordinary man and a warrior is that a warrior takes everything as a challenge, while an ordinary man takes everything either as a blessing or a curse." – Don Juan

"From my experience, common sense is only common in the area of your expertise or experience." - JLH

After about six to eight months, I was allowed to come home. It would be an extreme understatement to say I was happy to be home; it was more like ecstatic. It should be noted here that my mom had tried to sell the house in East Van as a way of getting us out of the shit we were always in and to be clear away from my brother and his gang stuff. Right motive and great idea: move the family to a small town on Vancouver Island by the name of Ladysmith (too funny, but at that time it was the home of a teenage girl by the name of Pamela Sue Anderson) and shake loose the connections to the past. I went with my mom to see the large white Cape Cod style house, situated on a hill with a great view of the ocean and a long white picket fence. She made an offer that was accepted, but unfortunately it was not strong enough to handle the total revolt from the rest of my siblings. Of course, they were all entrenched in peer groups of despair and didn't know shit from Shinola about how that move would have helped our family, so she caved in and got her deposit back, which sealed the family's fate. Now back to the timeline.

I couldn't wait to get back to my so-called normal life and sleep in my own bed, in my own room and not have to sleep with one eye open. As for forgiving my mother for sending me away, well that would take a while, but no question she made the right move in sending me there. Whatever lesson I was supposed to learn, though, I can tell you was left at the curbside as I got out of yet another faceless social worker's car. In fact, the whole experience only made me more detached and antisocial, ready to fight at the first signs of trouble or disrespect. As problematic as that would be for me, I had bigger fish to fry. While I'd been on vacation at the Perry House of Horrors, there had been a new addition to the family; a new sleepover "uncle" had entered the scene. I can't say he was a greater loser than the others that came before him, but he was to become a permanent fixture in our household, eventually leading my mom, with me and my next closest sister in tow, onto the express train to the Great White North. First stop, the country town of Quesnel which I of course called Loserville.

His name was Percy Joe Barrard but he preferred to be called PJ. I secretly called him The Cowboy, and you will soon see why. He was around 6'1" with bloodshot blue eyes, wrinkled leathery face and slicked back Brylcreemed salt-and-pepper hair, tinted with shades of nicotine from years of chain smoking Player's Navy Cut cigarettes (apparently the choice of sailors). He had shed his Royal Canadian Navy uniform years ago and gone back to his roots of ranch living: checkered shirt with fake-pearl snap buttons, wife-beater undershirt, jeans, a belt buckle about the size of a side plate you'd find at a restaurant, and, of course, well-worn brown cowboy boots. This worked well with his daily pounding of a twenty-sixer of Smirnoff vodka. Yup, my mom hit the jackpot when she rediscovered this jewel from her past.

What was the story, and how did they reunite? Well the Cowboy, as fate would have it, moved into a basement suite across the street from our East Van house. Because the entrance to his Hobbit house was around the back and he worked nights, he was virtually never seen - the perfect tenant! On occasion, though, he was spotted hanging with his landlord's dog, Sailor, a 110-pound German Shepherd with a suspicious pizza-looking skin condition on his ass. The dog's hair was usually worn off from his constant rubbing of his butt, like a bear, against the big wooden telephone poles or just about anything he could get to stand still long enough for a couple of rubs; car tires, bushes and of course, to the unsuspecting, your leg. As he was mean looking, it was best to let him finish. Him and the Cowboy got along like peas and carrots, or, in his case vodka and soda.

After a few visits down at the Legion, my mother suddenly realized she already knew him. As it turned out, he was the biological father to my oldest sister and one of the reason we had left her hometown. Mom hadn't seen him in twenty years or more, so nobody (not even my sister) other than her siblings or deceased parents knew this little family secret. They broke the news to us over a weekend that included wrestling with a forty pounder of gin. That was a shocker to me, and one I really didn't comprehend at the time other than to ask something like, "So she's not my sister?" It must have been like an atom bomb going off for her. After all, she was only in her late teens or early twenties and life was complicated enough without getting that kind of update on your heritage. I guess my mom had met and dated PJ briefly back when she was a teenager and, as these things go, she ended up pregnant, and being unmarried and living in a small town in the fifties was not cool to say the least. So as they did back in the day, her strict English-Scottish father sent her away to have the baby at a home for unwed mothers. This, I suppose, was done not to bring shame upon the family. All I can say is, what are the odds that that dude would move in across the street into my buddy Kenny's basement? Can you say Impossible?

I would say he stalked her out, but then there was no proof of that, and besides, he wasn't that smart. One thing for sure, after seeing my mom's setup (her own house and some cash in the bank) it must have been a tempting package for an old cowboy who was tired of riding the range. He had no attachments on his part, just his navy duffel bag with some clothes and a red primer-coloured 1958 Ford pickup truck. After telling us what was what, he started staying over the odd night, then more and more often, and thus he seemed to move in without much fanfare.

In the beginning, everything was rosy for my mom. Seemed like she'd found that strong silent type man and father figure she'd been looking for. The rest of us, as expected, were not happy about the situation from the beginning, and it just got worse. We lasted in the house for about four years and one by one, my sisters started leaving. The oldest not too long after her new-found dad moved in, moved to Toronto; my youngest sister, about two years older than me, so that would have put her at around thirteen or fourteen, ran away from home. I remember her calling and telling my mom she was in Calgary, a city some thousand miles away, working at a restaurant, and asking, "Can you send me money for a coat?" because it was winter and she was cold.

My mom had no doubt been worried sick and wondered where she was. But she had no problem in exercising some tough love replying, "You made your bed, now you have to lie in it." She came back home after some months but was not the same little girl she had been. The next oldest went on a trip to Northern Canada, met a guy and never came back. My brother, he hung in there as he didn't care about the Cowboy and he was not afraid of him, if anything, PJ was afraid of my unpredictable drug-taking brother and his wrecking crew.

So you've got the big house, kids have moved out, empty nesters, almost perfect time to suggest to my mom they could have a better life and start fresh if they moved out of the city leaving all her troubles (and offspring) behind. Live out her (his) dream: build a log cabin on a piece of land on a creek, listen to country music and sing "give me a home where the buffalo roam and the skies are not cloudy all day," drink 24/7, and maybe practice a little wife beating to keep in shape. They got married at city hall with the JP for PJ as it were. I found out he was my new "DAD" (Drunk-ass dude) some weeks later.

I can only imagine, as I was too young to kick out, the upside of having me living with him (it takes a big man to raise another man's offspring) was that it somehow was financially beneficial to him, or more likely my mom was just being a good mom and taking care of her youngest. What he didn't know was that my mom's money was in a trust fund controlled by Lloyd's of London. It must have been like getting a frozen hockey puck in the ankle when he found out that all the proceeds from the sale of the house (after he persuaded her that it was in her best interest to sell) had to go back into the trust fund. Bam! Zero dollars for the Cowboy. The devil's in the details, don't ya know? He had missed that fine print in the unwritten pre-nup.

The day came for Easter vacation (wasn't called spring break back then) and as far as I knew, we were going to stay on his brother's ranch in the small cowboy town of Quesnel for two weeks. "Oh boy," I thought. "My first real vacation!" I couldn't wait. My buddies would be so jealous when I told them I'd be going to a real honest-togoodness ranch, probably run into John Wayne or Clint while I was up there, of course. A bonus was that my next oldest sister, the one that ran away to Calgary, came back just in time to come-with. My two older sisters had, as mentioned, moved out by this time, which should have been a clue, but with all the other stuff going on, (bro and his gang; mom and her binge-drinking with my new DAD) it was hard to notice.

Did I mention my brother, Wayne, hated PJ more than any of the other uncles we'd had over the years! So he made his life as miserable as possible, which was probably an underlying motivator for his head-north-for-a-fresh-start-suggestion? On the eve of our departure my bro, who like my two oldest sisters, knew about the sale, stopped by with a couple of buddies for a farewell party, leaving old leather face with a couple of scars as going away gifts.

We left late from the house (I had a cool room), piling into an unwashed rust-bucket Ford Country Squire station wagon that belonged to some old-time Navy pal of the Cowboy's, as I recall. Pretty sure that was the same car I was in on the fishing trip with them. It was dark, raining and cold, fitting for a trip that I didn't know at the time was a one-way deal; yet, I was excited, and I think my sister was as well. We headed to the Greyhound bus terminal in the downtown core, me with all my favourite stuff squished into my one and only little ivory- coloured suitcase, more like an overnight bag than suitcase (I still have it to this day). This would have been the same bus station my mom had arrived at with kids in tow so many years ago. I guess her world hadn't changed that much after all. The rags-to-riches-to-rags story, or something like that.

Our nightmare Greyhound bus trip took about twelve hours because we'd taken the "milk run" which means it stopped at every small town, First Nations community, middle-of-butt-fuck- nowhere bus stop and railway crossing along the way. And for those of you who are not bus people, for some reason it is a safety regulation, or was at the time, not only to stop at the track crossing, but also to open the front door as the bus crept across the tracks. As you can imagine, this continuously woke up all those who were sober. I am sure that is where the term "we traveled cattle class" came from. Lots of fun arriving with blood shot eyes, a sore neck, and hungry, as there are no food stops open on the red-eye night bus. But it probably saved ten bucks per head, so who needs to eat? Especially if you have a twenty-sixer of Smirnoff tucked in your jean jacket. Add to that the rock-hard seats on the latest model 1970s bus, and you had the recipe for a real comfortable ride. Seemed to work for the Cowboy though. He probably thought it was luxury compared to sleeping on the hard ground while herding cattle up the valley.

The bus was packed, as to be expected and add insult to injury it was during the age of "its okay to smoke in buses, airplanes and everywhere else for that matter." The recycled air did little to clear the sweaty windows that didn't open. The air-conditioning was off because everyone was supposed to be sleeping. At least there was non-stop entertainment provided by a dozen or so drunken First Nations people and another half a dozen white trash trailer parkers. They drank and played cards and smoked all night; the cigarette smoke floated lazily around their painfully bright reading lights.

They'd occasionally burst out with some exuberant dialogue like, "Whoo! I won!" or "Hu! Ya! You cheating mother fucker!" plus the occasional "Fuck!" "Shit!" "Bastard!" My sister seemed to find it as entertaining as I did, but as the hours drew on, I think it was more annoying than anything. That would be the last time we would have any resemblance to a family or see our one and only house. Like most lottery winners, we too were broke not very long after.

We arrived at what was our roadside stop around dawn, and everywhere we looked there was snow, even though it was April. The big bus came to an unceremonious halt with a jarring pishhh sound of air from the brakes. "Sales Road," yelled the driver, as if that was supposed to mean anything to anyone. Apparently it did to the Cowboy, because he got up and said, "Let's move out." I had just fallen asleep, so I woke up confused because we were in the middle of the highway with no time to think, just grab my stuff and get off the bus. The sun was beginning to break, making the frozen snow glisten like billions of diamonds.

Outside it was about -15° F as the four of us hobbled down the steep steps of the bus, bags in tow. The driver pulled our other suitcases and bags from the belly of the diesel-stinking bus. He dropped them in the snow and was off in a big puff of black smoke, as if to say, "See ya suckers!"

There were no cars anywhere, only the fresh tracks of our chariot as it drove away, its taillights quickly a distant memory of warmth and security. Surprise, surprise, only one house in sight and a lot of trees. It was deathly quiet for a few beats as the silence roared in our ears. We all just seemed to stand there looking around waiting for the man of the house to give direction. I'm sure my mom and sister were thinking the same as me: "What the hell have we gotten ourselves into?" The out-of-the-frying-pan-into-the-fire thought must have been ringing loud and clear.

"Okay, let's go," commanded our new father figure, dressed in his blue jeans, check shirt with the phony pearl snap buttons, his well-worn cowboy boots and jean jacket. The basic dress code for my new town.

"Go where?" my sister barked.

"My brother Bob's house is just down this road."

I think he meant to say trail, since it was covered in two feet of snow. I didn't say much; I was still in shock, and beginning to shiver uncontrollably in my city-slicker brown corduroy pants and matching jacket, t-shirt, and plastic zip-up disco boots with platform soles. I was ready to take on the wild, wild west, no doubt about that. The Cowboy grabbed his Navy-issue green duffel bag and a small red suitcase and was off. He trudged over the four-foot snow bank created by some strategic highway plowing and down the so-called road, to some distant farm house we could not see.

My mom and sister weren't dressed any better than I was, but we took off following our fearless leader. We hadn't walked too far down the snow-covered hill before we saw a pretty farm house, painted white with a forest green trim. Thick white smoke billowed out of its red chimney, letting all who could see know that they were up and ready for the day. It was surreal no question, especially with the backdrop of Dragon Lake frozen in the distance, framed by the snow-covered hills turning a bright orange before my eyes as the morning sun gently woke this little ranching and pulp mill village. Although I was cold, hungry and angry at having to pull my little white suite case through the snow, I couldn't help but see the beauty in this new land. It was truly magical and I had that innocent feeling that this would be the bestest Easter Holiday, ever!

I saw a trailer about three hundred feet from the farm house. It backed onto the slope of one of the bullpens. I wasn't impressed and certainly didn't imagine it was going to be my home for the next six or seven months. It was a dirty cream colour with a brown stripe down the middle and a tinge of green from mold. The single-pane glass windows were filthy. A TV antenna had been attached to the back side of the trailer, but there was no cable, and (as I found out later), just two shitty channels, and both came in fuzzy.

It was basically everything you could imagine in some stereotypical movie like 8 Mile about trailer trash, except for the panoramic backdrop that made the trailer seem out of place. Here I was on a little ranch by a lake, thirty miles out of the small cowboy town. To set the record straight, Bob and Edna and their family, who owned some of the ranch and worked the rest of it for the guy whose name (Sales) was on the small road we slid down, were super nice people, hard-working, salt-of-the-earth ranchers. They should have been on a Canadian coin, stamp or bill they were that good; non-church-goers from what I can remember, but nonetheless, good folk. Bob smoked a couple of packs a day (and died at a young age of cancer) and just like his brother, had that Johnny Cash thing going on. You would never see him in anything but cowboy boots and a cowboy hat. Auntie Edna had a beehive hairdo and wore simple country-type dresses and smiled a lot. She was, or seemed, happy in the true sense of the word. I, on the other hand, was in shock and denial; cowboy boots, farm house, horses, chickens, cows, no street lights and, for crying out loud, no TV. Nightmare in Paradise would be the name of the movie I was living.

The plan was for the four of us to stay on their property in the trailer for Easter. I'm not sure how enthusiastic they were about this scenario, because they would have known that this was to be a permanent arrangement while my mom's new husband tried to find a job. This was probably why the welcome was warm but somewhat guarded when we arrived. I think they were wondering how long we'd be staying.

My new digs were simple at best, with my bedroom being about five by eight with peach and grey walls and an eclectic assortment of 1960s furniture. The water had a rusty flavour to it, but ninety percent of the time I mixed it with my powdered milk, so it was no big deal. The hot water tank was small so two people couldn't take showers in a row, and there was no bathtub, which was good because you couldn't have filled it up with hot water anyway. The TV, as I mentioned, was a small black and white thing. We'd left behind our big new colour one back at the house because we were just going on vacation; and while we were enjoying our vacation, someone broke into the house and stole the TV a week after we got to the ranch. That's the story my mom used as the segue into delivering the news about our move.

"Oh, by the way,", she said, "We put the house up for sale and we're not going back." Pow! Shot to the gut!

It took a long silence before what she said registered with us. As I sunk back into the gold polyester armchair, my mind was racing with all the things I'd left behind that I would never see again, things I'd miss out on: our cool house, in our new neighborhood, the normal friends I'd made, (although somehow I doubted they'd be missing me). I'd never even had a chance to say goodbye. Now we were going to be stuck in this stinking trailer with some lowlifes, and a cowboy loser for a father figure.

I hated my mom for betraying me. I was so mad that the tears were starting to flow, and I didn't want her to see them. Even though I was still in my pajamas that morning, I ran to the door, grabbed my coat, put on my boots and took off down the snow-covered road. The cold air burned my lungs as I ran, stumbling along, kicking at frozen wasteland and swearing like a sailor at the fallen branches that crossed my path. My tears turned icy on my cheeks. No one came after me. A few days later, my sister caught a Greyhound back to the coast. She wanted no part of this chapter of my mom's life. I was on my own.

For the first few weeks, I cried myself to sleep under the orange glow of my old electric clock. I would tell my sorrows to Miss Kitty, my black, long-haired cat with a white diamond-shaped patch of fur on her chest. She held her head close as I spoke into her big green eyes. She purred as she stared back, telling me she understood, and it was all going to work out just fine.

When we moved further north the Cowboy convinced me it was best for Miss Kitty if she stayed on the ranch. I lost my only friend, but maybe he was right.

I heard years later that she lived another 14 years.

Chapter 20

Life in a Northern Town

Tyger Tyger burning bright
In the forests of the night;
What immortal hand or eye,
Dare frame thy fearful symmetry?
– William Blake; 1794

Vacation time was over before I knew it, and it was time to start yet another school: Dragon Lake Elementary, a one-story K-7 school with about three hundred students. I wasn't looking forward to it, especially as it was halfway through the school year and friendships would be set fast with no room for the new kid; but I had played this role many times before so would adapt and survive. To the girls, I was this cool boy from the big city. They loved me. To the guys, I was a city slicker and a threat. They hated me. Bullies live everywhere; it's that plain and simple; and by the way, in case you haven't noticed, a large percentage of the times the best-looking girls generally like them, which complicates matters just that much more. Why?

Interesting article in the Globe following a very public and tragic teen suicide, where a girl showed notes about why she was going to kill herself because of relentless attacks by high school bullies. The thesis of the article: human females are attracted to dominant males, and that means schoolyard bullies and, yes, office bullies as well. It's been my experience the office ones thrive in the corporations. Go figure.

There was still snow everywhere and it was below freezing most days. My teacher was a young Japanese guy called Mr. Yashita. We never hit it off, as I was too cool for school, or so I thought; sure classic defense mechanism, I suppose, wearing my chocolate brown corduroy summer jacket with brass buttons, matching pants and light brown zip-up faux leather three-inch platform boots. Freckled face and curly hair, almost on the side of dread locks. Yeah, I blended right in like a Rottweiler at a cat show.

As usual, I showed up after the kids were in class. I went into the principal's office with my mom, got signed in, and then the principal took me to the classroom. The kids were all nicely organized in their cute little rows of desks. All clean-cut, with white teeth and pleasant smiles. Mr. Yashita was heavily into some topic, jotting feverishly on the board when I walked in. He seemed genuinely happy to meet me and introduced me to the class. I took my usual spot at the back and faked interest in the subject at hand. I searched my surroundings and stared back at the kids who were either staring at me or glancing and whispering to each other behind their hands.

I'd only been settled in there a short while before the bell rang and it was time for recess. The kids got up in an orderly fashion and shuffled out. Mr. Yashita asked if he could talk with me for a second. I said "sure" and lagged behind, all the time wondering what I would run into on the playground. He asked the usual-suspect questions: where was I from? where did I live? who my family was, brothers, sisters etc.? I answered in short statements until he got that hint I was not a Chatty Kathy and said we could talk again sometime. Never happened.

I went out into the schoolyard, where it was way too cold for my dress code, but I didn't really care. Three girls, two of whom I recognized from my brief time in the classroom, were standing nearby the orange steel fire door I came out of. It took only a second when the chubby, in her big blue winter coat and mukluk boots, said, "Where are you from?"

I said, "Vancouver."

"Oh, the big city, ha! I was there, once."

"Interesting," I said, looking away just in time to catch the eye of one of the others, a brunette with big lips and big blue eyes (my favourite) who chirped, "I'm going to go to university there some day." I thought this looked promising.

"Oh yeah? Whereabouts?"

"UBC," she said.

To which I quickly quipped, "Really? Me too! I have actually been on the campus many times," I proudly declared.

Being on the campus was true but getting a post-secondary education was a lie. That was the first time I had ever thought about it, and I really didn't think about it much from that day forward. The recess bell rang, but not before one of the UBC wannabees asked, "Do you want to sit with us at lunch?"

I instinctively said, "Sure. Why not?"

In retrospect and based on all the other schools I had already attended, it probably wasn't a good move, as I guess I should have sat with the boys, who were all glaring at me. Not having a lunch didn't help, but the girls were more than happy to share theirs. Regardless, even then I found girls more intelligent and generally open-minded, plus there are those other physical attributes that add to the fascination.

I chatted with the girls for most of the lunch period, which was odd as the lunch room was pretty much empty by the time one of them suggested we grab our coats and go outside. Not too long after, that particular girl became my girlfriend, which really only meant that she was a girl and was my friend; there was not much else to it, especially in a small town. I, of course, had other ideas of what it meant and was determined to educate the young lace.

Her name was Heather and she was Irish. For grade seven, she had what I would have called at that time a great body; now you would say a nice rack. We hung out a lot, although I lived halfway around the lake from her, which was at least two miles (divide that by 1.6 to get the kilometres) away. There was no public transit to speak of at that time, so I would ride this rusty ten-speed to her house or her mom (single mother of course), or my new uncle, Bob, would drive to pick us up or take us downtown to the old movie theatre. It was a cool experience for a city kid I must admit.

She was a sweet girl, living in a beat-up tiny two-bedroom bungalow on the outskirts of the town. She was far closer to town than I was, but still there were no street lights or highway lights for that matter, so it was really dark when we would drive home. I can recall sitting in the back seat of her mom's old station wagon, holding her hand. For some reason, it was one of the first real sensual experiences I can remember. Who would have thought? It was innocent, but somehow totally erotic to this preadolescent male.

Most of the folks living in this town were just simple, hard-working types: farming, ranching, logging and the big draw – working in the pulp mill. They all watched Hockey Night in Canada (a law in rural Canada), ate meat and potatoes and thought spicy was a bit too much pepper; milk, coffee and OJ for breakfast and beer or Canadian Club, a.k.a. C.C., rye whisky for dinner. Mostly everyone smoked. They loved pick-up trucks and dogs. Cats were a necessary but disposable asset; good around the barn, but "sometimes ya just had to shoot a couple of them to keep the others in line." Or stuff the head of a tomcat or two into a big rubber boot and use your trusty Buck Knife to make him a soprano and cut down on the cat population in the process. It's my guess that's where the saying "he squealed like a cut cat," came from.

A little chewing tobaccy wasn't too bad neither. Drinking and driving was like breathing and not wearing seatbelts. Pick-up trucks were the mini-van of the region, and everywhere you went you would see the back of the truck filled with either hay or people: not a good combo, drinking, driving and riding in the back. Just ask Rick Hansen, who grew up about sixty miles south in a town called Williams Lake. Sunday, the town was closed. There wasn't much going on at night either unless it was the stock car races, rodeo or annual fair. People just went home, ate dinner, watched some TV and went to bed. Early to bed, early to rise was the way of life.

As crappy as it was to me on so many levels, I can still remember having some neat experiences. One that stands out clearly is the time I was driving a snowmobile with three kids from the closest house hanging on tight behind me. For a city kid, it didn't get much better than that; flying through five feet of snow across an endless field chasing a red fox that got caught out in the open. That little guy was as fast as lightning, swerving left then right in perfect ninety-degree angles and somehow never falling through the snow.

I tried to keep up with him but made one sharp turn too many, catapulting all of us off the machine and through the air, landing like ten feet away, all the time laughing so hard I almost peed my pants. Mr. Fox stopped briefly, pondering what we might do next. Then, seeing no more danger, he sauntered across the field and into his den on the side of a snow-covered bank. It was a classic moment in time for me. I'll always remember it.

On my second day at school I had a run-in with the local bad-ass; every school has at least one. I went to so many schools that I even found some that had two or three. Excellent! In general, they were bigger than the other kids, usually a sports guy, you know, a jock, perfect word to describe the level most had as IQs; but sometimes they were bad boys, somewhat good looking and a bit too much testosterone. Why do they always test the new kid? Who knows? Maybe they feel they need to protect their reputation and the girls who they always seem to consider their property. What's the saying for Alphas in the animal kingdom? "First Meat; First Mate."

This little hick town scuffle wasn't a big highlight of my schoolyard education; in fact, it was pretty short and sweet. The kid, who I think was called Calvin, was a blonde kid with the stylin' feathered hair of the day, blue jeans and runners. His thought process, I think, went something like: pick a fight with me in front of as many girls as possible (standard procedure) by some form of verbal put-down. Challenging by physical contact, such as bumping into you with a shoulder so you drop whatever you are carrying is one of their tried and true techniques. This, I assume was the best way to introduce a city slicker to the simple country life.

This guy went with, "Nice freckles."

I came back with, "Is it true your mom and dad are brother and sister? What's that like at Christmas?"

What happened next is pretty self-explanatory. I was about to run because he outweighed me by probably twenty pounds, and also chose to run in my direction in the classic head-down tackle position. No doubt it is a good technique for football, but not so good for excelling in schoolyard fights. I grabbed his hair and kneed him in the face; he squealed and that was the end of that. I was in the principal's office before I knew it, and the self-fulfilling prophecy began again.

Ground Hog Day!

"We all preferred beer when we were broke." -JLH

Chapter 21

Home Alone

"As for violent crimes...well, if 'anger blows out the light of reason,' what can you expect?" – JLH

Six months later, I had a real-life Home Alone experience. I was used to hearing my mom and the Cowboy's drunken arguments, which seemed to always start on Friday and end on maybe a Tuesday or Wednesday. Regardless, they always went late into the night, and no question this affected my school work and sleep pattern. There were many times when I had these spontaneous conversations with my mother about him being a total prick. I hated seeing the bastard knock her around. But love is blind (if love is even the right word), so it never seemed to make any difference what I said. She sure as hell shouldn't have needed an eleven-year-old kid counseling her on men choices, that is for sure. But there I was trying to protect my mom the best I could.

One morning, the Cowboy decided to drive down to the coast for the weekend to apparently wrap up some unfinished business in Vancouver, (no idea what that could have been other than selling our house, furniture etc. as he didn't have anything from what I can recall.) Come to think of it, I found it strange that he had basically zero personal belonging when he moved into our house other than his Navy issued green duffel bag with his initials PJB written in black felt pen on it. Well, that day he stuffed some socks, underwear and a couple of fresh wife-beaters into the duffel, pulled on his old brown cowboy boots, put on his jean jacket and got into his old pickup truck and was off. No matter how you slice it, that was a long drive to do in a couple of days, especially in that beat-up truck. Well, the weekend came and went and no PJ. After about five days my mother was concerned, and did what any good wife would do: chase after him. So without giving me any warning, she was gone to the coast to get him and would be back in a couple of days. That was the story Bob and Edna told me anyhow after school that day. They were to watch out for me while she "popped down to the city over the weekend" to see what the holdup was and to bring him back. No big deal.

I pretended that it didn't bother me when they told me, but inside I was scared and hurt and wasn't looking forward to sleeping in the trailer alone, that was for sure. The upside, if there was one, was that I would have the trailer to myself for a few days, which meant watching my shows on the two TV stations and getting some sleep. But, like the Cowboy's game plan, the weekend ended and Monday came and went and she hadn't come home yet. I still got myself up and went to school those first few days, thinking she'd be home when I got back from school … maybe even a little fantasy of me getting off the big yellow school bus and running down the dirt road into her open arms, just like a Disney movie. Never happened. Days went by, and still nothing. After about three weeks of living by myself in the trailer but going to eat dinner at the main house most nights, I began to feel like Oliver Twist asking for more food. I can't honestly recall, but I assume Edna made me lunch each day, although I do remember a daily staple of peanut butter and jam sandwiches with powdered milk (you mix it with water if you don't know … you gotta get the consistency right or it just doesn't taste like, well, watered-down milk. Oh yeah, stir it with a fork so you can crush the powder chunks against the inside of the glass while you stir) and breakfast of puffed wheat with my powdered milk of course. I really don't know how I felt those first few weeks, but my emotions were running wild, so a safe bet would be angry, confused and lonely. I mean at that point I thought she wasn't coming back, because she didn't call to tell my new minders what her plans were. No question, I was forced to keep growing up faster than I wanted to.

Bob and Edna must have wondered what the hell kind of people they were to just up and leave an eleven-year-old boy by himself for the most part, and not give any indication of when they were coming back. As they were honest salt-of-the-earth types, they must have felt it was a huge burden of responsibility to be put in that position and probably resented the whole situation. Even simple folk like them know when they are being used. I can't say, however, that they ever made me feel unwelcome, but I still felt uncomfortable hanging round their house after the occasional breakfast or nightly dinner (no food in the trailer for me or Miss Kitty). I always grabbed her an extra few pieces of steak or chicken, but she too had to learn to adjust to our new life, which she did far better than me I might add, becoming an excellent mouse hunter in the barns. I would usually go back to the trailer not long after eating. I can't say they weren't nice about it, and in fact they would encourage me to stay, especially if there was a hockey game on. Just nice people.

Concentrating at school was a bit more of a problem than usual, as to be expected. Sleeping became a challenge because it was really dark way out there in the boonies. To an adult it must have seemed pristine with a billions stars to look at, but to me they were all eyes watching and waiting for me to doze off while they hatched their plan to get rid of the city boy.

Thank God for Miss Kitty, who was there to keep me company as I fell asleep to her gentle purring in unison with the hum from my beat-up electric clock; The warm orange glow from that little electric Westclox lit my little room as I watched those tiny black hands tick their way to my future, a soothing and hypnotic pace. I must admit that it lulled me to sleep each night, even if it was a restless one, because every time I heard a car pull up, which wasn't often, I would subconsciously jerk awake and run to the dirty trailer window and peer out, imagining my mom pulling up with an armful of presents. Never happened.

Finally, after another four or five weeks, the Cowboy and my mom did show up. No gifts in hand, just my mom sporting a poorly-covered black eye, brown paper bag with some groceries and her cheap overnight case. The cowboy was in tow with his green duffel bag casually slung over his boney but broad shoulders and a twelve-pack of Old Style, his favourite beer, tucked securely under his arm. I never asked her how she got the black eye but assumed she would say something like, "I bumped into a wall" or "I hit my head on the truck door." Whatever. All I knew was that it seemed to happen quite often. I never really got mad about it because she never made a big deal of it, so I figured it wasn't a big deal either. I was just glad she was home.

A couple of months went by and life was as normal as it could be: school, bus back to ranch, homework if possible, dinner most nights, sleep, repeat. I guess this is my life, I thought. I mean, if you're a worm, a day is about twelve inches, not very exciting. Then without any warning, my mother announced, "Good news, we're getting away from this trailer." I thought "back to Vancouver!" The next words were not what I wanted to hear. "PJ got a great job in Prince George," (hundreds of miles even further north). Yeah, our world was about to change all right when his apparent plum job was being the janitor at a high school. Woohoo!

I was completely sick of moving by now, but at the same time, I was still getting into fights at Dragon Lake Elementary on a regular basis and the teachers thought I had a bad attitude. So I figured maybe a break wasn't that bad of an idea. Besides, what choice did I have?

We packed our sparse belongings into the back of the pickup truck, said our goodbyes and headed off to parts unknown. The trip was long and uncomfortable with the three of us plus the cat stuffed in the small cab of the old truck. The continuous smoking didn't help either; I think me and the cat both threw up at some point. We arrived in the middle of the night and as expected there was no plan as to where to stay, so we basically checked into the first cheesy motel that we came to. I can't remember the name but I do recall it was blue and we shared a one-bedroom, so not much of a step up from the trailer from my point of view; plus now I was sleeping on a pullout couch in the middle of the small living area.

This is about when the migraines and acid reflux started; can't imagine why. I would bet the chain-smoking of my parents, lack of sleep and not-so-good diet played a bit of role. The migraines were just small headaches at first, pressure behind the eyes, that sort of thing, and occurring once a week; then they started coming on a couple of times per week. I can remember needing to get into somewhere dark, like a vampire, to lessen the pounding; keeping a little yellow tin of Aspirin with me at all times (stolen from the local drug store) helped, that's for sure. I enrolled in Connaught Elementary School for the balance of grade seven, which was only for a few months. That was uneventful, thankfully, with the highlight being meeting two boys, one named Elmer Chow and a native Indian kid called Charlie. We hung out throughout the summer doing this and that, all pretty harmless but boring, except that is the big summer festival in Fort George park which I went to and happened to win a new Sekine ten-speed bike, while Elmer won a Harley Davidson mini-bike; yeah, so that was a good day for both of us.

Summer ended and I went to the high school right next to the elementary school which happened to be of the same name. On about the third day, I was walking down the stairwell from the second to first floor enroute to the bathroom, minding my own business, when I saw something on the ground. It was a hundred-dollar bill. Suddenly it was like time stood still and a thousand angels were singing Hallelujah, as the light from the northern sun blazed through the dirty window, casting a bright yellow halo around the spot on the grey cement floor. I bent to pick it up, my heart pounding like a trapped chipmunk, but as I picked it up I realized it was nothing but a cool business card that looked like a hundred dollar bill. The angels stopped singing and then I realized the singing was laughter. Well, without realizing it, a native girl who was coming up the stairs had spotted it a split second after me and was convinced it was hers. Like most schools back then, there were cliques or gangs of kids that had similar values, interests or whatever. The problem in that is being the new kid and a loner meant you were at an obvious disadvantage. This particular native girl (or butch) was part of such a group.

She didn't waste a second and blurted out, "Hand it over or I'll beat the living shit out of your skinny white ass." She weighed a good forty pounds more than me, (Well, everyone weighed forty pounds more than me) so there was no surprise there

"Sure, no problem," I said quick and innocently. The big stairwell was empty and as quiet as church, with all the kids in class. (Hmm, no witnesses around, this could be fun.) She held out her chunky hand as I pretended to give it to her, but at the last second, I bolted back up the stairs. As might be expected, this pissed her off and with surprising speed and agility she was on me before I made it to the top of the first set of stairs, her fat fingers immersing themselves in my thick locks. This pulled my head back with a snap. Did I mention I was a light weight? A friggin' pigeon could knock me over. Now, at this point she did not know it was a fake bill and for some reason I did not want to tell her. I guess I just didn't like being told what to do even then. So what happened? Well, I guess a chunk of my hair came out about the same time as I did my version of a lucky mule kick to her fat gut and the law of gravity took over, sending her airborne backwards down the stairs.

She let out a non-human screech as she floated to her destiny; it was a thing of beauty, landing with a kind of thud sound on the cement landing. This knocked the fight out of the big cow, so I casually walked down the steps to her as she gasped to catch her breath, and pried the fake business card from her hand. I looked down at her shocked expression and said, "That's mine," and continued to my class thinking this was the end. The whole altercation lasted about fifteen seconds if that.

Unfortunately, that wasn't the end; no, only the beginning of weeks of ducking beatings from First Nation gangs. She had an entire tribe, it seemed, using all their tracking skills to catch or set me up. I managed to outsmart them most of the time, but on a few occasions I still got the shit kicked out of me. I remember one time it was because I was being a smart ass and taunting this white Indian dude (aboriginal, red-haired, missing front tooth, trailer trash wannabe, and, of course, bigger than me), who moved like the wind on his one-speed bike. By the time I even thought to bolt on my new ten-speed (the one I'd won from the local radio station) it was pow time. He then hit me with his left, sending me ass-over-teakettle down an embankment, then turned and casually rode back to the clan, their laughter echoing down the dirt road. I had no idea what happened but decided it was best to avoid him and the rest of the gang after that.

"All ideas are great; it's just the timing that isn't." – JLH

Chapter 22

Braving the Elements

Between the crap that was going on at school, living in a one bedroom no-tell motel (I'm sure they rented by the hour), my mom and the Cowboy drinking pretty much every day, there was no such thing as peace or privacy. It was just not an option. Amazingly I was still able to pass all of my classes maintaining a C-or C+-average. Nothing to brag about. I will admit. As for food, well, on occasion we had the real deal, I mean other than my trademark dish of Kraft Dinner with thinly-sliced Oscar Mayer hot dogs topped off with splash of Heinz ketchup. I can smell it now! So usually a real meal was at some cheap diner or Chinese delivery (I still love Chinese delivery as long as the menu doesn't say "Chinese and Western Cuisine"), but on occasion my mom or the Cowboy would attempt to make a meal, as the motel had a small stove and fridge. On this one particular night I was trying to be a good student and do my homework, but as usual it was challenging to concentrate, having not eaten since breakfast and my drunken guardian units singing loudly to Charlie Rich and Johnny Cash; nothing against those legends, just to be clear. But at this time I had just had a bath and was sitting in white briefs (didn't have pajamas at the time), on my hard brown wool-something pullout couch/bed. The street lights were trying to rip through the white sheers, long since changed to a light brown from years of cigarette smoke and diesel exhaust from the hundreds of semi-trucks growling by the ice-encased single pane windows, and it all seemed to harmonize with Johnny Cash's We're Going to Jackson. Since the first concert I ever went to (only good thing Cowboy did for me as far as I can recall) was Johnny Cash and June Carter, I gotta admit I love that song!

Anyway, it was around 7 p.m. and around twenty below zero Fahrenheit in Canada's Capital of the North that night, with at least three feet of snow blanketing the forest city of Prince George. The smell of steak my mom was trying to fry engulfed the small motel room in billows of beautiful-smelling smoke. No, there was no fan over the stove. If I was a dog (or tiger for that matter) I would have been drooling on my text books. (Wow, steak! I was thinking. I haven't had that in about a year!) No sooner had the beautiful piece of art been laid before me by my mom, the Cowboy stumbled out of the bedroom and walked up to me and cut my steak in half and headed back to the bedroom, I followed like his shadow as he put the other half on a small white plate for my cat. Now I loved that cat, just to be clear, but that crossed the boundaries of our feline-human relationship and I think she knew it as I plunked my other half of that succulent meat of legends under her nose while yelling, "Why not give it all to her?"

The cat went one way and me the other, with the Cowboy, wearing white briefs and matching wife-beater T, in close pursuit. I guess I misjudged how drunk he was, because he reacted with surprising speed and agility closing the gap in three strides of his bony ivory legs and grossly- long dragon-like toenails. He caught me by the hair (this was a running theme in my altercations for some years; when it comes to fights, bald men have a distinct advantage … same goes for bald women I suppose), jerking me backwards off my feet. Time stood still as he dragged me to the front door, cursing the whole time, "You little ungrateful son of a bitch, I'll teach you!" One hand was tangled in my hair while the other yanked the door open with such force that the brass doorknob punched a perfect hole in the cheap wood-paneled wall. In a flash, both of his sinewy tobacco-smelling hands were over my face as he picked me up by my head and tossed me like a piece of garbage into the snow. That was a wake-up call for sure as the cold instantly seared my bare feet and legs like walking on hot coals.

The door slammed with a bang! I scrambled to my feet, brushed off the snow , scrambled up the stairs and began pounding on the door with all the might my mini-fists could muster. I heard some yelling from my mom, and the Cowboy then used the classic wife beater move which includes the smack, shriek and thud, as the female hits the floor. No doubt if a police report was ever filed by a hospital it would have said slip and fall, not smack and thud. I knew in a few seconds this was a waste of valuable time and that if didn't get indoors quick, I'd probably freeze to death or acquire some nasty frost bite on parts I was hoping to keep for a while longer. So I ran to the next motel room over and banged on the hollow wood door.

"We don't want any trouble," came a raspy voice from inside, followed shortly after by the standard, "Go away or I'll call the cops!" Pointless to try to explain that was a good idea, as I was naked and about to freeze to death, since he was most likely a Cowboy replica and had just thrown some other young punk out into the snow himself.

This couldn't have been the first night they'd heard the crashing and yelling sounds from their various white-trash neighbours including us. I felt my feet starting to burn but I was somehow not cold yet. (Funny how really hot things and really cold ones feel the same on bare skin. Makes you say, "Hmmm?") Well, I , made a break for Elmer Chow's, who lived basically on the opposite side of the huge Fort George Park, which was not far from our motel. I guessed it was only about half a mile or so, and without any understanding of the effects of frost bite, I bolted for it. I mean, what choice did I have? So off I went. The time between hitting the snow and making a run for it was probably no more than thirty long seconds, running as fast as I could, sometimes knee-deep in snow other times on top of the snow like an Elf from Lord of the Rings. There were no cars or people around, lucky me; just as well, since I was prime meat for the ever-hungry pedophile carnivores.

I was scared; the cold biting into me like ten thousand starving black flies hoping to bleed me out. I started to shiver before I crossed the highway in front of our twenty-room home. The tops of my ears felt like someone was putting a cigarette out on them and, to make things just a bit more memorable, I seemed to have no feeling from my waist down. It was like running on stumps that did not belong to me. I have always been a fast runner but that night I literally ran like a jack rabbit, skimming across the top of the snow, barely leaving footprints.

Not sure how long it took me but it seemed forever to finally reach the Chow family home, one of those small post-WWII-style bungalows churned out by the thousands for the returning troops. It was a cute, well-kept, yellow-with-a-brown-trim house. I imagined it had three bedrooms, but I somehow doubt it. By the time I got there, I couldn't feel my legs or my hands, so I immediately began pounding on the door like a rabid albino chimp, using both hands to get some impact. After several whacks, the door swung open with one of his rather attractive teenage sisters looking right over my head to the street, then glancing down and gasping with a facial expression of shock, horror or humour - hard to tell - as a skinny, naked white boy (Well, I was more pink than white at the time), asked, "Is Elmer home?" like we were going to head out and make snowmen. It was the last thing she would have expected. As she stared at me, I casually stepped inside the blissfully warm house, trying of course to look cool, which is hard to pull off at the best of times for me, never mind when shivering uncontrollably in my underwear. She yelled for her mom, and I suspect a lot of Cantonese went flying around. The other sister, also cute, came running around the corner with a grey wool blanket as she wrapped it around me. I thought, "I love her!" Then I sat, or kind of collapsed, onto the light brown lacquered wood floor, not really knowing what to do next but feeling a combination of embarrassment and thankfulness that I had a friend named Elmer.

It would have been more than thirty seconds when his dad came on the scene. He managed to get me up and said something to the mom in Hong Kong Cantonese as he sat me on the small brown and yellow flowered loveseat next to the TV. By what happened next, I guess it was "run him a hot bath," since Elmer's mom led to their small bathroom, cluttered with the tools that help make pretty women pretty. She directed me to the bath with a combination of Chinese and universal hand gestures. I got the message just as one of the daughters brought me a pair of Elmer's PJs. The door shut, I dropped the blanket and I quickly slipped into the soothing liquid of pure joy. It was the best bath I had ever had. Afterwards they tried to get out of me what happened. I made up some story, covering for my mom like any kid would. I did not want her to get into trouble over something that was my fault. But really, was there any answer I could give a so-called-normal parent that could satisfactorily explain how I ended up there at 7:30 on a school night in my underwear? Nope.

I might have given the number or name of the motel to the dad or mom, but I doubt it. Even if I did, who would have come to claim me? The Cowboy junkie? I don't think so. I slept on the loveseat, getting up early and wanting to leave the situation quickly. They insisted I share some awkward silence and Cheerios with Elmer and his sisters. I ate and said my thanks and headed back home wearing Elmer's clothes from head to toe. (Well, except for the underwear; they were mine.) When I got back to the motel my mom and the Cowboy were having the breakfast of champions: bacon, eggs, vodka and OJ. Perfect! What every growing lad needs to kick-start their school day. My mom said something like, "Jake, where have you been? I have been worried sick," like I'd just popped down to the store for some mixer. Truth be told, she probably was. I didn't say much, I mean, what would have been the point? I just got changed into my own clothes, slapped a PB&J sandwich together and went to school.

When I got home after school, things were pretty much the same, and I doubt they even remembered what had happened. That night, I lay in bed listening to my little transistor radio that I kept under my pillow, a Vancouver AM station fading in and out as I dreamed of being at the upcoming sold-out Welcome to My Nightmare Alice Cooper concert at the Pacific Coliseum.

It was 1975, and I was living my own nightmare.

Chapter 23

Escape to the Army…the Salvation Army

A few weeks later, we moved into a furnished shit-box two-bedroom apartment a few blocks from the motel. It was a urine-yellow, three-story walk-up on a side street; a big plus was that it was a hell of a lot quieter than the motel on the highway. We were on the second floor of the dimly lit, and as usual, cigarette-and-piss-and-vomit-smelling building. Inside was the standard teal-coloured bathroom set, old furniture, and a couple of cool but tacky Mexican black velvet paintings. I actually like those. It was a palace compared to where we had lived, but then again, as a kid, if your mom and dad said a cardboard box was your new home, you'd be thinking, "Far-out! Do I get my own room?"

Another huge plus was that I actually did have my own room. It had a child's single bed, a small night table and nothing else; simple, but good enough for me. As usual, the first thing I did when I moved was put up my four blacklight posters that I had somehow managed to keep with me. My favourite for some reason was of a couple who were hugging as they floated towards the setting sun in a large balloon that was

being pulled by two giant flying cranes. My second favourite was a werewolf, which I still have to this day and is pictured here. I don't remember what the others were, but wherever I lived, those posters were always unpacked and put up first.

We still didn't have a TV, but the Cowboy came home one day with a used Hi Fi record player so they could play their mix of country and Louis Armstrong type music; nothing like the classics to help get in the mood for some good ole-fashioned drinking and wife tossing. You know, men beat women because sometimes you just have to tell them twice, that kind of thing. Not! It's just the way it was, but like most sons and daughters I was keeping score and one day it would be payback.

As you might have guessed by now, the Cowboy had quite the Jekyll and Hyde thing going on: hard-working, cow-puncher type by day and hard-drinking woman-puncher by night. Dinner on the table? It better be, or else! Who needs a real reason for an argument when you're hammered? Anything will do.

From my room, I could hear his muffled never-ending rants: "Those damned kids of yours … we coulda stayed in Vancouver … your brats are all alike … pompous, stuck up bitches, the lot of ya… without the Canadians you'd all be speaking German……get me another beer … I think your son is drinking our vodka and filling the bottle with water … why are there dishes in the sink… empty that fucking ashtray; it's overflowing onto the floor … what the hell's wrong with you? Has anyone fed the cat?" (Okay, he gets one brownie point for liking the cat more than me.)

I wanted my mom to yell back, to tell him to leave. But I could hear her just politely replying, always trying to make peace. She kept asking why he would say the things he said, slurring her words with her English accent getting stronger. "Now that is not nice," she'd say. "Why do you talk like that? I want to know. Why?" she would whine over and over, until the boiling point, when bam! He'd deliver a backhand (Remember. the slap is abuse, but the backhand is to make a point.) Sometimes, though, it was an open-hander to the side of the head.

I stayed in my room a lot, but there was no way to completely drown out the sounds of the ever-repeating songs coming from the rotating turntable and the escalating arguments. I feebly attempted to do my homework night after night with the never-ending interruptions; not much chance of nailing a 3.9 GPA or even a 1.9 for that matter; no Ivy League university options in my cards. Well, what can you expect? I never actually knew anyone who went there other than that live-in student who almost took a bullet to the pumpkin during one of our regular drive-bys.

I'd sit there and think, "I wish I could fly, escape and never come back," like in Peter Pan when all the kids take off with him. "Second star to the right and straight on till morning." Capturing that feeling would be like a whisper heard in the wind; you'd turn to see where it came from, but it would be gone, leaving just the lingering sweet fragrance of freedom and the fleeting moments that make up childhood. Then I'd hear more yelling and loud crashing, and the bubble of a youthful dream would burst into a million tears.

One night after a particularly bad fight, I remember coming into the living room and seeing my mom getting up off the floor. "I just slipped off the chair," she said. But her eyes told me what really happened: she got punched in the bread basket by an expert bully. "No scars allowed," according to the Wife Beater's Handbook.

Later on that evening, we used the old Star Trek's Captain Kirk tuck and roll maneuver and escaped while he was passed out on the couch.

My mom came ever so quietly into my room and said, "Jake, put on your coat and shoes. We're going for a walk." I was momentarily confused but figured it out pretty quickly.

That was about it. No clothing, just my pajamas, shoes and a coat, and off we went into the Prince George night. Like the old Johnny Horton song goes, "When it's spring time in Alaska, it's 40 below." Not quite, but it was damned cold in Northern Canada. I don't know what time it was as we walked along the old highway towards the centre of town. The occasional semi-truck blasted by, and a few beat-up pickup trucks slowed down to try to scope out the situation.

"Where are we going mommy?" I asked. "Can I bring my stuff? How long are we going for? Can we move back to Vancouver? It's a lot warmer there."

Her face didn't show any signs of bruises or blood - just determination - as she pulled me along as fast as I could walk. Her hair was disheveled and she was still a bit tipsy, but she was sobering up pretty damn quick.

(To me, it was exciting; another adventure into the unknown. Maybe I could get a hot chocolate or a PB&J sandwich. I wondered if there would be other kids where we were going. Maybe even a girl or two perhaps? Yes, I had noticed girls were different by this point.)

We arrived at a large red brick building. It reminded me of a community centre, but with a security check-in at the front. I thought that was odd and wondered why they needed that. But I was cold, so it really didn't matter. I'd seen the sign before - Salvation Army - and knew they were good people. After all, they had more than once dropped off a food basket and some presents at Christmas. Looked like they were coming to the rescue again.

We went through the security check-in where my mom answered some basic questions and I soon found myself in a gymnasium-sized room full of cots and lots of women, and, yeah, some kids. A quick look into some eyes told their story: they were tired, hurt, angry, scared and thankful. The mosaic of desperate souls was made up mostly of aboriginal women, but from what I recall, the balance were what those who have not suffered much would call "trailer trash," and I suppose my mom and I were two of them.

We found two beds near the back of the hall. I feel asleep when my head hit the hard, smelly pillow as my mom stroked my head, saying, "It will be all right. Sweet dreams."

On the third day we were there, my mom and I were up early and eating a pretty good breakfast of bacon, eggs and toast in the school-style cafeteria setting when she told me we had to go and collect some things from the apartment. It was late morning when we arrived, my mom first making sure his old pickup truck was gone before we climbed the stairs to the apartment. The thick old blackout curtains were still closed as she quietly opened the door and walked into the living room. It was dark as night, with only a sliver of light cutting its way through the cracks of the curtains. The only sound was the hum from the fridge and the old clock in the kitchen ticking away. The smell of stale smoke and beer hung in the air like a hangover you never forget.

Everything looked the same as we left it, until we got to my room. When I opened the door, I was hit with an immediate adrenalin rush. My room looked like a bear had ransacked it looking for scraps of food or a sleeping hunter: my blacklight posters were ripped from the walls; all the drawers of my little dresser were pulled out; my collection of the fossilized fish and plants I had excavated during an archaeological dig of my own from high up on the wall of an open quarry in Quesnel lay in ruins on the carpet; but worst of all, so was my prized electric guitar.

"My stuff! My stuff!" I yelled as loud as I could. "It's smashed up! He smashed my, my, my guitar. He broke my guitar in half!" I was hyperventilating and sobbing as I sat on the edge of my overturned bed and picked up the splintered ruins of my guitar. I was numb.

My mom came in with tears in her eyes and said, "Oh, Jake, I am so sorry," as she sat down beside me and gave me a big hug. I wasn't mad at her. I knew it wasn't her fault. She just for some reason was attracted to a certain type of guy commonly known as the rugged, good- looking asshole.

She then grimly grabbed the pillow from my bed, ripped the pillow case off it and told me to stuff all my clothing into it as fast as I could. She disappeared into her room and I heard the clicking of a suitcase; I assumed she was packing our own things. I looked around at the mess in my little room and realized that there wasn't much for me to pack, now that most of my treasured things were crushed. As I shoved a few pieces of clothing and toys into my pillowcase and rolled up my posters I thought of several scenarios where I would get revenge on the Cowboy; this included smashing everything left in the apartment; waiting in the dark for him to come back and ambushing him with a bat (which I didn't have) and beating him unconscious; or coming back at night and slashing the tires on his piece-of-shit truck. Well, I ultimately did nothing, because I was a kid, and it was just too much for me to handle.

The score had just gone up and I vowed to get that bastard and I did. I'll talk about that later.

"I have several things I feel define success…one being a fridge full of food, including desserts." - JLH

Chapter 24

Tilly the Hun to the Rescue

Tilly, my mom's old drinking pal from the Projects, came to our rescue, convincing some beer-bellied unsuspecting sap to drive his  little two-door Datsun B210, 11 ½ hours north to get us and my cat. She was a five-foot-four dumpy, pear-shaped half-aboriginal woman, weighing in at 235 pounds, more or less. She wore a pair of bad-fitting false teeth that she kept rolling around in her St. Bernard-sized jowls. And of course she stunk of BO, because who has time to shower when there's so much food and alcohol to consume? Basically, she was in the dictionary as the definition of "fat, stinky trailer trash." We squeezed ourselves plus all the stuff we had grabbed from the apartment into the joke of a car and headed on the epic journey south. Well, as to be expected, or as luck would have it, halfway to Vancouver, the motor blew or something like that. Bottom line, Fat Boy and the Hun were stuck and pissed in 100 Mile House. Tilly didn't waste much time; she got the Greyhound bus schedule and the three of us (and Miss Kitty) were on it later that day. Not so for the fat patsy; he was stuck waiting to get his car fixed. Tilly eventually made my mother pay her for the guy's bill, and I would bet anything he never saw a dime of that money.

Somehow the Hun convinced my mom it was best for us to just move in with her. We did, and as it turned out, things did not get better, just different. Her house was on the border between the good side and the bad and ugly side of the city, only a stone's throw from the Projects we had left not that long ago. It seemed like we'd gone full circle, trading the row house for a room I shared with my mom in a small house with five dogs. Tilly was a big woman, to put it mildly. (Think Star Wars' Jabba the Hut meets legendary singer Aretha Franklin; no offense to Aretha.) She tolerated me for the most part, but only if I did exactly what she said. She pretty much over-rode my mom's parenting whenever she felt like it. After all, her boys were pool players (one was famous at that time, apparently the number one snooker player in the world ... like I said, "apparently"), and she knew Hells Angels members and gangsters on a first-name basis. I guess she figured if I played my cards right, I too could be like her boys even though I was not allowed to go downstairs and use the pool table - ever! As things seemed to go for us, our little sanctuary didn't last too long. Besides the non-stop partying, Tilly seemed to have a thing for my mom. Yeah, that was way before this type of stuff was so open. I was young but not stupid, and on more than one occasion thought this toothless bag of goo was just a bit too touchy-feely with my mom. Then came D-Day and our biggest falling out at the classy Mr. Mike's Steak House. So this is how I remember it. She wanted me to sit in the restaurant part while she and my mom sat at the bar section through a door and out of sight. Her logic was that they don't serve food in the bar so I couldn't be there and she could get rid of me for a while. I protested; I really didn't want to eat my mac and cheese by myself and I really just didn't like this fat bitch. But she wouldn't listen to me or my mom and eventually told my mom to "shut up and get into the bar". To my surprise my mom followed her instructions and went off to the other side of the restaurant while the Hun lagged behind to give me some parting advice: "Listen here, you little prick," she said in her acidic whisper, "You sit your ass down in the restaurant and let me and your mom talk. We have some business to discuss."

Yeah, right. She wanted to hit on my mom or get money from her. Either way she would be sure to get my mom to pay for her food and drinks. Well, I gave them about twenty minutes until my food arrived, and then I innocently asked the waitress if I could take the food into the bar and sit with my mom.

"Sure, sweetie," she said, "No problem. I'll take it in there for you. Let me get a tray. You go in and I'll be there in a minute."

So off I went like a proud puppy, wagging my little tail with a smug expression on my face. I sat down beside my mom and smiled. Tilly just glared at me with daggers in her eyes. It took about two seconds until she burst out with, "What did I tell you?" she hissed.

"The waitress is bringing my food in here. She said it was fine," I said, but before I could even finish my sentence, she took her tall, ice-filled glass of rum and coke and splashed it into my face, but she did with such gusto that the glass hit me hard on the bridge of the nose, leaving a neat cut. I fell sideways off the big-bench booth and hit the floor crying, the shrill of my nearly-adolescent vocal cords echoing across both sides of the restaurant.

"You fucking little bastard. How dare you!" She yelled, as her giant Jell-O like body seemed to move in waves of angry emotions with the speed of the comic book hero (that never made it to print) Fat Flash. In a blink she had oozed off the shiny burgundy-coloured vinyl booth and was gone. I was on the floor looking up, and all I could see was her earth-shadowing butt blacking out the distant windows as she squeezed by the other patrons, all not knowing what was happening, but somehow suspecting they had just been the victims of an invisible, 5' 4 ", 235- pound elephant attack. Those who cared to check would have seen only the puff of blue smoke coming from the back of her ruby-red and rusted 1968 Ford station wagon with classic wood paneling.

The waitress showed up a few seconds later, as my mom and I sat there stunned, a bit of blood running down my nose. She just stood there for a second or two, obviously wondering what the hell had just happened. She quickly gained her composure, gave me a napkin, put down my food, and said sheepishly, "Is there anything else?" Ha! "How about a new life?" I wanted to say. But all that came out of my mouth was a simple "No." My mom asked her if she could call us a cab when we were finished. The lady smiled gently and said, "No problem, dear." We left twenty minutes later, not exactly knowing where to go, but my mom put on a strong face and we headed back to the Hun's. She was out. so we watched some TV on the little black and white portable in our room and went to sleep early. Nothing was said about the incident again, but Tilly not only looked like an elephant, she also had a memory like one, so my days were numbered there for certain.

A week or so later, my mom and Tilly were having a few cocktails in her original 1960s teal-coloured kitchen, with the added personal touch, as expected from a group of chain smokers, of walls and ceiling transformed from light yellow to light brown after years of smoke from unfiltered roll-your-own cigarettes. The floor was also original first- generation linoleum, but the colour was hard to describe; best guess: it was once white but was now stained light brown from her filthy pack of dogs. Not sure if they were trained, but two things were evident: one - none of them liked me and two - they were never too far away from her, which is fine except for Captain, the 190-pound male black Great Dane with his watchful eye and twitchy trigger finger.

After living there for a while, I thought the dogs and I had reached an understanding that I was their leader. Well, not being all that familiar with dogs other than having had them chase me on occasion, I didn't have that pack hierarchy thing worked out quite yet, but I suspect they did.

So one night, a couple of days before starting yet another new high school, I was just hanging around the kitchen watching and listening to the chatter of my mom, Tilly and a couple of their regular alcoholic guy friends. They didn't say much of interest other than the usual complaining about money, cars, money, booze, money, politics, money (as in lack of it) and gossip about people that weren't there. These conversations seemed to go well, provided no one seriously disagreed with or challenged the Hun. Then it would change instantly from senseless but friendly drunken banter to daggers flashing from her bloodshot eyes and poisonous venom spewing from her fat red-smeared-lipstick mouth, with cheap beer sometimes showering the unsuspecting person until they backed down or walked away. Well, since they were all engaged in deep discussion that evening, I thought I would entertain myself by (stupidly) dropping to my hands and knees and pretending I was a doggy too. (Why? Who knows, maybe I was just trying to get attention from my mom or whoever else was interested.) Well, it worked fabulously, except the only attention I got was from the Captain.

All was working well until I made the near-fatal error of crawling under the Captain's belly. That mistake only lasted about a tenth of a second when wham! he snapped his neck around while opening his gaping jaws full of huge yellowed teeth and made a valiant attempt at grabbing me by my air-filled head. Intuitively, (John C. Maxwell says you are intuitive in the area of your giftedness, and, considering the many situations I have been in over the years, that required getting out of harm's way; it's one of my gifts), I jerked my head out of his mouth, but not before his canines snapped shut on my left ear. I don't remember much other than pain that was equivalent to a cigarette being butted out on your arm. Try it sometime. Fun stuff.

I screamed like a girly-boy; not proud of it, but after all I wasn't a Spartan kid being trained for combat or death, so the shock of my voice probably startled the big dog enough that he didn't try to get a better grip on my freckled face and chicken-leg-sized neck. What happened next I am not sure, but from what I can recall the Hun, with the unexpected speed and agility of a starving hippo, flew to my rescue, but not before pounding back the remainder of her drink and slamming the glass on the table. Cigarette dangling from her toothless mouth, she grabbed the big mutt with both hands, one clutching the back of his neck and the other his spine. He yelped with a screech that would wakened the dead as I screamed again, rolling over on my back and cupping my ear. It was ripped in half, and blood was oozing through my fingers. The other dogs scattered to all corners of the stinky house.

Tilly lifted the dog off the ground and flung all hundred and ninety pounds of him against the kitchen cupboards. His nails uselessly clacked on the linoleum trying to find some traction. She then dragged him across the floor, threw his yelping ass down the basement stairs, and slammed the door with a bam! The entire event took probably less than fifteen seconds, from my scream to the big dog's yelp as he flew down the stairs.

My mom was in shock over what had unfolded before her eyes and honestly didn't know whether to take a swig or wind her watch. This was no doubt a lot of action, and it was definitely not part of the evening's agenda, but as moms do, she quickly snapped out of it and yelled, "Bloody hell! He's bleeding!" as she yanked a dirty dish towel from the oven handle and pressed it on to the side of my head while I rolled around on the floor, blood dripping in big blotches as I did. Seeing the blood on my hands and floor only made me squeal louder; this of course had all the other dogs barking and howling while Tilly flew around swearing in French as she corralled the other mutts into her bedroom. For me, it was my second out-of-body experience (the first, as mentioned, was my Halloween drug candy fun night) and probably the Captain's first. Since this happened so fast, my mom did really know where the blood was coming from, because the precious life-juice was smeared all over the side of my head and face. At this point she told the Hun to call an ambulance, but no sooner had the words dropped from her lips, Tilly bellowed out in her deep raspy dominatrix voice, "No! It will be faster if I drive him to emergency!" Apparently she had a thing about ambulances coming to her house, or, more likely, the police being called due to the type of incident.

So off we went to the hospital: me and the lesser-known Canadian Olympic Team athletes who excelled in the Drunky Drawer events (which include singing, driving all types of motorized vehicles at whatever speed feels right, fighting, swearing and let's not forget my all-time favourite, projectile vomiting. (I think the record is about 12.5 feet and held by someone I know.) As expected, the emergency waiting area was full of unhappy-looking people, but that is what you get with a universal healthcare system; you get what you pay for. Tilly went to the counter, smelling like a brewery no doubt, and gave some story to the nurse about what happened. My mom and I did what we were told by Tilly and sat down on one of those uncomfortable waiting room chairs. I wasn't really paying attention because I was still holding my ear, but I heard the nurse ask Tilly, "Are you the mother?"

"Nom" said Tilly. "I'm his aunt."

"Where is the mother?"

"She's there with the boy."

"Okay. We'll need some information from her."

Tilly didn't really like this and had been trying to coach me and my mom on the drive there, saying, "It will be best if you don't say anything about you being attacked by the dog. I don't want any cops coming to my house. I will handle it!"

My mom reluctantly asked, "What do you want us to say?"

The Hun came up with some stupid story, like I was cutting my own hair with some scissors or something. That was the story we told the doctor when he asked me what happened. I think he knew something was up, since it wasn't a clean cut that would have been done by a blade, it was more of a ragged rip and he probably knew the difference; plus my hair was long and curly, obviously not cut. Well, he gave me some freezing thing then put in a half a dozen stitches.

He gave a prescription for antibiotics, and we were on our way back to the Dog House.

Chapter 25

Back to School

The next day I started grade eight (high school) with my ear stitched together and a few choicely-placed bobby pins "to keep the hair out," as my mom said, no matter how much I protested. This was one of those forks in the road for me. My mother had enrolled me in Eric Hamber, an upscale West Side school in an upscale West Side neighbourhood. The kids at Hamber, like their parents, were all well-heeled with good teeth and tans. The boys played rugby or tennis or golf. Most of them had brand-new cars and, from what I heard, they had loads of house parties as their parents seemed to always be away or maybe they figured that if their kids were going to do drugs, drink or have sex, they should do it at home. There is some logic to that I suppose. I was only there a few days when the school realized I lived on the wrong side of the street, which was at the time meant I was not in their district catchment's boundary - as in one side of street West Side was okay; other side East Van, not okay. So they were more than happy to break the bad news and send me to the "right" high school, Sir Charles Tupper Secondary School, which just happened to be one of the worst schools in the city at the time.

Like so many inner-city schools, it was overcrowded (seventeen hundred-plus kids approximately) and under-staffed. It was the first school I had ever heard of that had a fulltime cop (Mr. Wright) stationed there. The kids were all from blue-collar or, like me, from low-income families, plus a large number of first- generation East Indians, Chinese and Vietnamese. For most, I'm sure, the goal was to be the first in their families not only to graduate from high school, but maybe by some miracle, from university as well. Well, that may have been their plan, but to be honest, anything past high school never crossed my mind and for certain was never a conversation around the dinner table. That never fazed me, as my plan was to either be an actor, pilot or if all else failed, join the Air Force.

My mom told me that no one would notice the bobby pins holding my hair away from my stitches – not! On my first day there, I encountered Count Zeffer, as some of the teachers called him, and his minions. He was a blond, dreadlock-looking teenager, not too tall, but his stocky frame and wild nature made up for his vertical challenges. He wasn't the best-looking guy with his teenage trademark zits and B.O., but he made up for that as well with his greaseball look of a storm-rider jean jacket and Dayton Boots. Not sure what his home life was like, but at fourteen or fifteen he was already a stressed out, chain-smoking and angry wayward punk as far as I was concerned.

The first day of school, I was sitting in remedial (basic) math, not really paying attention to the teacher because I was more concerned about all the eyes glaring at the new kid. I was used to this by now, but it was never comfortable. The math teacher, Mr. Hack, left the room "just for a few minutes," as he would always say, but as time went on I noticed he generally came back about five minutes before the end of class. On this my first day, the Count had clearly noticed my hair appliances, not to mention the shiny new Mickey Mouse binder that my mom had thought would be cute. Cute, not so much; noticeable target material? Oh, yeah! Before the light green hardwood door hit Mr. Hack's chubby ass, the Count turned to me saying, "Only fuckin' fags wear bobby pins" while simultaneously kicking me in the side of the ribs with his Dayton's. A second later, Rob Rose, psycho kid, kicked a hole in the side of my desk with his steel-toed running shoes. He was very proud. The next second, a few of the not-so-feminine girls grabbed the front of my small desk and flipped it up and backwards, sending my head into the hard classroom floor. The rest of the class burst into laughter as I lay there on my back, desk on top of me, trying to figure out what the hell just happened. Whispers of "Bobby Pin Boy" and "Mickey Mouse Binder Queer" floated like mustard gas across my face. As usual, these things happen in seconds, not minutes like in the movies. I would have pegged this one at about fifteen to twenty seconds, tops.

I didn't feel any kind of pain at the time due to a combination of the adrenaline rush, the shock of my head hitting the floor and the utter humiliation of the event in front of my new peers. I was lucky, I suppose, because I would have probably gotten a few kicks to the head if the teacher hadn't come back into the room a few seconds after I hit the ground. Mr. Hack heard the noise from the hallway as he sauntered back from getting a spiked coffee, I suspect. The big door opened fast with him yelling in an East Indian accent, "What's going on in here?" Seeing me upside down under my desk gave him a bit of a startle, and I thought I caught a slight trace of a smile across his big fat lips before he gained his composure and said, "Who did this?" The class was, of course, dead silent for a second or two, but the snickers couldn't be contained for long. So, before things got too weird, I calmly explained, "No one. I did it myself." I knew better than to rat out to a teacher even then.

Mr. Hack, a well-meaning, soft-spoken, pock-mark-faced, bald-headed, combed-over, EA (as we use to call educational assistants) must have lost a bet to get this class of misfits and ESL kids. All in all, he was a very nice guy, but he had no interest in trying to teach the majority of the kids in that class math equations no matter how simple - especially when they called him "Fuckin' Hindu" and "Paki Rat Bastard" to his face. He would challenge the boys and some of the girls, who dressed more like hookers than students most of the time, but limited it to "You not allowed to talk at me like that. You leave at this room now." Funny thing was, he never reported these events to the school VP or anyone else. Not sure why, but I found out pretty quickly that several teachers had been beaten up on a number of occasions both on the school property and off for pushing it too far with certain groups (gangs) in the school.

He was a bit of a perv, managing to get the so-called "early bloomers" (as in big guns and no brains to aim them) with their low-cut tops to sit in the front rows where he could keep a bloodshot eye on them no doubt. For them, he always had time for some close-up and personal one-on-one teaching. The classic move (back in the day) was that one arm would go around their shoulder and drape/hover a hand an inch or two from their high-beam nipples. I suspect that is why he had a policy of no wearing sweaters or jackets in class, and coincidentally his class seemed to always be the one with no heat on; no proof, just saying. He would often diligently help one or more of them in hushed tones for the entire class and yes, they were, as expected, all "A" students. Students like me rarely asked him or any other teacher for help during or after class due to the unspoken rule that it is better to be thought stupid than to ask the teacher and let the other kids know you need help. Oh yeah, with Mr. Hack, like many teachers, there was always the breath factor, as in his smelled like a rancid hockey bag left in the back seat of a car all summer.

The buzzer rang and I lagged behind a bit, letting the Count and his crew swagger out into the fray. Mr. Hack came over and gave me some of his sage advice. "You'd better watch yourself with that lot," he told me. "No shit, Sherlock," I thought, as I barely managed to turn my aching neck to look at him. I peeked out the door and no one was waiting, thankfully, but this was not what I had in mind on my first day of grade eight. So much for keeping my head down and blending in to the woodwork.

The Wallflower Principle: Someone, usually in high school, who sees everything, knows everything, but does not say a word. They are not loners; they are introverts.

Nope, I had caught the attention of the tough crowd and had to be careful not to end up like one kid, Jim, who some years later got on the wrong end of multiple pairs of double-soled, tractor-tread Dayton boots. Yeah, he was left unconscious and with permanent brain injuries, and as luck would have it for those involved, it was just off school property, as in across the street, and of course there were no witnesses. So it was a city crime, not an official school one. The kid never returned, a smart move by his parents, I would say. As for my fate, there was really not much I could do about it other than make some fast friends and watch my back regardless; there would be plenty of opportunities for them to take out their teenage anger on me over their pathetic home lives and zero prospects for a bright future.

I managed to avoid them for the most part but had other challenges in the form of so-called jocks. Not sure how I got in their bad book,s but I did, so they were generally keeping an eye out for me as well. So now I had it coming from both sides: the bad boys and the star athletes. Talk about feeling like a loser. Wow, that first year of high school simply sucked! Never mind trying to think about homework, PE or girls; I was dodging beatings by running, talking and fighting my way out on a daily basis. Upside? It wasn't South Central L.A., so no one I knew had guns (that came later), and it taught me how to sell my ideas very quickly.

I managed to start a change in my reputation with them by setting off a pipe bomb in the third floor washroom. The explosion destroyed the entire washroom; thankfully no one had to pee at the moment or the outcome could have been a lot different. The police and fire department were all over the school and I was suspected due to casually walking into the counsellor's office about fifteen seconds before the explosion. My thinking was it was better to be sitting with him, and several "Blue Gooners," as the jocks were called, than seen scampering down one of the three stairwells. Anyway, the year ended with me, surprisingly enough, getting to know a couple of the bad boys to some degree; but let's be clear, at this time I was more chummy with the nerds/outcasts as I was somehow one of them and that fit my lifestyle at the time . Well, that eventually came back to bite me in the ass and stab me in the side, kick me in the teeth and shoot at me with a gun. So there was that silver lining on the black clouds for a brief moment in time which gave me some glimmer of hope that I could fit in with not only the cool kids, but really any kids.

You see, I never felt like I fit in. I always felt like a wolf amongst sheep. It took me decades to accept the reality that most of the population are sheep and need to be led and to learn the stark conclusion that other wolves can sniff you out in any herd no matter what Armani suit you're wearing. High-rises and technology have advanced far faster than male evolution. That is as much a fact as night follows day, regardless of what women and the politicians preach. Malcolm Gladwell has it down. That dream of fitting in and getting to be part of something (gang or whatever) only lasted a few months as my mom announced she was back with the Cowboy and we were heading north, once again.

I was not cool with this and now knew I had to plan my escape.

Chapter 26

First Love...She Was Cool, Blonde, and Her Daddy Had a Rolls-Royce

Because I was the new kid at so many schools, I was forced to consciously and subconsciously develop a kind of school social survival strategy (all kids do this by the second week of school, by the way) to try to, as Bruce Lee would say, "be like water." My interpretation was to try and relate to everyone (including teachers, not so easy) but in my soul I felt like I never fit in with any clique, regardless of whether they were nerds, greaseballs or others—the ones who try so desperately not to fit in that they fit in perfectly, right down to the clothing, shoes and hairstyles, of the rest of those trying not to fit in. At the end, I chose what Yoda would call the Dark Side, since I felt I had always been heading there anyway. Path of least resistance, less painful, easier, call it what you will, they were easier to relate to, cooler and definitely funner to hang with. But as I would soon find out, fun had its price. Looking back, there is no question that choice altered the course of my life for good or bad; in all reality only God knows that for sure. As for me, even with the monumental mistakes I made, it always seemed like I was given another chance to be a better man. Don't kid yourself, the POA (Power of Association) is as real as electricity; both can kill you if you don't obey their rules. There are many great books on the subject and most are well worth the investment of life's most precious commodity, that being time, for those who still think its water, oxygen or (you gotta be kidding?), money.

Girls were always friendly, an upside, I suppose, to being raised with three sisters, but since I was usually the new kid, they generally kept their distance; well, at least in the beginning anyway. Regardless, my default demeanor was being aloof. No easy task for a hormonal-surging adolescent male. It worked for me, though, as a strategy until I got the lowdown on who was dating who, but that by no means was ever the real me. The coolest one I met by far was Fiona, the daughter of a wealthy art dealer. She sat beside me in a couple of classes during my grade nine stint at the upscale Lord Byng High School. For some reason, she just liked me, probably one of those "push back as far as I can against the way I was brought up and the types of boys my parents would approve of" teenagers. Who knows? But one thing is for sure, we became fast friends. She was a beautiful blonde with big blue eyes, full lips and tight jeans and the laid- back demeanor of a California surfer girl. What else could a fourteen-year-old boy ask for? I knew that there truly was a God and He answered prayers, that's for sure. She was a bit eccentric for her age, and I liked it. Not sure how it happened, as we didn't talk much in class; some eye contact then one day she offered to help me with a math question she saw I was struggling with. Then the next class she simply said, "Do you want to come to my house for lunch?" (I probably didn't have a lunch anyway). She was out of my league, and I knew it but replied with a cool, "Sure that would be great." That was that, we were tight from then on. In retrospect, of course, her parents were right, I was definitely a bad influence on her: getting her to skip school; getting half-naked on her parents couch every other day over lunch, and other stuff. Concentrating on school was tough enough for me without the distraction of her. I loved it!

Her dad didn't much care for me once he found out I lived in that house, the one he and the other snobs had or would have protested against, feeling, rightfully so, that it would bring down property values and raise crime. But to his credit he never said a negative word to me, although he didn't hire me to work at his art gallery when he was looking for some part-time help. Ironic as it was, he could tolerate me doing who-knows-what with his pretty hard-body daughter, but he drew the line when it came to his pieces of art. Priorities - what can I say? I was too high a risk, I guess. Instead, he opted to hire his nephew from New York, a tall, curly-light-brown-haired lanky guy with a strong New York accent. That turned out to be a mistake, and he ended up stealing about $300K+ (as I understood it) worth of paintings and selling them to support his and his girlfriend's various lifestyle addictions. I think I was the better bet, just saying.

As I said, we were good friends for a short time, and I used to tell her I was going to buy (more likely at the time, steal) a customized Chevy van with a TV, bed, stereo, big mag wheels and a cool paint job, and when I did, we would take off and head south across the border, hit California and never come back. No thought about money, school or anything that complicated. Truth is, at the time she would have gone with me in a heartbeat and as luck would have it around that time I actually drove (yeah, it was stolen) a van like that. It was purple with a painting on the side by the awesome Frank Frazetta.

The challenging part is that the owner probably wanted it back, so crossing the border would have been a problem.

The end of the school year was also the end of our fun. We saw each other a few times in the beginning of the summer holidays but, as usual I was getting grounded on a regular basis by my very cool group home parents, Jon and Reko, and topping that off with going to Juvie, again this time for six weeks, the result of an epic adventure starting with borrowing a car from the local Mercedes dealership. Enhance that stupidity with a string of B&Es in the hamlet of Abbotsford, a town some sixty-five kilometres away. But wait, there's more! To cap that stupidity off properly, you need to initiate a high-speed police chase by stealing none other than a police cruiser of course, and then do this in what the British call a "peasouper," i.e., a dense fog you could not see twenty feet ahead of you in and you need to do a hundred miles per hour with cops right on your ass, somehow pushing you to go faster.

They remind me of the greyhound dogs chasing that rabbit, I mean, really? The only purpose for that archaic strategy is to force a crash. No? Why else would they do that? The logic of consciously or unconsciously pushing an idiot like me at the time to drive faster with the end result of me being stopped by running into something like, God forbid, an unsuspecting civilian trying to get home from picking up some last-minute items from the 7-11 is difficult to grasp. I'd get that mentality and motivation if I was some killer, kidnapper or the like. But stealing a cop car? Do you really need to go lethal over a car? You have lots.

Yeah, that pretty much confirmed for me that urban myth, that police candidates are actually vetted or even screened for specific levels of aptitude and intellect. Saying that, there is no question my level at the time was the same or lower. I mean, why else would I steal a police car to jumpstart (with my partner in crime, Dale, a mentor in the art of stealing cars, B&Es and getting girls) and steal an iconic 427 Corvette convertible? I rest my case on that one.

Anyway, it was over just as simply as it started. It didn't help that our lifestyles were so different; she had money and I had none. She took trips with her family all the time and would call me and I'd be jealous. One night she called me from the States and said she was going out with this guy – an old friend of the family – and he had an Opel GT car, so I guess we shouldn't go out any longer. I agreed and made a few choice comments to seal the deal and try to keep my pride, and that was that. I was replaced by some Tad or Biff with his sweater tied around his neck; I would have liked to choke the life out of him if the opportunity had arisen. Yes, he was older and I guess driving the GT gave him dibs on driving her as well.

Practical girl in the end, as I just had my dreams and my thirty-four-window limousine, otherwise known as public transit.

Chapter 27

The Cowboy "Reloaded"

"Good judgement comes from experience, and a lot of that comes
from bad judgement."
– Jason Statham; Actor

Yes, back to PG, Prince George. What a nightmare! Apparently PJ had changed. "Give up the booze in a one night stand," as the Gerry Rafferty song goes, and my mother, being the eternal English optimist from her years of living in London under the Nazi Blitz (you know the "keep calm and carry on" mantra that helped to save them from a fate worse than death. Interesting that now it's just a funny sticker or t-shirt with all kinds of variations written for profit by people who have never been in a war; but what the hell, it makes those wearing it on their body or pasted to their car feel like they are unique; yeah about as unique as a piece of straw in a haystack, in my opinion). Anyway, she did her best to paint a picture of happily-ever-after, like everything would be different this time. Not! I was so fed up with moving and I protested, but my mom had made up her mind and that was the end of it. She would follow her man to the end of the frigging earth. Nice quality if the man's character matches the quality of her resolve. So of course I was going. Where else could I go? There was no way I was getting left behind with Tilly the Hun. So once again we packed our bags and caught the Greyhound for that painful journey north.

And once again we moved into a one-bedroom apartment; no more No-Tell-Motel as my address; yeah, not the coolest thing to tell kids in high school that you live in a rundown motel on the highway. PJ had big plans to work as a custodian at a sawmill. I guess there were no janitor jobs in a major metropolis like Vancouver, so better head to a small northern town. Whatever. Plus he had to get my mom away where it was safe; the "knight in rusty armour" routine. Yeah, right. I enrolled in yet another new school where, as usual, everyone had grown up together and the new kid had to be tested and put in his place. Pretty regular stuff. I think my picture is under "bullied" in the dictionary

Things were uneventful for about the first two weeks. Then payday happened, so to celebrate, PJ invited my mom to accompany him on a trip: a two-day, non-stop vodka bender. I was asleep as I should be on a school night, when suddenly at 2 a.m., PJ burst through my bedroom door piss drunk, wearing the standard uniform of the day: wife-beater t-shirt, boxer shorts, and his pride and joy, a new pair of black with mother-of-pearl-inlaid cowboy boots. Well, for some reason, that only a full-blown alcoholic in his prime could understand, he came in swinging my tennis racquets down on me. By that point I'd learned to sleep with one eye open, especially when they were on a drinking binge, so I rolled out of bed before he knew what happened and to the Cowboy's surprise, I had my jeans and logging boots on. Yes, I seem to have intuition in the area of being attacked.

Oops! Sailor boy didn't see that one coming. I was a year or so older since our last altercation when I hadn't stood much of a chance, but this time I wasn't going to take any more bullshit from him. No, this time I was going to deal it out! Before he could say "Jack Daniels," I had sprung up on the bed, bounced once and landed a solid steel-toed kick to his left rib cage. He was visibly shocked as he gasped for air, tennis racquet flying from his nicotine-stained hand and hitting the small dresser mirror but, surprisingly, not breaking it. No time to gloat as I threw a flurry of punches, sending him stumbling back and tripping over two twelve-packs of Old Style empties stacked neatly in my little room and waiting for their return trip to the mother ship. The bottles shattered like the ringing of church bells as they scattered across the wood floor like cockroaches running from a can of Raid.

In his hasty retreat, he found himself stepping on them, and it was like a scene from a movie where a strand of pearls breaks on a marble floor and causes one of the main characters to go ass over tea kettle; in this case, it was him crashing through the cheap rattan-framed glass coffee table. That caught his attention as he lay there for a few moments in his now-white-and- red blood-spattered underwear, his cowboy boots looking not so intimidating under the circumstances. He paused as if contemplating life, and I suspect it went something like, "What the fuck just happened?" I stood there looking down on him like a victorious gladiator, yet with another side of me feeling sorry for him like you would if you ran over a dog by accident. For him, it probably felt like a few seconds on his back before he sprung to his feet like a startled tiger caught napping by a poacher. My mom was screaming at this point for us to stop but it was not going to end until he was a TKO. Bing-bing-bing! Round two: too drunk to know he had a small chunk of glass stuck in his right ass cheek, he got up and somehow pulled it together into some sort of drunken boxer's stance. Deep breath … he then slurred, "Come on you little prick. I'll kill ya."

To his credit or drunkenness, he was ready for a full second round, as was I, but before I could move, my mom stepped in between us, which was admirable and stupid, as he forcibly pushed her out of the way, sending her hurtling into the 1960s couch with its wooden arm rests. That hurt her, and she let out a small whimper. Without missing a beat, he threw a useless kick at my balls. His black boot fell short of its target by six inches; not so lucky for him though, because my boot collided with his saggy nut sack, dropping him squarely to his knees right into the middle of the broken table, hands clutching his manhood. That took a bit of the fight out of him as he sat still for a moment, moaning like a tomcat calling to his lover the moon. At this point I was wild with rage, adrenalin and hormones, so I had little control over what I was doing, never mind saying. Yet I mustered up some words in a low raspy voice, that seemed to be someone else's, saying, "Stay down!" I thought it sounded pretty convincing and a bit scary, but the rusty old dog had other plans as he slowly dragged his boxer-shorted,wife-beatered, blood-spattered middle-aged ass up to a semi-standing position.

It was obvious he was so drunk that he felt no pain and was not going to stop, so I grabbed two handfuls of his slicked-back Brylcreemed hair and yanked him forward, causing him to slip on the rubble that was once our coffee table. This sent him slipping down into the layer of flesh- eating beer-bottle shards, landing on one knee and earning a sizeable gash as a parting gift from the table. Unlike him, I had traction in my big boots (Note: always wear appropriate footwear … you never know what may happen when you slumber), and although far lighter, I managed to drag him across the floor to the door in one clean jerk. PJ was swearing and throwing wild punches over his head at me like a kid in a schoolyard fight. I paid no attention. My mom had recovered and was sobbing and heaving at the same time with the words, "Stop, Jake ... stop!" I didn't, because this was going to end tonight, or so I thought.

I grabbed the door handle with one hand, with the other still gripping the Cowboy's hair; blood was everywhere, but he got up pretty fast for a drunk and landed a good one into my left kidney. I crumpled to the side but felt little as I let go of the door handle and re-grabbed his greying hair again, driving his head down as my knee came up. It landed with a solid thud as it broke his nose and knocked out one of his front teeth, which dropped to the floor like a discarded chicklet. I returned my focus to the door handle and my goal of getting him out of the apartment, my pulse running like a rabid dog pursuing a postman. I pulled the door open so hard that the doorknob pushed past the door stop and punched a perfect round hole in the wall. Thinking I was half way there, I was stunned to look up and see this big aboriginal dude from upstairs standing there with this righteous look on his face. If that wasn't enough, I could detect the sound of sirens off in the distance. The big Chug, as we use to call them back in the day, had second thoughts after he bellowed out, "What the fuck is going on?" He had probably been ready to lay a beating on whoever opened that door, but the scene was not what he expected. Or maybe he had seen it many times before. Who knows? All I can say is with him looking at me with blood smattered over my hands, chest and face and my eyes filled with psychopathic tendencies, he didn't know what the fuck to do. His jaw just dropped and his porcelain-clear eyes went as big as tea cups. I stood there for a second or two looking at him, thinking what he must be thinking, then replied, "None of your fucking business. Get out of my way!" The Indian dude, who outweighed me by at least a hundred pounds, locked eyes with me - one of those "whoever blinks first is a pussy" deals. I didn't blink as we both took stock of each other. In a moment of pause that somehow turned into this distorted version of respect. I smiled and said, "He had this coming ... now get out of my way," my skinny body twisting the greasy head of hair in my hand for a firmer grip. To my surprise and relief, he laughed and said in a deep baritone voice, "You're a fucking crazy white guy," and turned heading back up the staircase, his bulk causing the wooden planks to cry out in agony. I looked down at the blubbering mess of a man I was dragging and wondered why I had been intimidated by him for so long. What was he anyway? He was nothing but a pickled old cowboy living off the quickly-fading reputation of a man to be feared.

He blurted out some feeble threat, still not backing down as I dragged him into the dimly-lit hall with its persistent foul odour. Suddenly my prize regained some sure footing and once again stood up to be a good five inches taller than me. But, as the saying goes, "the right plan and the wrong time is the wrong plan," and his plan proved to be flawed as I spun to my right while pushing him backwards down the stairs. As far as I was concerned, that saved him some time on his inevitable exit out the front door of that piece-of-shit building. He rolled backwards ass-over-teakettle twice, his momentum catapulting himself straight into the big glass door to the apartment. It exploded with a mighty crash as he went through it like a bowling ball knocking down pins. Glass showered him as he continued on his journey down the four big cement stairs to the sidewalk, scaring the living shit out of two RCMP officers who had just pulled up. As to be expected in that town, they approached with hands on guns; no question they would have pulled them in lightning fast unison if they had the least reason. Why they didn't, I'll never know, as I must have looked like a Jack Nicholson from The Shining standing there in jeans, no shirt and logging boots between the greenish glassless wooden door frames. But, as the saying goes, this was not their first rodeo in that backwater town, so this was probably just business as usual.

Today it is a bit different, but back then cops tended to walk away from what they labelled a "domestic dispute," like it was some universal term that gave the guy a get-out-of-jail-free card so he could regroup and refocus, only to lay waste to his family another day. The first words out of their mouths were, "What's going on here?" As I have said before, police forces the world over generally shy away from recruiting high-intellect thinkers - and for sure no rocket scientists - but come on, there was no police guess-work needed to figure out what was happening at that moment. It was black and white: I had sent him through a plate glass window. Guilty as charged, your Honour! The Cowboy decided that was the perfect moment to start yelling from his hands and knees, "Jake, Jake, I never meant to do that! Jake…Jake … it's okay ... I'm sorry … just a misunderstanding … Jake!" The cops told him to shut up or they were going to arrest him for disturbing the peace. He shut up for a moment then started to grumble under his breath something like, "You little fucker…hahaha … huuu … urggggg! You little prick …. hahaha!" One of the cops helped him up as he apologized to them saying, "No problem here boys … we are fine … just a little misunderstanding … we are fine … we are fine … no prooooobbbbllllleeeemmm." Yeah, they knew he was pissed but thought the best advice to him was "You need to go sleep it off there, buddy." That was it. They asked me nothing, gave me no trouble; no taking anyone down to the station to make a report. They just helped him back up the stairs to the apartment, looked around and then said something like "go to bed and stop fighting with him. He's just a drunk old man. We 'll come back tomorrow to talk about this," Yeah, right.

The door to the apartment closed and the Cowboy staggered towards his bedroom with my mom holding him up. I felt a little sorry for him, mainly because of my mother's loyalty, but that soon faded like the sound of train whistle off in the distance. Round three came about an hour or so later. I was once again lying in my bed, covers over me but with jeans and boots still on, when the Cowboy came stumbling through my door, I suppose with some classic American superhero movie-type plan of approaching from behind and knocking me out. It never happened. This last round was over before it started, because this time I had the tennis racquet and broke it over his sweaty head. I left him lying face-down on my bed, honestly not knowing or caring if he was dead or alive. He lay still and silent in his warrior gear: blood stained t-shirt, shit-stained boxers and black boots.

I realized in that moment of psychotic clarity that my mom and I had to go. There were many reasons, of course, and amongst them was not being accidentally killed in my sleep by my stepfather, who would plead self-defense or temporary insanity. In a flash, I stuffed a few clothes and possessions (including my new Bruce Springsteen Darkness on the Edge of Town album) into my small, ivory-coloured suitcase with its crimson lining, corralled up my mom and walked off into the darkness, eventually selecting yet another roadside motel to be our sanctuary. My mom was still drunk and didn't say much other than that she was sorry. I didn't blame her for a second. It was just how it was. The night manager of the motel was a slight woman with greying hair and friendly eyes. My mom told her of our plight, explaining that she needed a room but had no money. The woman sized us up, not knowing what to think, I am sure, but said, "Okay, when can you pay?" My mom said that she had money in the apartment and would get it once he had gone to work. The lady smiled and said, "No problem, dear." Perhaps she had been through a similar situation, who knows? She helpfully added, "The diner is open for another forty-five minutes." We went there before heading to our room. I'm not sure what I ordered, but it was awesome going down and not so good when it came back up. We headed to the room, which had a bedroom and pull-out couch, and my mom told me to take the bedroom. I did and was asleep before my head hit the pillow. As if the night hadn't been stressful enough, I woke up two hours later puking my guts out from food poisoning that knocked me out of commission for the next twenty-four hours. I came around to my mom gently shaking me saying, "Jake, you have to get up. There's a bus leaving for Vancouver in thirty minutes." I got up, still groggy and dehydrated, grabbed my bag, and we once again made our way through the small town of heartbreaks and lost dreams, but this time heading in the direction of my escape. As we neared the idling Greyhound, my mom handed me a bus ticket she had bought while I was passed out. I asked if she was coming, but she said she couldn't; she needed to go back to the apartment to work things out. I boarded the Greyhound at the Husky gas station across from the motel. Destination? My sister's place.

Dawn broke on the mountains in the distance as the diesel-spewing whale sailed me south and away once and for all from this never-ending bad dream.

Chapter 28

Leaving …on a Greyhound

"Mistakes are the price of progress and failure is success deferred." - JLH

My mom knew I was leaving her for good, so to say it was awkward would be the ultimate understatement. But what could she do? No job, no education; just a good English girl who did her best to raise five kids on her own. In my books, as I have said, she did pretty well; other than my brother, we all turned out okay in the end. It was obvious I could never move back in with her and the Cowboy again. That was clear after this last incident, so there was no big discussion about it. I bet she felt like a bad mother, and on some levels she was, but in the end if it's anyone's fault, I would have to blame it on my dad. Even though he had no role model and grew up in an era of ultimate turmoil, he should have "stood in the gap" to start. Maybe he did to his best ability, I don't know, but he needed to try harder and just maybe he could have prevented this from being put into motion years earlier.

The goodbye was scary and exciting, since I knew that was the end of being under my mom's wing - as in forever this time. But it was an incredible weight off my back to get away. I got on the Greyhound and settled in by the window. I could see my mother outside waving, looking sad and disheveled. There was a lump in my throat as I waved back, though she probably couldn't see me through the diesel-and-dirt-tinted windows. I was scared, but I had nothing to lose and nowhere else to go other than to my older sister's place on Commercial Drive (known locally as "the Drive") in Vancouver's East Side.

Someone once wrote or said (might have been John C. Maxwell) years later, "If you have faith in the future you'll have power in the present." So it goes without saying that at that time I didn't have a lot of power. I hadn't really thought about what I was going to do in the future other than the simple in-front-of-my face goal of somehow graduating from high school. Yeah, staying in school was my internal compass, the only stable thing I had, I guess. But now I had another pressing goal: finding a place to live. I had visions about how great my freedom would be, and why not? With no one to depend on or telling me what to do, it would be great, right? Nothing but sex and drugs and rock 'n' roll. Oh yeah, and school would have to fit it in there somehow. Well, that was the only horizon I could see from my very limited vantage point, but as the saying goes, "be careful what you wish for," as I probably got more than I should have at that age. But it posed other challenges, as you well may imagine and by luck or God's will, I managed to dodge yet another bullet in my path. As I said, I always figured if all else failed I could join the Air Force. They took just about anyone. Food, education, housing, travel, heck, they'd even let me fly an F-18 fighter jet. Hell yeah, right! Cleaning the toilets was more likely for C+ Boy.

I'm sure when the Cowboy sobered up, licked his wounds and did some deep reflecting on his actions (not likely), he was very happy to see me go, especially because he knew, beyond the shadow of a doubt, that I would never return: The last of his non-biological offspring was out of his life. That deserved a drink! As for him handling my mom, I'm sure it wasn't that difficult beyond putting his arm around her and saying in his cigarette-inspired baritone voice, "Now, honey, he will be just fine. He's living with his sister (she was a year older than me). It is for the best..." He could have no concept of what a parent could possibly be feeling after having to choose her meal ticket over her fourteen-year-old son. Like I said before, I don't blame her; she had the cards stacked against her from the get-go. I replayed the fight again and again in my mind, with everything seeming once again to be in slow motion. Like the first time, I enjoyed every second of the heart-pounding adrenaline rush and tried to compare it with the altercations I had been in before, but there were none that came anywhere close to that milestone event. It was nothing less than some modern version of a rite of passage test - becoming a man.

Truth be told, if my brother had been in that situation, he would have killed him with about as much thought of the consequences as getting caught picking your nose in public.

My sister didn't meet me at the bus station when I arrived after the long journey. Then again she was just a teenager herself, so not keeping schedules was forgivable. It was around seven o'clock when we pulled into the Greyhound bus station; my experiences back then are probably why to this day I still hate buses. I was from Van, so I knew how to catch the trolley bus to the Broadway-Commercial stop near her house. She lived in an illegal suite in the attic of an 80-year-old, three-story house on a narrow side street bordering a 60-foot ravine that housed a set of railway tracks (now a Skytrain route). She was cool with me living there for the most part, but it wasn't the greatest set-up for either of us. Food was limited and so was space, so I slept on the seat cushions from her old couch. It was comfortable enough and beat the Cowboy alternative of sleeping with my boots on. Her boyfriend was a big goof. He was about six-foot- six, and weighed about a hundred and forty pounds soaking wet. He had straw-coloured hair that looked like something between Albert Einstein and Bob Marley, and he believed it was cost effective to light a cigarette off the one you were just about to finish. Yes, he was a chain smoker, probably a carton-a-day man. I worked for a family company many years later and the son, my boss, was a two-carton-a day man and damn proud of it. He wore a leather biker vest, yet the closest he had come to being a biker was getting chased by some. He wore these beat-up platform boots that gave him another three inches in height, so he basically looked like a character out of a Tim Burton movie. He told me he was a black belt in karate and actually carried this raggedy card in his black vinyl snap-button biker wallet that hung from a chain attached to his belt. I asked him why he had those cards, and to my surprise he said, "By law, I have to hand these out because my hands are registered weapons. It is to protect any dude who wants to fight me." Yes, he actually believed that, but of course it was utter bullshit; the guy would hand the cards out to avoid get a shit-kicking from some tough chick, never mind a guy. Anyway, he was entertaining to have around, but a total loser nonetheless. I never saw my sister do drugs, but I would imagine through the power of association she could have been doing anything, and because I was a young selfish world-resource-sucking, it's-all-about-me-teen, I didn't really care anyway. It was really all about me. Or so I thought.

I met a local neighbourhood gang pretty quickly, soon after chatting up two blonde girls who were walking by the big house I lived in. I seemed to assimilate with them quicker than the "Borg. taking over the Star Ship Enterprise, and we got along great for about a two months, as I was fresh and exciting and far different than the other boys. The leader was a good-looking kid, part-white and part-Chinese, but we had a falling-out not long after, because one of the blondes I met that day took a liking to me and soon after became "mine." For that age, she was, by all accounts, matured with a nice figure and a large set of breasts, (maguiffins, as my cousin Joe likes to call them). That was fun for me from the get-go, but for the other guys not so much. They thought it was less than cool because she was their so-called property, so they decided to teach me a lesson. The plan was to take me to their secret hideout, a cave they had dug into the soft clay on the side of a ravine, which to say the least was tricky to get into, and push me down to the tracks below. I'm sure they didn't intend for me to die, but if I did, all the better. Fortunately for me, my girlfriend gave me a heads up just as I squeezed under the wire fence and started along the cliff wall. I put two and two together, pretty quickly thinking, "Yeah, why are they letting me go first if it's their so-called secret hideout?" I didn't let on or back down (stupid, I know), but continued to scamper like a mountain goat along the wall far faster than they had anticipated, only hesitating for a second before making the short but scary jump across a portion of the wall that had been rained out. At that juncture, the leader's plan was to simply push me from behind. That didn't happen because I jumped sooner than he thought and then continued on up the embankment and was gone before he could figure out what the hell I was doing. I didn't see her after that, so I knew where her allegiance was and I can't blame her. The pull of the pack mentality is strong, even on the best of us. In all honesty, I have never been much of pack follower (leader, yes; follower, not so much). Like the dogs pulling a dog sled, if you're not at the lead, the view never changes. That's not for me.

The challenge of course, was that they lived in the area, so I got into a few scuffles with them individually and had to outsmart and outrun them when they were together after that. Didn't matter in the big picture, because I was trying to figure out where I was going to live and how I was going to finish school; both of which didn't fit into my current sleeping-on-the-floor-gig in my sister's single-room apartment. Don't get me wrong: it was interesting living there, in addition to being one block off the super-hip Drive. The basement floor had a big suite where a gay hairdresser lived with his lover (back then a partner was someone who owned a business with another man.). Needless to say, this was not normal unless, say, you lived in Frisco, that is. One of them always looked like he just came from surfing and the other was a doppelganger (term I learned from my buddy Dallas) to the Greek pop-singing movember-wearing god of the nineties, Yanni. Lots of floral dress shirts, tight jeans, no underwear and hissy fits. They were both very nice to me, but to be sure they were never going to be the big brothers (or sisters for that matter) I never had. As mentioned, being openly gay wasn't all that common back in the early seventies, so I, like most of the population, found it weird to see two guys kissing and grabbing each other's asses. Those dudes seemed to do everything to excess, whether it was telling jokes, laughing, drinking, singing, barbecuing, you name it; and of course a lot of wild mood swings. Not sure if he wore one of the then-super-popular mood rings, you know the ones that magically turned different colours like red if you were mad, or blue if you were sad, but if you can you say "hormonal therapy," then you're on the right track. My sister told me he was getting ready to go to Switzerland to have what they called back then "the operation." But one morning after a night of heavy partying, the Yanni dude woke up and found his silver surfer stone cold dead beside him, having choked on his own vomit. The breath of fresh air was that the Yanni guy's two sisters lived on the main floor. Both tall brunettes, Greek or Italian as far as I can remember. They had this long thick hair; you know, the kind Rapunzel would have had to have had, and legs up to their shoulders. Yeah, those girls were incredibly beautiful and yes, I can say I had more than one teenage fantasy involving them, me, nylon stockings and whipping cream. You get the picture.

As for doing school work or sleeping much for that matter, well, since there seemed to be a party every second night, this was tricky at the best of times.

Chapter 29

Ward of the Court

"Life is too short to live small…get good at something and stand tall. Once your relatives realize the Lottery is not going to make it happen, they will give in and start asking you for money. Give it freely to their children and grandchildren only." - JLH

Sleeping on the floor in the cramped one-bedroom apartment was not a long term plan of mine, or my sister's for that matter. She couldn't support me and I knew I needed to have some kind of stability if I was ever going to make it through high school. Yes, as I have said before, finishing high school was a goal and one I was not about to miss due to minor inconveniences like not having a bed, never mind bedroom, of my own. September came and school had started and I wasn't enrolled in one of them. There was no chance I was heading back north to a small town and Team Messed-up, so I got a phone book and found the address of the nearest social services office where I walked in and told them my story ending with something to the effect of, "I'm fourteen and have no food, no money and nowhere to live but want to go to school. Can you help me?" This got their attention. The receptionist asked me to sit down as she quickly walked through a door behind her. I wondered what the outcome would be and had thoughts like they would arrest me and hold me until my mom and her man came down to get me. I wasn't worried about that because I knew that would never happen, yet it was one of the only things I could think of. After ten or fifteen minutes, a side door opened and in walked what I would describe as a Jewish hippie, with long black curly hair, long sleeved baggy dark purple top, not-so-matching skirt that almost touched the floor and occasionally revealed her black socks and brown leather Birkenstock sandals. That was the first time I met this super-cool woman, my new social worker, Ruth Hestolgin. She became a friend to me for sure and seemed to always know when I needed to go for lunch or chat over tea.

There was a process as expected, which included a court date to officially go before a judge so I could become a ward of the court. Chances are good that becoming such a thing at any other time in history (or in just about any other country) was not a good thing, but this was Canada in the seventies and it was all about the kids. My mom had to sign some papers, basically like adoption papers, where the government became my parents. She was a good lady and great mom in her own way, and it must have hurt to see her youngest child put into this situation, but there it was. She had made her choice and I had to make mine. To her credit she called me and asked if this was what I wanted. I said yes. I mean, what was the alternative? Back with her and the drunken Cowboy? Me sleeping with one eye open? Not going to happen.

I knew I'd have to go into another group home or a foster home, and that made me nervous. Forget about bullies in the schoolyard; I lived with them 24/7 and it sucked, to say the least. I guess I always liked the unknown, or, more likely, I didn't have a choice; so if you can't get out, go further in. I still like the unknown today. Pioneering is ever so much more fun than homesteading, and the pioneer/hunter made sure the land was safe for the farmer. It was fun most of the time, to be sure – a little like Pinocchio when he lands on that island with all the other lost boys ; yeah, and if you stay there long enough, you do turn into a donkey.

Picture this: no parents, just staff working 8-hour shifts, most of whom were hippies, Vietnam draft dodgers, Ph.D. students, anthropology , sociology and psychology grads, plus a sprinkling of nymphomaniacs and the occasional gay guy. Most of them were pretty liberal, I mean you could do no wrong really other than break some simple rules like no stealing; no smoking pot in house; no sex in house; no drinking in house. That's about it. My fave group home by far? Tolmie House just outside the gate of University of British Columbia [UBC].

Why? Well, many reasons: some I get more into later, but the fact some of the women staff liked to give us long massages in our beds at night was one huge reason. It was rough being a teenage boy at that place.

Over a six-year period I lived in five different homes, including two foster homes. For those of you who don't know the difference, foster homes are home-based businesses, typically run by a husband and wife. They get paid a flat rate, per-head, per-month. The challenge with that biz model? To make extra money (you understand that you can't do anything about what the market will pay; in this case, the government will pay you per head), you save money by skimping on things like food, clothing and activities. Simple really. Just spend as little as possible on the stable of discarded youths to make a better margin. By far, the Perry home I spoke of was the best run business unit. I mean they could have run a training school on how to make the most from your stock. The baby tigers weren't really that different in foster homes compared to group homes , other than a foster home typically had fewer cubs, typically one to a max of say, five. The main difference was group homes were run by staff on a rotating shift of eight to ten hours unlike foster homes, where the owner/operators lived in the business because it was also their own home. In both cases, it was not unusual for them to be co-ed. This, as expected, resulted in many opportunities for, you guessed it, sex. There weren't exactly locks on the doors or guards walking the hallways. No matter what the rules were - no smoking, no drinking, no swearing, no sex - they were rules that everyone broke, daily. Also, I was now a teenager and better able to deal with the other Trainspotting nightmares than years earlier.

Being a ward of the court came with a whole new level of freedom, which for some reason meant I needed to grow up a bit and be responsible, and to me that meant staying in school. No easy task I assure you, especially when no one cared if I went to school or not, and the reality of being the only teen that was enrolled in high school at most places I lived. This put me on the hit list of the young "thugs" I lived with. They didn't appreciate my reminding them of their choice to be losers by attending school every day and carrying a school bag with homework, not to mention the tenor saxophone I was learning to play. I was popular out of the gate, especially at Tolmie House. Then again, why try to keep your head down and blend in? Why? So you don't make others feel uncomfortable in their complacency? Who gives a shit about them anyway? They will die and be forgotten before the ink is dry on their death certificates. They are fertilizer for the people trying to make a difference.

On a regular basis they would steal my homework, pick fights with me, wreck my room and generally try to make my life a living hell. So it didn't take me long to figure out that I was either going to have to join them or live on the streets, living at the mercy of strangers who would no doubt be happy to take care of me in exchange for some sexual favours. Yes, the staff intervened if they saw something, but most of the time they weren't around; and besides, they got paid by the hour so no one took it very seriously. Since I knew a number of kids, including my brother and one of my sisters, that chose the street life, and knowing that the average life span of a kid living on the streets is seven years, that did not interest me. So I decided to try to manage my environment the best I could, as in "When in Rome, do like the Romans."

Side note: I ended up in the group home after getting myself kicked out of the Hansons', a huge mistake. The Hansons were new foster parents, and I was the first kid to live with them, so they didn't really know how to handle it. They were just trying to give back by helping provide a home and some values to a kid that never really had either. I must admit I liked living there. It was like I had magically jumped through the TV screen into a modern version of the Brady Bunch, definitely a life I had never known but always craved. They were a nice couple. I can't recall the mom's name, but she was a cool-yet-tough lady who wore her hair up most of the time and loved raising boys - hence taking me in. They had a big custom-built house with a panoramic view of the city and mountains. They had two sons of her own, Bret and David, and a yappy super-friendly wiener dog, named Baron. The Old Man, as the younger son called him, was a still in pretty good shape, sixty-five-years old, who you could tell was a big buffed dude back in the day. To me he was the dad every kid would want (other than Bruce Lee, Steve McQueen or Sean Connery of course), as he had done a lot of interesting things in his life, included things like being one of the founders and builders of Vancouver's prestigious Hollyburn Country Club; been an offshore speedboat racer with the name, SeaBee; owned one of 12 houses (now gone as I understand it) on "deeded property" in the middle of a National Park called Golden Ears that was only accessible by boat. That was cool on its own, as he had a superfast speedboat. He also had been a gold miner in this spooky area called "The Valley of Headless Men" see picture below…forty-four people were either beheaded or disappeared there; hence the name.

As cool as that was, his stories of being the private chauffeur for Billionaire Howard Hughes (see pic below) whenever he would come to Vancouver were far more interesting.

Anyway, back to the story. While enroute from the Hanson's, I was told by the social worker that I was going back to the Perry Home. To say the least, I went hysterical, yelling, "I'm never going back there. Ever!" and jumped out of her moving car as it pulled away at the Nanaimo and 2nd intersection. Not too smart I know, but fortunately all those James Bond and Bruce Lee movies paid off, because I did the "tuck & roll" as I hit the asphalt, giving my shoulder a nice road rash for my efforts. The Tolmie House turned out to be the same or worse; same dog, different fleas, so I tried to make friends with various boys. To be honest, it was lonely always being the new kid or the outcast. Sometimes you just want to come in from the cold and belong. Do you know what I mean? If not, then lucky you if you were one of the popular people or just such a geek it never crossed your mind. By the way, what does popular in high school look like when you're forty, normal and average? For those of you who were more like me, hang in there.

Why not a gang? Webster's defines "gang" as: "a group: as (1): a group of persons working together (2): a group of persons working to unlawful or antisocial ends; especially: a band of antisocial adolescents. 2: a group of persons having informal and usually close social relations." What's not to like about that? As a former wayward young male looking for direction and leadership, I ask you. After all, it's just like a sports team, just with a different end-game.

At the Tolmie Group Home, that is what we became: a gang (or a ball club, if you think like a jock). Even in and amongst the hourly-paid government workers and counsellors, we jelled into a crime unit. Funnily enough, I usually started out fighting with whomever the lead dog was; that just seemed to be inevitable. In this place he was named Dale, and he was basically a dark Peter Pan and leader of the Group Home Lost Boys. He had his own specific version of Never–Never Land and decided how we would fly there. Stolen cars were the cocktail of the day. It was like I had some smell or scent that got the hair on their back up, causing them to pretty much hate me the first time they met me. By the way, this happens in the corporate world as well, for both men and women. Gender equality is one hundred percent when it comes to managers' feeling threatened by new hires…who soon become new fires. The stats on what that costs countries in lost productivity is in the billions in North America alone.

Pretty soon, I was back at my usual level of anti-social behavior, but this time it was amped up just a bit. Besides the shoplifting and B&Es, I added in stealing cars, high-speed police chases, experimenting with various narcotics, and (needing money) eventually armed robberies - not to mention countless street fights. This resulted in my being in and out of jail more times than I can remember, but to everyone's surprise, including my own, I was determined to go to school, so I kept my schoolwork up to date, barely passing for sure, but passing nonetheless. The challenge was that I would hang with the group home boys at night and try to do the schoolwork when I got home or before class.

Yes, that proved to be a bit more difficult than I had thought, as it's hard to get your ass out of bed when you've been out all night and none of your bros are getting up to attend school. So my schoolwork suffered, but I was getting a good education in some of the less appreciated arts and having a gas doing it. I should mention that Tolmie House was smack-dab in the middle of one of the most expensive areas of the city and country, the West Side Varsity district, as it is called by many. Oh, I can just imagine the locals were not too keen on having this place in their midst. No question, the crime rate must have jumped after we arrived, and especially when we came together as a gang. I attended grade nine at Lord Byng while staying there. I suppose placing this eyesore house of untamed tigers (see pic below) at the gates of the prominent University of British Columbia was not dissimilar to the groundbreaking experiment of busing American inner-city blacks to predominantly white neighbourhood schools back in the sixties. It worked like Monopoly; I got a card that said "Go straight to wanting what they had: money." No lessons about the steps to get it when you are apparently not part of the "lucky sperm club." I may have said this before, but for those of you who were born into money, please get over yourself and stop trying to preach the sermon of "be satisfied with your station in life." No, the station is where we used to wait for the train so we could kick your ass and take your wallet.

Now the interesting part of this transplant program, and what made it even worse for the locals, was the impact our association had on the rather naive sons and daughters, who were wide-eyed and looking to be bad and to somehow get back at their parents for no reason other than they just had too much of everything. And we were all happy to teach them whatever they wanted or didn't want. So they too were either introduced to a new level of excitement or new level of pain and despair caused by any number of situations including car theft, high speed police chases, and let's not forget the many uses of narcotics, barbiturates and Mother Nature's own recipes for cannabis and mushrooms. And this all led to the basics of picking up West Side girls who were attracted to East Side boys; rich girls looking to express themselves sexually, and who were we to try and stop them? One thing for sure, if they hung around too long they would be sucked into the vortex of our spiral dive and the inevitable crash landing just shy of the runway to Lostville.

One other thing Tolmie and the Ross House did was to combat antisocial behaviour. The homes rewarded you for participating in any outing with the group home staff. That meant gold stars on a board. The events were not like picking up garbage along the highway, although they should have been, I suppose. They included movies; go-karts; dinners in good restaurants; going to gym; ice-skating, and going to museums and concerts. Unbelievable but true, and as you may guess I seemed to win the most stars week in and week out, which meant at the end of the month I could pick an outing and they would pay for it. I always picked dinner at one of the best restaurants in Vancouver. That got the other boys pissed in the beginning, but as time went on and I got to know them, they basically all started attending the activities. The staff knew I influenced them and told me I was a leader, so I needed to try and act accordingly. Never happened! They also had this system of vouchers for clothing, shoes, and other fashionable attire. Now, that worked well for me right out of the gate because I discovered a small loophole in their system. How it worked was that I would tell the social worker that I needed clothing for school, and she (they were usually female) would then give me one or more vouchers, which were basically the same as cash as far as the major department stores were concerned, except they would not give you any leftover amounts back in cash. I asked, trust me. So I would take a voucher, which was a printout of miscellaneous clothing items that maybe totaled $800 or $900 and buy one or two really upscale and expensive items instead of 20 cheap ones. Example: one time I bought a full-length brown leather jacket, a pair of tan dress pants and a cool copper-ivory wool turtle neck sweater. I guess that is where I learned to love better restaurants and nice clothing. Like I said, there were some serious upsides to being under the government's care in Canada at the time.

But, in all honesty, that type of association (like jail in general) had about as much chance in getting me on the right path as putting out a camp fire with gasoline. What makes it even harder is that insecure street kids are down on what they are not up on, and that was me many times. I liken it to the time recently when I took my fiffy-pound Bouvier puppy to a ranch, where for a small fee, he could get some exercise herding sheep. The sheep were instantly spooked when my puppy entered the corral. The ranch handler said, "Huh, that's unusual … the sheep picking up on your dog's prey drive." I think many humans are like those sheep and instinctively pick up on high- prey-drive/Alpha men and women. On the street or in a nightclub, it leads to a fight; in the work place in leads to being fired.

I don't fully understand why, regardless of the distractions and commotion going on and how many times I moved, I never quit school. I was struggling and needed help around grade nine and ten, and it happened that my brother knew a guy from the Big Brothers association who offered to tutor me in math, English and science. The guy's name was Steve Morrison., and he was all right because he could somehow manage to keep me interested in the subjects and even make them exciting. No question, he is the only reason I was able to turn around my marks considering how much I screwed around. For instance, I failed in English due to having an FM radio in my pocket and wearing an earpiece, thinking I had convinced the teacher it was a hearing aid.

Well there were basically two highlights to Steve's teaching. One was passing my courses. The other was attending something called the Habitat Forum, which was held in in a refurbished Air Force hangar on Jericho Beach from May 31 to June 11, 1976. The conference was attended by such world-renowned personalities as Margaret Mead, Mother Teresa, Buckminster Fuller, Paolo Soleri, and Maggie and Pierre Trudeau. It turned out to be a once-in-a-lifetime event for me because I got to sit in on intimate talks with both Margaret Mead and Buckminster Fuller.

This one morning I was standing by myself in the hanger with these amber stained windows forty feet above, so dirty the light only made them glow. Remarkably, only one of them was broken, letting in a single precious shining ray of golden sun. As I turned to leave, I literally bumped into a tiny little women dressed like some kind of nun, who was shining against the backdrop of blackness in that single pure ray of warm sun like some magical unicorn. I stared at her for a second, not knowing exactly what to say other than, "Where did you come from?"

The little lady, with the dark rings of no sleep and pain under her eyes and a face as leathery- brown and wrinkled as a cowboy from an old Spaghetti Western movie, flashed an infectious smile, a sparkle of magic dancing in her eyes, and replied softly, "Oh, me? I've always been here." I just looked at her, still wondering where she had come from and feeling mesmerized and a bit uncomfortable under her soul-piercing gaze. Instead of something interesting, I just said, "How you doing today?" She looked at me for a second and then, in an accent I couldn't recognize, grabbed my hand, her grip surprisingly firm, and said, "I am doing fine dear. Just fine. How are you?" I said "Doing good thanks," and then some other small talk. As ignorant as I was, being an East Van boy, I still somehow knew I had just clasped hands of greatness. Years later, I would realize I had been chatting with Mother Teresa.

The following pictures are of Lord Byng high school, where I tried to get through grade nine, the other is the infamous Tolmie House.

Chapter 30

Last Year of High School

"The advantage of emotions is that they lead us astray." - Oscar Wilde

I went into the last year of high school thinking it would be easy and fun, but it wasn't. The workload was heavy (at least for me it was) and a new group of young bucks were trying to make their mark in the school - as they should, by the way. As I always say, "The world doesn't need another wallflower. It's got enough to cover the entire surface of the planet".

Last year of high school, gotta make it count. What to do? Why not run for office in the notorious East Van High School? I think I wanted to be in control and to have some fun in the upcoming final year and hoped that me and my best friend FJS, a.k.a. The Viking, would nail it. Who was FJS? Well, we met a couple of years earlier upon my returning to Vancouver and to Tupper Secondary. He was a high-energy, fun but intense kid from pure German ("Aryan" as he would call it) stock - your classic features of blonde hair and blue eyes. Not sure how we met exactly but we shared one or two classes together and I thought he was a cool, intelligent dude. We became fast friends and were inseparable throughout high school and for several years after, until yet another gang fight and subsequent court scene, which like a road sign, told me, "You're on the fast track to a dead end." I'll get to that later.

As it turned out, FJS's bro had been school president a year or two before, so I thought, "Hmmm, maybe we could leverage his bro's rep, speeches and last name to get elected. Works in real politics, just look at George Bush Jr., so why not?" We chatted about it for a few weeks and then decided to go for it. I thought it best if he went for the presidential seat and I tried for the vice-president position. Not that strategic really, as he was smarter and more organized in certain things than me, plus his brother could help. Also his dad was a successful senior exec and could put in some money if needed. No question, the Viking and I would have made for a memorable last year of school by all accounts, but most likely not that great at the actual job of running the student body. Oh yeah, getting girls - that was another motivator. What chick doesn't want to bed the president or VP? Just watch TV or movies, and besides, what else would be expected from teenage boys? As a matter of fact, as part of my election speech I actually promised monthly wet t-shirt contests - as a fund raising initiative, of course. I did this in conjunction with a precisely-timed opening of the school's giant crimson velvet stage curtains, revealing a thirty-foot, "Vote for S&H" banner held by two perky, well-developed grade ten girls in black bikinis and red pumps. Yeah, that happened, and I can tell you the principal and vice principal and most teachers sitting or standing in the audience didn't see that coming and choked on their donuts and coffee in front of half the school.

Surprise, surprise, come election day some four to six weeks later, the vice principal called me and FJS in to his office to explain we didn't get a single vote, yeah, right, and that the winner for president was a girl I knew; she was cool but a bit butchy for my tastes, and, as it turned, out she was gay and is now an officer for the RCMP. No idea who the VP was, but the two of them actually did a great job. All's fair in love, politics and war, someone once said, so we didn't feel it was too wrong to put a few hits of acid in the big, easily accessible, stainless steel staff coffee maker as our vote of disapproval.

The summer came and went and was full of all kinds of fun and games. Then came the last year for high school and for many the last schooling they would ever do. My grade twelve year in 1980 started off much like all of them, except for this air of being the official top dogs for once. Even the teachers seemed to treat us with a degree of respect not afforded the younger grades. This was great, but it wasn't long before it was business as usual for me and the crew, half of which were still one year behind me. The highlights of grades eleven and twelve were surprisingly split among the classes, the school teachers, and the weekend parties; not that the teachers showed up at the parties, but they did drop some pearls of wisdom on my scratched and chipped school desk: Graphic Arts, Law, English and Social Studies to be specific. A rare combination for me of cool topics delivered by cool teachers. Thanks to those teachers for doing a great job, the result, I suppose, of loving what they did. That ride ended about four months before graduation though because, yes, once again I ended up getting kicked out of school.

How did it happen this time? Well if there is a theme to my school years, it is breaking rules and fighting, generally combined. One weekend, my crew and I attended an East Side house party. We showed up in two separate groups, due to transport being a challenge generally. I got the invite from a kid who looked up to me, which is great, but the house party sucked, as in a sausage fest at an East Side dump. So we hung out for about half an hour and then headed west. Someone in the crew had a line on a West Side party, which was always a preference for me. To make a long story short, about an hour after we left, the balance of my crew showed up and wrecked the house. That was also kind of typical of the time; not sure why, but doing things like throwing the fridge or stove through the large front window of the host's house as a signal we were leaving just became a signature move; well, at least that's what we were taught coming up in the Riley Park area of East Van.

The social gathering on the West Side turned out to be a non-event because they would not let us in (smart), so we headed off to track down (pre-texting days) a few other party hunches in the Viking's dad's cherry red VW Microbus. Nothing really panned out, so we aimed our sights on where we had started; back at the East Van house. Who knows? Maybe it was rocking by now? Not the case, plus we literally walked into an ambush, as it were. We pulled up out front, I think there was about four of us, and we grabbed our liquor cache and headed to the stairs, thinking positive about the night. Then, out of nowhere like a pack of hillbilly ninjas, these dudes descended on us from every bush and doorway possible, two of them pulling up shotguns on us. For those of you who have watched the classic movie Deliverance, I'm sure this family was in it, actually they were the stars, only thing missing was a banjo playing in the background because I swear I heard, "I'm gonna make you squeal like a pig, boy." Did I mention that out of the ten or so of the agile Neanderthals, eighty percent of them were about fifteen years older than us? Yeah, we were just learning how to shave and what to do with a morning dog and these guys had all done long stretches of time in some backwater prison and knew exactly what cost the most cigarettes and what went where and when.

Unbelievable as it happened, these inbred lemmings of generations of married siblings had this one planned out pretty well. No sooner had the sliding side door of the VW slammed shut, the coordinated attack began with two cars pulling up out of the darkness, boxing us in on the dimly-lit narrow side street. "Oh, fuck!" came slowly from me and FJS in unison. "Not good" was the other thought forcing the hairs on the back of my neck to stand up so straight they pushed out my jean jacket collar.

The car-bound Deliverance gang members foamed at the mouth as they clawed over each other to get out of the windows of their rust-bucket AMC Ambassador American V-8 (car of choice for the hillbilly ninja crowd apparently). This was about the time I realized I should be in sales as my mouth kicked into high gear saying whatever it took to persuade the pagan squad to let us go. We slowly walked backwards to the van keeping eye contact, me continuing to talk like we got caught in the tiger cage during feeding time..."nice kitty, good kitty." We had hardly got in when I guess one or more had second thoughts about what our punishment should be, and a five-foot steel rock-breaking bar came through the sliding door like a hot knife through butter, nearly impaling one of my companions. The Viking popped the clutch and jerked the van to the right as I yelled out the classic "Punch It, Chewy!" FJS hammered it without a second's delay. As usual he was great under pressure, slipping the van easily between the parked cars and directly at the trolls who had thrown the spear. The Hillbillies didn't see that coming, and they seemed dazed and confused as they tried to decipher the bright lights coming towards them. Thankfully, at the last second they scattered like pigeons being chased by a hungry meth-head on East Hastings.

We flew across their lawn, smashing through their neighbour's fence with a boom! Wood panels flew into the early morning sky. With none of us wearing seat belts, we were bouncing around like a box of raisins, but the Viking stayed the course, blowing through a dozen or more hedges and fences until hitting the end of the block, the VW jumping into the air and coming down hard on the asphalt road, barely missing the parked cars on either side of the road. Yeah, he could fuckin' drive, that boy! We all yelled in excitement as the adrenaline of our escape hit us hard; that was until I saw the two hillbilly limos' smoking tires, one in reverse, bodies hanging out every window, as they come after us. "Shit!" I yelled. "These boys are on us"

Yeah, we had a few bats and all carried knives, but no guns. Down the street we went, the now-screaming Microbus redlining all the way, left then right, down an alley, up a street, across a small playground, but we could not shake them. That's when I thought "Why not head to the last place we would ever go? Or them for that matter." The local cop station. Why not? Their motto, "To Serve and Protect," should be put to the test anyway. We came screeching around yet another corner and there it was up on the left; only thing between us and their compound was a grassy road divider. No problem; we had been ripping up lawns and boulevards for the past twenty blocks anyway. FJS cranked the wheel and whoosh, we slid sideways across the island and straight into the big parking lot, sparks leaping from the front as we bottomed out the Microbus. The few cops standing outside had no idea what was going on as we skidded to a stop with the knuckle-dragger cars coming in right behind us. Probably oblivious to where they were, they hammered the brakes, trying not to run into us. That worked for us, but not so lucky for them, and the second car slammed into the first with a bang! That got the cops' attention and shocked the drunken inbred swine out of their haze of rage. The looks on their faces as they realized where they were was priceless, and even better, they both put their cars in reverse, tires literally screeching, with no regards for the then-half-a-dozen police looking at the scene in amazement. Off they went swearing and yelling out the windows like Cheyenne warriors trying to scare General Custer at the Battle of the Little Big Horn. Well, there was no question that we were freaked out, but the cops not so much, as two of them hopped in their cruisers, lights flashing into the night as they gave pursuit.

We had to do some fast talking with the police officers that stayed behind (something like, "Sorry, made a wrong turn…have no idea who those dudes were …" and we were out of there. We didn't actually talk much before the Viking dropped us off, but it was an adrenaline high that I could see getting addicted to, and I wasn't ready to let it go quite yet. No idea what my buddies had in mind, but for me, no sooner had FJS's taillights turned the corner, I was loading my pockets with thumbnail-sized steel ball bearings and my Wrist Rocket slingshot, thinking a solo mission was in order. In no time flat, my ten-speed had me staring at the house from the darkness of a neighbour's yard. I could see most of them all laughing, drinking, slapping each other on the back, and probably saying what chicken-shits we were, which we were that night for sure. That made my blood boil and I don't recall much after that other than some dreamy vision of me letting fly those silver little balls of joy, hitting speeds close to a bullet, the first one taking out their big plate glass with a mighty crash! Yeah, that took the smiles off their pock-marked, unshaven faces.

My pocket empty, I suddenly realized I had no escape contingency that included them all coming out at the same time, some jumping through the broken window the rest slipping and sliding down the cement stairs. Oops! Exit stage right was the plan, but those boys were on me like white on rice as I pushed the ten-speed's pedals as hard as my skinny legs could manage. Those good old boys would have surely buried me in the basement of their East Side rental after lighting me on fire, doing shots of Jack, while roasting hotdogs of my burning corpse as they said, "I hate white rabbits" each time the smoke got in their eyes, and singing along to Lynyrd Skynyrd's, Sweet Home Alabama. As much as I like camp fires and singalongs, I had to pass on this one. I thought I was in the clear, but here's where my second guerilla military maneuver went awry. I came racing out of the protection of the alley into the street lights of death, thinking I would be long gone before they got mobile, especially as my route home was down a very steep hill. But no, those fuckers came Tokyo Drift-style around the corner, not more than half a block behind me. As there were no cars on the road and for sure, no skinny white dudes pedaling their ass off down a super-steep street, I was their huckleberry! Can you say "loser"? Sure you can, and at the time I was fairly confident there was a picture of me in a dictionary by that word - pictured on that bike, head down and sweating bullets. Upside? I wasn't dodging bullets as of yet. As they pulled up beside me, I noticed that two of them seemed to be waving at me. Not! They were swinging axes at me. Hmmm. Not good. By this time, I was doing between forty and fifty miles an hour down the super steep hill at the south end of Main Street heading towards Marine Drive thinking, "I can't even turn because I'm going too fast. If I slow down, I'm going to take an axe to the head. I die turning or I die with an axe in my skull, so what the hell." I leaned hard to the left, crossing straight in front of their rusty piece of shit. I guess there is a God and He wanted me to make that corner. The rim of my bike tire was scraping the curb, but I held fast as I squeezed the front and back brakes with all my might, one hundred percent focused on making a sharp turn into a small alley some hundred feet in front of me. Once again, I made that miraculous turn as well, the sound of their car skidding as they backed up to make that first corner. For me, I was down the pitch black alley for no more than seventy feet when I spied another alley going to the left, I skidded and pushed my way up it for about fifty feet, the lights of their car lighting the night sky behind me. Shit, they turned left, as I did, up the small alley. I thought for sure I would lose them with that move. No, they were tracking me like hound dogs on the scent of a wounded convict who got cut on razor wire as he escaped from a maximum security jail. No way was I going to make the end of this long dark alley. They would run me down in no time and think they were doing society a favour. At that second, I jumped off the bike and dragged it as fast as I could into some house's carport; thankfully there was no light sensor, so it was as dark as a murderer's heart.

Without thinking, I tossed the bike over the adjoining fence and stuffed myself under the car in the car port. I barely made it, but there were no options at that moment. Skidding tires and feet all around the car a split second later. Lots of "Where the fuck did he go?" along with "Fuckin' guy just disappeared." Thank God (I was praying, don't you kid yourself) for monkeys with limited intellect as none of them thought to look under the car at their feet. As quickly as it started, it was over. They bumbled back up the driveway and were gone, no doubt on to MIT graduate studies in anthropology. I stayed there for another half hour to make sure, then squeezed out only to find my bike gone. Not sure what happened to it but better it than me.

As expected, the weekend fun and games spilled over to the Monday morning school week, and it took no time at all for it to get way out of hand. The big kid who had originally invited me to the so-called house party came around the hallway corner where my locker was; this wasn't necessarily bad, because he and the three other punks with him had lockers not far from mine. The problem was that they were packing knives and bats and were eye-balling me big time as they walked by, one of them pumping me like I was a junior. I could have let it pass, as I was outnumbered, but when this Asian kid said, "What the fuck you lookin' at?" that was it. Like the glass says on the box containing a shotgun at one of my favourite Gastown restaurant/bars, Chill Winston's, "Break In case of hurt pride"; my pride was hurt and I broke it. Pretty much by the time he finished his sentence he was spitting out teeth like Chiclets from a fast punch to his slack jaw.

What happened then is a matter of perspective, as in mine and the other shocked Monday- morning-dazed teenagers. From what I recall, I did a combo of spider monkey and Spider-Man on the two others, feeling there was no turning back now as they would engage for sure. They never got the chance (lucky for me). I kicked one in the balls so hard he thought it was Christmas, while spinning sideways and grabbing another by the hair and slamming his face into the grey lockers; he dropped as the other guy did. The big hillbilly kid, who I had hoped would have run by now after seeing his buddies lying in the hallway, was standing there with blood in his eyes and a small bat in his left hand as I turned. He hesitated. I didn't. I lunged at the bat hand as I drove the top of my head into his chin, the bat dropping to the dark purple-tiled cement floor with a hollow sound. Stunned, he stepped back and I followed his momentum, spinning him around and running him as fast as I could, face first, into the emergency fire exit doors, which opened gladly upon impact. He dropped unconscious on the pavement five feet from the door. The entire event took about ninety seconds max. Two left the school in an ambulance, and I left the school forever being threatened with charges if I entered property again.

The school used the opportunity to do some gang cleansing, so to speak, and expelled about twenty of us with the option to come back if our parents could successfully plead our case for why we should be allowed to graduate from that school. Well, the vice principal knew full well the family setup of most of the chosen ones, so only about a quarter of us got back in. I was not one of them. The Viking, whose dad was a senior executive at a large company, had no problem in persuading the principal and VP to reconsider their position when it came to his son. Me, well I asked my mom, who happened to be in Vancouver, to go for it, and to her credit she did. Very cool she would do that for me, but it had little if no effect as they were convinced I was the ring leader of the wayward circus.

As I recall, many of our group just didn't go back to school. That was not my game but no schools wanted me except for one, Killarney High School. They had me sign a contract that said, never mind fighting, if I missed a class, did not do homework or even farted in the school, I was out. I learned something about myself during that time, mainly that I didn't need a gang for success. I was a one-man gang in my own right. It was simple as I knew basically no one in the school, so I just focused on the end game, getting a 'P' for pass on all classes and the Dogwood Certificate, which meant I met all the criteria for graduating from grade twelve. I got it mailed to me some time later. Small victory, but it was one of my big goals. The downside was that I couldn't attend the Sir Charles Tupper graduation ceremony and hadn't attended the Killarney School long enough to want to go to theirs, but in the end I did go to the Killarney party because it was held at the famous Commodore Ballroom. The theme I recall being either the Beatles' Long and Winding Road or Follow the Yellow Brick Road from The Wizard of Oz. The upside? My graduation present from my mom was a pair of legendary Luigi Sebillin hand-made-in-New-Westminster black leather biker boots, that I just wore to ride my H-D 4300 Kilometers across the U.S.A.

"Don't grow up. It's a trap" - Fairmont PacRim bar coaster

Chapter 31

Odd Jobs and Trying to Stay Out of Jail

"I can resist everything except temptation." - Oscar Wilde

During my last years of high school and the first few years afterwards, I tried all kinds of jobs, where plenty of exciting, and sometimes life-threatening, incidents occurred along the way. There was the pizza delivery job (rear-ended a semi on Christmas Eve – cut the entire roof of the car off, but luckily left my head attached to my body); also being a stowaway, on a cruise ship (Not really a job but who cares? Not sure what the plan was there, but hoped they would at least let me work as a cook, deckhand or whatever);the dishwasher/busboy job at a classy restaurant, and the driving a tow truck in the city centre, a job that ended rather quickly after I ran into another tow truck in the yard, unfortunately being driven by a Hells Angel member who tried to come through my window to punch me out, causing me to run into his truck a second time. I was sixteen, so what can you expect?

As good as I tried to be, the past seemed to track me like a dark shadow. One night after getting off work at the tow yard under the Granville Street Bridge, I miraculously happened to run into DC, one of the lead dogs from the Tolmie House. He had in tow his latest Padawan learner protégé. It was a lightning-fast reunion and it was truly good to see him; that is up until he asked me if I could lend a hand in driving a truck for him from downtown to somewhere south. He said I could earn a quick couple of hundred bucks. The dilemma was he and his young partner had another two vehicles needing to also head in that direction. Hmmm. Sounds plausible if you are a car thief heading to a chop shop, but of course I said, "Sure…why not?" Thirty seconds later I was standing at the door of a new red Ford pickup truck. Just before touching the door handle, I paused, thinking I better put on my gloves. DC and the kid took off in their cars, and I followed not giving much thought to the fact I was once again driving a stolen vehicle. Well, as Forrest Gump's mother used to tell him, "Stupid is as stupid does," and I was dumber than Gump. We didn't get far over the classic old Burrard Street Bridge when a silver four-door Crown Victoria pulled up beside me with two sour-looking dudes giving me a look that said they either knew me or the truck; I was betting on the truck. They then slowly moved up to the car in front of me, a black Mazda RX7 that had DC in it, and gave him the same once-over. This is not good, screamed my inner voice. Then the inquisitive guys in the Crown Vic moved up to the Mustang GT that the kid was in and eyeballed him for a split second. By this time, we were all coming to the end of the bridge, and two choices came to mind: one follow the pack, or two wait for the last second and blow out in the opposite direction. I knew something was going to happen, betting, if I was going to bet, that they were cops. I picked door number two and hit it like a Great White (a.k.a. in Aussie language, White Pointer) taking down a surfer! It worked - almost. DC and entourage headed south on Burrard to points only they knew. They were either oblivious to being followed or not sure what to do at that second. The almost part? No sooner had I cranked the wheel, heading west on Point Grey Road, my only thought being to bail from the truck as soon as I could, when I just happened to glance in the rearview mirror and to my horror, I saw a second Crown Vic, this one white, about five cars back, so I pulled hard to the right, making the same turn. Fuck! My heart jumped about fifty beats while my butt puckered in preparation for the fight-or-flight scenario that was about to unfold. As luck would have it, a big city transit bus pulled out from its stop, slowing my new buddies down to a crawl. They must have lost sight of me or I was just paranoid, because no one was following me as I drove another block and then made a slow right down a beautiful tree-lined side street by Kits beach. Then I punched it and made another quick right, pulling the truck into a spot between a van and a car parked in front of a very nice house. I jammed the truck into park, shut it off, left the keys and bolted out the passenger door and across the well-manicured lawn, then sent myself diving head first into a thick bush where I hit my head on the side of the house.

No more than five seconds later, the mystery second car came flying around the corner, the two guys in the front seat somehow missing the truck; not sure but it could have been the van temporarily obstructing their view. I didn't wait for them to come back. I got up, pulled off my gloves and toque, turned my jacket inside out and started walking in the opposite direction. I took a long circle route to get to Broadway, hoping to blend in with some commuters. No sign of the car, I thought, "Perfect. I'm out of here." I got about two blocks heading east on Broadway and casually glanced over my right shoulder as I walked past a side street and, sure as a bear shits in the woods, there were both the Crown Vics, blue and red lights flashing and DC over the hood of the silver car. Priceless! They were undercover cops after all. I instantly squashed my impulse to run, thinking DC or one of the undercover dudes would recognize me, and I got to the bus stop just as a bus pulled up. I once again got that Get-Out-of-Jail-Free card and went whistling past the paddy wagon, court house and jail cell. No, I didn't learn the simple life lesson of "be careful who you hang with or you might get hanged." Not me. Too cool and smart for that. Needed to get burnt, beaten and stabbed before that hit home.

Let's roll it back a few years to the end of grade twelve when I got a call from one of my sisters asking me if I wanted a job at the Easter Seals camp she managed. Well, this was in the resort area of Kelowna on a hundred-mile pristine lake, so it took me all of five seconds to say yes. She was the camp director and bus driver and I guess was short a counselor or two for the summer sessions, which ran from June 23 to September 3. I thought "What the hell, nothing but same old, same old going to be happening in the city, so why not? Could be fun." It was an absolute blast! And yes, I took advantage of sister being the boss and played on her not firing me for doing harmless (to me) fun rule-breaking things. For instance, the camp had a giant yellow school bus to take the campers on outings to the lake, to musicals, for ice cream and all kind of clean fun stuff, so of course that was boring as all get-out for me after like a week. Upon arriving back at the camp after one of those excursions, I lingered back in the bus with a few of the cooler campers. Some had mental challenges, as in serious "I see dead people," but for others it was mild, or they were just in a wheelchair or had cystic fibrosis. Anyway, this time I thought what the heck, my sister who always drove the bus, had got off, and the other staff were helping the others down the stairs and corralling them in the direction of the dinner hall. I said to the four or five with me in the back (who had got caught smoking pot and drinking beer with me and Lance two days earlier) "Anyone up for a joy ride?" They all started yelping and whooping to the point where one of the counselors paused and started heading back to the bus, thinking maybe I needed some help. Not! I jumped up and yanked the cool steel-handled lever that pulled the big yellow door closed with a solid swoosh! At the same time, I pulled hard on the emergency brake and turned over the diesel engine and ground the bus into what I figured was first gear. That got everyone's attention. What's the worst that could happen? Get fired? I don't think I was even getting paid, so who gives a shit? And besides, most of them or me might be dead that time next year. I popped the clutch and the big girl leapt for joy, knowing this was good! My sister, on the other hand, was yelling at the top of her lungs and running full speed as I punched it. She actually caught up to the door. I recall her hitting it, but it was too late by that time; me and the boys (my new crew) were going for a cruise; not sure where but we were all laughing like it was the last day on earth. I didn't go far, just a quick spin to give them a memory that would last; and, to be honest, it was a lot harder to drive the forty-eight- foot banana with no power steering than I thought. Also a crashing thing and getting arrested for not having the proper license would have dampened the mood just a tad. As expected, she freaked out, but in the end only threatened to fire me, as deep down she knew, as I did, that this was really good for me. I thank her for that. It was just another one of those baby steps or dry stones to land on in a fast-flowing river that kept me moving in the right direction and gave me the added confidence that I didn't need peer approval, not that I ever cared, and that I was destined for another horizon, possibly one of my own design. Wouldn't that be something?

The hot summer came to an end and it did so too quickly for me, as I loved being there. I was sad it was over because that meant I was dropping into my old life, and I was less than excited about that for some reason. So, what to do? Well, I was having a beer on a patio and heard a Neil Young song playing over the speakers, and the lyric that got me was "Think I'll go out to Alberta, weather's good there in the fall. I got some friends that I could go to working for."

I didn't have any friends in Alberta, but there were oil rigs and, who knows, maybe a job. If not, it would still be a great way to continue the adventure. So I jumped on a Greyhound and headed off to Edmonton. Fortunately, one of the female counselors had a brother that lived there with some buddies, and they were cool with me crashing on the couch until I got myself set up. The trip lasted about six weeks, and one of the highlights was that I saw the just-released Blues Brothers movie. For kicks I climbed from the river to the top of the biggest bridge in the city. As for the rigs, it was early eighties, which for those who were still in diapers or weren't even born, it was just like 2008 and 2012, where many sectors were crashing: no jobs, no money, just layoffs and plenty of repos. I was just about out of money, so it was time to use what I had left for a bus ticket back to the coast. Took about five minutes in Vancouver before I dropped back into my usual-suspect's circle of shit, but I did get a job working on the docks for a while, then a lumber mill, none of which seemed to last, but me and most of my buddies found collecting welfare and doing cash biz on the side worked just fine.

As for association being a factor on your life's ascent or decent, yes, it is as strong as gravity. I met many people and groups over the years but some of the most unusual and I might say coolest in their own, came about when I was introduced to Jessie, a massive twenty-something guy and head of (what we knew them as) the Egicote. Who were they? Members of an aboriginal band that I believe originated on the Queen Charlotte Islands off the west coast of B.C. These boys were so wild they would fit in well in any Genghis Kahn tale or third world country, or for that matter, a big U.S. or Brazilian city ghetto; a throwback to a time when men were real men, not just rough, but in touch with nature and life as a whole. Yes, they seemed to us like something out of a time warp; a tribe living breathing, drinking and fighting just like they did hundreds of years ago. They wore their own brand of colours when they were going to battle or when they were just heading out looking for trouble. They carried weapons of old including hatchets, Bowie knives and the occasional gun and don't kid yourself, they would use them with the slightest provocation. I met them via one of my high school dropout buddies and, as I will explain, spent a bit of time at their camp due to my natural ability to blend, mirror or be chameleon, call it what you will; I could basically fit in with most groups: bikers or preachers. That was simply due to God's gift of a lightning-fast mind and a silver tongue connected to it. Both of these got me into as much trouble as they got me out of, especially when I combined the two with alcohol or drugs.

Interesting enough, I read a story by Emily Carr, the famous artist, who wrote about the Haida Gwaii, as they are known, and called them the "Vikings of the West" due to their size and history of conducting voyages of acquisition; raiding, pillaging, killing men and capturing the women; travelling in massive canoes made from some of the largest trees in the world across open oceans with no sails, only paddling, which is not the same as rowing. Think: dragon boat races. The unfortunate villages that came under their contemplation could do little to retaliate or save their women; their strongest warriors and best canoe-makers could not pursue them, as they were not physically strong enough to paddle the great distance in the open ocean. Anyway, I met him and his many brothers at a biker party and immediately I could see these boys were different. I likened them to the movie Lost Boys with Kiefer Sutherland, inasmuch as they were impulsive, friendly and willing to drain your blood without losing a minute's sleep. Pure animal instinct guided these dudes; no question they were tight crew and always watching each other's backs with no regards for what the more so-called 'Cool Hoods' thought of them, nor would they back down from a fight.

They dressed the way they felt, and could drink any man under the table. The thing that was unsettling somehow was that, other than Jessie with his dark complexion and uncharacteristic blue eyes on top of his six-foot-four frame and weighing in at over three hundred pounds, the rest of his gang were average-size guys. The crew, about six of them, were all slim (other than Jessie's "little" brother, Lover, at two hundred and twenty pounds), but tough as nails with cable-like tendons, rippling muscles, and veins popping out of their skinny arms; and this was not because they went to some pansy health club; no, the boys worked, and worked hard. This was unusual for me to see, compared to the circles I travelled in at the time, I can almost say these guys set some sort of good example for many of us. How? Like you can work and party. Wow! What a revelation. We hung out with them on occasion, like every other weekend, and they were friendly, but you always knew you were not one of them, the family, and you never got in between them. I made this mistake one night while partying heavily by myself drinking Jack, Bud back, my signature combo back then, with Lover and a couple of the others. It all started harmlessly, but one of their crew, a half-white kid and family member named Dean (who looked like James Dean, really, and wore tinted aviator glasses at night) was out of town at camp working, but his hot little blonde girlfriend came to party with us for some reason; I think Lover invited her. Now I don't know what she was thinking, and I doubt she was, but Lover got real drunk and real horny for her and she was being what was classically known as a cock-tease: flirting, rubbing up close to many of the boys, not realizing that if this was a banquet, she was going to be the main course for a bunch of starving pirates. She said it was time to go and Lover said, "I don't think so," and grabbed her by the waist and flipped her over his shoulder like a big bag of dog food. She screamed and began to kick, her red pumps flying like knives, one of them hitting a lamp and sending it crashing to the floor. We all just looked at the unfolding situation. I instantly knew this was out of my control as she began to punch, bite and pull the long black hair of the giant young bro. In reality, when I think about it now, it was probably a total turn-on for him or should I say, foreplay, as he purposefully moved his big frame towards the stairs that led to the main floor and five bedrooms of the massive, turn-of-the-century, four-level wood house. The music kept pumping loud, so there was no way in hell someone was coming to her rescue. I watched this unfold and even in my drunken state still thought it seemed a bit unfair for her to be treated this way, regardless of how she was enticing or acting like she had wanted to fuck all of us for the past three hours. I was a guest in their house, so who was I to step in when these guys would just as soon bury me in the basement as have me stop them from pulling a train on her?

We all followed him up the old wooden stairs, each one screaming as loud as her in agony from his sheer mass. Into the bedroom he went, and by this time the PYT (pretty young thing), had given up and accepted her fate, saying, "Okay, but just one of you at a time." Being a male teenager, I heard those words, as did the others and thought "Hmmm that could work." The bedroom door closed and Lover, I guess. was getting down to business when the Liz, queen of this tribe, came home and saw three of us standing around the bedroom door. She then said, "I thought 'Veronica' was coming over." We all looked at each other as if to say, "never heard of her," but I, for some reason, spit out, "She's in with Lover, and I'm next." Her eyes went huge, the whites blazing at us like a tigress about to rip the throat out of a

Capybara. She yelled, "No fucking way are you boys taking turns on her when Dean's out at camp!" With that she headed straight for the door, aiming to push us aside like so many bowling pins, but just before she got to it, I stepped in and said, "She asked for it and said it was okay, so back off, you bitch!" No delay, she open-hands me across the face, spinning my head to the right so hard I hit the door. Now, you got to know Liz was Jessie's girl, and she was not fat but just a few feet too short for her weight. I instantly raised my fist to drive her big nose through the back of her bleach-blonde hair but decided not to follow through, as I was drunk and horny, but besides was it really worth all this work? No. She pushed me aside and burst the door open to find young stud boy with his pants still on kissing her. She stalled for a beat and then of all things, big Jessie walks in. Now I'm not a coward but this guy was just a plain scary-looking dude who would kill you just as soon as he found a good place to bury you; like I said, three hundred pounds, Fu-Manchu moustache combined with an angry disposition, basically a human rhino. Even for a white guy (and I'm really white) at that precise second I went from white to an off-purple since all the blood drained out of my body and my pulse jumped to 180 bpm. The thing of it is, I didn't know whether it was fight or flight time so I did the next best thing: I froze, hoping he wouldn't see me or something stupid. He saw us and yelled, "What the fuck's going on?" His queen started chirping immediately about what happened and said that I was about to hit her, which was hard to deny since he pretty much walked in when my fist was raised. Damage control; I replied quickly and very loudly that it's true, but only because she open-handed me without warning. By this time Jessie was towering over me, his pale blue eyes flashing with anger. Bam! Another open hander to the same side of my head, this one sending me sideways so hard my feet came off the ground by at least two inches as I bounced off the bedroom door frame. "That's for raising your fist against my old lady," he bellowed. To my surprise he then turned to her, pointing one of his Bratwurst- sized fingers at her and scolded, "Don't you ever hit one of the boys again. I don't care what they do. You leave that to me. Got it?" She shrank under his gaze and said meekly, "Okay, okay, I got it." He then turned back to me, said nothing to his bro and said, "Come with me." Not good, as we headed back down to the partially-finished basement ending up in unfinished sections. No sooner had we got there, he turned and hit me again, this time on the other side of the head, the force knocking me hard to the dirty cement foundation floor.

This was not good. I could try and make a break for it but I would never make it because all he would do is call out for the others to stop me and that would be that. He said in a slow raspy voice, his breath heaving from the stairs and excitement, "I should kill you for what you did. Who the fuck do you think you are?" This is when my sales career really took off, just so you know. I started talking, and after about three minutes without me taking a breath he said, "Shut the fuck up! Don't do that again. Let's get a drink."

That was the end of that event. As for Lover and the hot young blonde, not sure what came of that since I felt it best to make my exit before things somehow got ugly again; and besides, I was having some challenges with my balance due to the two shots to the ear. I didn't see Jessie or his crew for about a year after that. It wasn't just the fact I could have disappeared, but I had my own crew and his was just a bit to mediaeval for my liking. We hooked once after that when the General was putting a team together for some reconnaissance, and possible abduction work, sometime later. Another case of association mistakes coming up here. It seemed some coke-head was into a bike club member we knew for substantial chunks of cheddar. Well, we had three teams set up to search the Lower Mainland for this guy, who had dropped off the grid. So since I had done this a few times before with the General, we put into action the same type of creative thinking that tracked down the others. I started to retrace his steps, associations, habits, likes, foods, etc., and put together a likely area that he may be in and, bingo, we nailed it. He was holed up in an old house in a small community about sixty miles outside of the Van. The General and I staked out his place over the course of a few days trying to get his profile and pattern down. We wanted to know what we were going to be walking into. The night finally came, and the three crews met at an empty parking lot in an industrial area, a marshaling yard is as good a name for it as any, several blocks from the dark country road where he lived. We knew he lived in the house with at least two women and two or three kids, along with the cliché pit bull. So it would have to be quick and controlled. No room for hot heads. Six of us and every one straight, lots of time to party after; if not, this could get really ugly.

We do a slow roll-up fifty feet from the driveway, lights out. The cars we are in are a new Caddy of the General's (or should I say his rich girlfriend's?); Jessie and the crew in his 'light-armoured' Lincoln; and then there's the Viking in his monster Ford truck that I swear if it ran over a gas-efficient car it would have felt like a speed bump. No neighbours, so no witnesses. The General and Jessie divide, taking one person with them each; one goes around the back to deal with the runner or dog challenge, the other was going to try a diplomatic approach via the front door. I went with the General to the front door since my gift even then was the ability to defuse most situations or at least buy some time until things could be swung in our favour. The Viking backed up Jessie as they went around the side of the house. The others kept the cars ready to roll. I will admit I was surprised that a few of them were packing heat; unlikely it would be needed, but like a parachute it was better to have it and not need it rather than need it and not have it; stupid logic under the circumstances.

Jessie has his sawed-off twelve-gauge tucked inconspicuously inside his trench coat. It is late October, so I can see the engine exhaust as we approach the front stairs. It's about 10 p.m. on a Wednesday night. We figure the kids will be in bed and he will be relaxing watching the mind-sucking box, oblivious to what is about to happen. Knock, knock, knock! The General's ring-filled fist hits the big wooden door of the old farm house. We both step sideways, just in case he's a bit more excitable than we think. We instantly hear a commotion and whispers and cupboards opening and shuffling of feet. The dog start barking uncontrollably and we hear a male voice say, "Put that mutt away."

"Who is it?" asks a female voice through the door.

The General shouts out, "I need to speak to Billy. He probably wants to talk with me too."

"Who are you?" asks the voice again.

"My name is the General, and I was asked to pick him up and deliver him to the guy he owes a lot of money to for the cocaine he has been consuming but has yet to pay for."

Hushed whispers in the background, angst moments and stress. The door opens a crack with the chain still on it, a female face appears, bleach-blonde hair, too much mascara, but before she can say anything the 265-pound frame of the General pushes the door open, sending her sideways into the shoe closet. We quickly step inside. "Where is he?" demands the General. Billy steps out from behind a wall that separates the dingy dining room from the dilapidated kitchen. I help the chick up and notice a sawed-off double-barrel shot gun just out of her reach. I grab it and smile. "No need for guns at this point. Maybe later?" I joke trying to lighten the very tense moment.

"What the fuck do you want?" snarls Billy.

"Well for starters" says the General, "I want you to slowly turn around and look through your back door window." Billy gets a confused look on his face, but obediently does as he's told. Faintly illuminated by the kitchen lights he can see the huge mug of Jessie who points to the door handle, motioning for him to open the door. Billy weighs his options and wisely concludes it best not to escalate things any further. He comes with us for a long ride and explains his case and agrees to a payment plan that includes doing anything it take to come up with the money in the next forty-eight hours. He is then told to hit the road. He does, but he never comes up with the cash.

I'm not sure what happened to him after that, but it probably wasn't good as for the member we did the pick for.

I was told a guy shot him and then killed himself sometime later during a similar episode.

As you can see, I had my involvement with the law.

Chapter 32

Blood Is Thicker Than Water

My brother Wayne was heavy into drugs in the years before he died and in and out of jail since he was twelve, so I didn't see much of him during his brief act on our blue marble. But on occasion we would cross paths, usually at some East Van party or biker bar like the American or Eldorado. I must admit it was always good to see him, even though I wished he was not such a screw-up and could have taught me more than his eclectic view on the finer points of street and jailhouse survival. I have listed some of them below. numbers 1, 3, 18, 23, 24, and 27 were his; the others I learned from my own mistakes, movies and mentors, including martial arts teachers like the world-renowned living legend, E. Chad.

They go like this:

1. Always stab on the right side of the chest - fewer vital organs.

2. Never pull a gun on a man unless you intend to shoot him, and never shoot him unless you intend to kill him.

3. If you need some quick cash, follow a likely mark into the bathroom at a bar or restaurant and while he's in mid-stream, come up behind him, reach your hand between his legs and grab his Johnson and yank down hard. Use your free hand to smash his face

into the cool white tile wall in front of him. Take the W.W.R (wallet, watch, rings) and walk calmly out, eyes down, make no eye contact (that implants image memory). Use the credit card within twenty minutes maximum. If you want the full meal deal, check the license. This gives you the option of hitting the residence if possible.

4. If you need to blow through a police roadblock or ram cars, always hit them in the back end - less weight.

5. In a fight, never worry about the kick; it is 99% of the time a diversion for the haymaker punch.

6. Use caution when parking next to a van.

7. Rule of Three: If you see the same face or vehicle three times in a day, you're being followed - especially when traveling in known kidnap countries.

8. If you see one police car, you will see one or two more within five minutes. They move in herds.

9. When using an alias, have a detailed back-end story memorized with name spelling, phone number, addresses, etc. Name should be nickname, dad's name and mom's family name, to be sure you remember it.

10. The one with the plan, no matter how dumb, usually wins.

11. If a person is nice to you but mean to the waiter/waitress, they are not a nice person.

12. If being choked or strangled, turn your head to the side; this opens the wind pipe enough to breathe. Then grab groin and squeeze grapes like making wine, or pinch and twist inner thigh or under armpit. If not, go for eyes.

13. The average fight lasts ninety seconds. You must have the wind to go three times that.

14. If being chased on foot at night, remember that as you pass under a street light your own shadow will quickly pass you, giving the illusion your pursuer is closing the gap. Think sundial. Do not look back; this often results in falling.

15. Ninety-nine percent of fights end up on the ground. The best street fighters are wrestlers who have done some boxing.

16. If you are knocked backwards or swept off your feet, the neck must be strong enough to hold the head so it doesn't hit the ground. This usually prevents being knocked out.

17. If you get, or even think, mace is on your hands, don't rub your eyes.

18. Stay in school, no matter what.

19. If someone pulls a gun on you and tells you to get in the car, it will only get worse. If possible, run zig-zag. Your chances of being hit are about 10 percent as opposed to 100 percent if you get in.

20. Never tangle with a man who doesn't care or has nothing to lose. E. Chad & Napoleon philosophy

21. Look at what the masses are doing and do the opposite.

22. The Government wants you to have attachments and a healthy portion of debt to keep you preoccupied and under control. Never pay credit card debt. Get control.

23. Crush up sparkplug tops that are made of porcelain. A handful thrown at a car window shatters it with very little noise.

24. Chrysler cars/vans have a glow ring around the ignition (or used to), which makes it easy to break off with a screwdriver.

25. Leather is best to avoid "road rash" after coming off your motorcycle.

26. Anger blows out the light of reason and will get you into trouble. Your pride will keep you there.

27. Never come to visit me in jail unless you bring some balloons.

28. Loose lips sink ships; keep your own counsel.

29. Sit with your back to the wall.

30. If you lose control of a car, turn into the spin.

31. Keep your friends close, your enemies closer.

32. All women want security; in the past it was meat on the table, now it's money in the bank.

Here are examples of what a typical evening out with my bro could be like; in other words, a not-too-uncommon situation to be involved in. That won't shock those from the wrong side of town, but maybe for the office bully, fat ex-school jock, after-work hockey stud and the tough guys behind the wheel of a car (they're my faves, you know, the ones who will give you the finger or want a fight at the next red light, oblivious to the possibility they may be grabbing a tiger by the tail and there will be no commercial breaks or referee stepping in to save their saggy asses. No, those guys are the ones we often read about in the paper as "nice guy in the wrong place." That is probably true nine times out of ten but seven out of ten times they just wouldn't shut the fuck up and walk away.)

So here we go. It was one of those very rare occasions that I went out with my bro (you just don't do certain things, or at least you shouldn't, like swat a polar bear in the face with a branch, but I did that too) and three hotties dressed to the nines: fishnet stocking, pumps and push-up bras. You get the picture. Not the kind you take home to meet the folks. The women were a few years older than me and that was exciting; one of them - her name was Shelly - had a thing for my brother. I was invited because I drove them in my dark burgundy 1968 Mustang; the car was small but my bro was more than happy to have one of those miniskirts perched on his lap. The scene was a bit surreal since all three were, in my estimation, out of our league, being, from what I picked up in about the first ten minutes, from Upper West Side homes; prime grade A Canadian meat with rich parents. We did a couple of shots at my brother's space (a dump of course, no idea how the that Shelly chick was into him. other than his Elvis/Eastwood style without the singing, acting or money.) We ended up at this new nightclub; you know the type: long lineup at the door; wall-to-wall people inside; music pumping out the latest hits; light show, strobe lights, fog machine, the works. We walk up to the front of the line like celebs; without missing a beat, my brother Wayne shakes the no-neck's hand and we're inside.

The girls were trying to figure us out at this point, but enjoying the first class treatment. The doorman probably gave a nod to someone and they took us to a table right beside the dance floor. Five minutes later, a round of shooters on the house. At this point, I was beginning to buy into my own bullshit. Wasn't too long before everybody was feeling good and the girls were beginning to loosen up. I can remember thinking I might just get me some tonight, when just about that time a bodybuilder hit on my brother's Kim Kardashian look-alike. There's bold and courageous, and then there's just unlucky or stupid; usually those two are walking hand-in-hand off a cliff. Bad move for him, but considering he was five inches and fifty pounds bigger than my bro, he probably felt pretty confident. Oh, and not to mention he had a crew of monkey boys giving him moral support.

That in itself wasn't a real problem. The problem was that Shelly was not interested, but buff boy didn't take no for an answer. My brother watched this for a minute or two, then casually got up, walked over to the dude, and politely told him to fuck off. That got his attention. He didn't say shit; he just pushed my brother hard, and Wayne staggered back a few feet. Then the bodybuilder made what could or should have been the final mistake of what could have been (if I wasn't there) his short life; he asked my brother to step outside. Hahaha! In retrospect I can only guess what this six-foot-five surfer-looking dude, in his skintight white denim jeans and matching t-shirt (come to think of it, he looked like Mr. Clean but with sandy-coloured wavy hair), was thinking, ("Outside, knock this punk out, come back have a shot, get the girl.") The classic Alpha male program of 'First Mate and First Meat'. Plus, I'm sure he was thinking, "This dude is too small and wasted to be any real threat." I'm sure the plan looked good on paper.

The problem was my brother had a plan of his own, similar but with a slightly more permanent ending for the lost Beach Boy. It went something like this, "I'll pop outside, kill the guy, come back in have a drink and dance with my new girlfriend, then head back to her place and bang her for the weekend." He clearly had no interest in trading blows with a guy who outweighed and out-reached him. Nope.

So outside they go, unnoticed, no one following except me, his crew of gym rats having way too much fun to pay attention to themselves in the mirrors and the female hard bodies bouncing everywhere, to those dogs it was like the classic distraction of "Squirrel."

My bro walks out first and heads towards the parking lot behind the club, gesturing to his opponent to follow. He does this feeling secure in his own manhood, which I suspect was based on a life of being a big fish in the small pond of Richmond, B.C. I slowly ease my way past the doormen and the crowd of people waiting outside in anticipation of the fun they'll have once they are privileged enough to be allowed to cross that imaginary, yet somehow mystical nightclub threshold of exclusivity.

The two of them ended up squaring off just outside the reach of the ever-watching parking lot lights. As my bro was leading the way, I knew it was not by accident. He definitely wanted the added advantage that, for those who know, comes with the cover of darkness: no witnesses, no cops. The big guy made the first move just as I came around the corner. He came flying at my brother with a flurry of punches and kicks; he might have had some training by the looks of it, but like the old saying goes, "you don't bring a knife to a gun fight," and you sure as shit don't bring a fist to a knife fight. Morale of that story is my usual saying "Remember where you're from but realize where you are."

I was about fifteen feet away as the parking lot Gladiators engaged in their twentieth century version of the arena fight. The gorilla got caught in the stomach with the five-inch blade of a Buck knife that appeared out of nowhere. The sound that came out of that guy was barely human, it sounded like the squeal of a two hundred and fifty-pound pig as it enters the first stage of becoming part of my favourite weekend breakfast. The white t-shirt went crimson red in an instant. I just stood there frozen for what felt like a half an hour, totally mesmerized by the sheer drama and pure unedited violence of it all. Then, Bang! I jerked back to the reality of the situation. The guy fell to the ground, but not before he received one more puncture to his abdomen for good measure, you know like the second atomic bomb that was dropped on Japan, as if they didn't get the message from the first one. The next thing I saw, as if I was sitting back watching it from the safety and comfort of a theatre seat, was me flying through the air thinking, Oh my God, he's going to kill this guy. I landed in the middle of them focusing all my attention on where the knife was. I lunged for it, but grabbed the blade instead, giving me a deep cut in my right hand as a permanent souvenir of the evening's entertainment highlight.

For a split second I recoiled from the pain that shot through my arm, taking my breath away like the time I dove into a glacier lake high in the Rockies. With my left arm, I locked his elbow and pulled with all my might, but his momentum and blind, drug-induced rage was way out of my league as we both fell on top of the poor fucker, this time the blood-stained blade opening a four-inch cut down the big guy's rib cage, those hundreds of hours at the gym and his nineteen-inch arms in the end being of little help.

Then things really got wild. Boom! Three rock crushers (bouncers) burst into the fray, like a pack of starving hyenas. There is a clarity and calmness that I guess I've always had, especially in stressful situations, not quite like the "keep your head when those about you are losing theirs" secret to leadership, but that time it worked out for both me and my bro. In a flash I knew the bouncers didn't know what was going on because there was so much blood on all of us. It was splattered on their faces, arms, you name it; and yeah, I had some on me too. I yelled at the top of my lungs, "He's got a knife!" and pushed the white, now blood-red t-shirt and its occupant back against the wall of the club with such force that it surprised even me. What happened next would have been comical if it hadn't have been dripping with violence. The three wild-eyed steroid poster boys unleashed their big 'roid rage (apparently they are small in other aspects) on one of their own, knocking him to the ground and going what we in Canada call "lumberjack style" on him. He should have known it's not the size of the dog in the fight, its size of the fight in the dog. And some dogs just don't fight fair; they fight to win. I know it's not fair - go tell your mom or better yet, tell your girlfriend or wife. Yes, all honest women want a man who is a winner and, if push comes to shove, who will kill or die for them. Just the way it is.

That veil of bloody confusion gave me that split-second opportunity to disappear into the night, my brother in tow, his fist still clutching the blade that was so covered in blood it looked like part of his hand. Fifteen seconds later we were burning down the highway, no words spoken until we got back to my one-bedroom teardown house on the far East Side, when he said, "Thanks."

My brother was one of my idols, as many big brothers are, until I realized he was a loser. He had chosen a path of drugs, jail, more drugs and more jail. It was never going to end, and within it was his self-fulfilling prophecy of "die young and have a good looking corpse." I had this thought stirring in the back of my mind for some time, and I finally said to myself in a dark whisper, "If that is your destiny, then it not going to happen because you chose it. It will happen because you died trying to break free from it."

Come hell or high water, I became determined to move on and map out a different road, a future path with no drugs, no jail, and no young corpse. Yes, the wife, kids and white picket fence became my dream. I had never been in Kansas, but I was going to get over that damn rainbow, if not in a hot air balloon, then at a hundred and ten miles an hour down the hot black pavement of destiny.

In case you're wondering, that was not the last time my brother tried to kill someone in front of me and set me up to get killed or incarcerated. As I may have mentioned (if not, I am now) that I lived with my mother on and off over the years, the last time in that one-bedroom house I wrote about. How does that work, you ask? Not too well, thank you, because I actually slept in the underground root cellar. Oh, and the best part was I had to enter from a trapdoor cut into the piss-yellow linoleum-covered floor of the five-by-ten-foot kitchen. I had to pull up the door by a brass ring-like latch and secure it to a small hook screwed into the wall. Then I carefully made my way down the eight almost vertical wooden stairs to what I called the "Tiger's Lair," well to myself anyway. I actually never told that to anyone other than my cat, and she totally approved. More than once, that heavy wood door came unhooked from the wall, probably because I lightly bumped it, and it came down hard on the top of my head, literally pile-driving me into the cold cement foundation. I was lucky it didn't break my neck, to be honest, but it did catch the cat trying to follow me once and almost severed her leg. I fixed up the lair somewhat, with a few flags as curtains, some junky carpet and a kid's-sized single bed. The highlight was I had a kick-ass stereo system, compliments of my brother, but for the most part it was dark, damp, cold and full of what my daughter D.W. calls "Ling-Hos," spiders, and the creepy little critters came in all sizes, let me tell you. I still love crushing the guts out of those little suckers. And, of course, there was the flea infestation from either my cool Manx cat named Kitty or from the carpet I had expropriated from the front of some house that was throwing it out.

My brother seemed to have an internal GPS that was triggered whenever I moved in with my mom and seemed to temporarily resurrect that thing, as delicate as the wing of a fairy, called a family. He would find out where we were and show up, usually high on heroin, pills, booze or a cocktail of his own design. I had not lived with him since around the age of eleven and had moved out of my mom's life at twelve, which I mentioned earlier, leaving her in the town of Prince George to live happily ever after with the man of her dreams (and my nightmares) the wife-beating, Cowboy. So by twenty I was no longer used to his brand of zero-to-ultra-violent situations that followed him like the smell of a dead dog rotting in the hot summer's sun.

The standard knock on the door (can't recall ever having a house with an actual working doorbell up until that time) came at about 10 p.m. on a Wednesday, and I was just settling into watching the movie of the week, in my life a rare but comforting ritual, as I had work on the North Van docks at 7 a.m., a two-hour bus ride from East Van. My bro W.A.W. was bigger than life after another jail stint, which made him a bit worse to handle after a regimen of three squares a day, plenty of sleep and fights and pumping iron daily. This constituted a tried and true recipe for breeding strong and unpredictable gang pit bulls. (Warning label that comes with dogs: Not good with children or civilians). His girlfriend Shelly, the Kardashian twin from the nightclub, was standing behind him. This time, she appeared ragged, with big black rings under her eyes. Whatever it was, she had definitely lost some her shine and was on the yellow-drug brick road and off to meet a different kind of wizard in a not-so-enchanted Emerald City.

He said, "Hey what's up?" as he pushed his way by me into our palatial twenty-square-foot living room, with Rain Forest theme wall paper. He was totally fucked-up wasted, probably on pills because he had no money for heroin, unless, that is, Shelly was buying it. She was a dental hygienist, at least she was the last time I saw her, and paying for his drugs was very possible as she was as naive as they come. He staggered in, pulling Shelly by the arm, and I noticed she was not that keen to follow him. As I stood there for a second, I noticed a taxi sitting in front of the house, not unusual except it had the name of a taxi company from Victoria.

"Not much. What are you doing here?" I said, totally pissed that he was there.

He slurred back, "I bin on da Island for a while and decided to come see ya, bro."

"Oh," I replied. "How did you find out where we live?"

He smiled and said what I thought he would say, "I called mom and she told me."

"Greeeaaattt," I said sarcastically, as they both made themselves comfortable on the threadbare brown tweed couch, which I think I got from the Salvation Army. He sat for a few seconds, then leapt up and went to the bathroom. There was an awkward silence as I continued looking out the slightly-ajar door and noticed that the taxi driver was getting out of his cab and coming towards the stairs. Shelly smiled and said cheerfully, "You're looking good, What's new?"

"Ah, not much," I replied coldly. Before she could say another word, my brother was emerging from the washroom and the taxi driver was climbing up the stairs. I thought, "Yeah, this is about to turn into one of Wayne's shit shows and it's going to play in my theatre. Fucking great!" I turned to look at my brother and said, "So, what can I do for you?"

He casually asked back, "You got any money?"

"No!" I snapped back. "What for?"

"To pay the taxi driver," he spurted out. At this point I was thinking I should just give him the twenty or so bucks for the cab fare and be done with it. The Indian cab driver was now standing three feet behind me and could hear me say, "Fine. How much?"

Before my bro said a word, the cabby spoke up. "It's $362. Don't worry about tip." I turned to W.A.W. with an astonished look on my face and yelled out, "Fuck that! I'm not paying. How the hell can a cab be that much?"

The mild-mannered man said, "I drove him from Victoria. Taxi ride plus ferry fee for three people. You have to pay me."

At his point my pulse had jumped to about two hundred beats per minute, so speaking got tricky, but I managed to get it out as I turned back to my brother, now sitting on the couch with Shelly. "To hell I do. He can pay you!"

My brother then did something odd. He said to the cabby, "Come in for a minute. Have a drink."

Taxi dude proudly said, "I don't drink. I just want my money or I call police." Mention you're going to call the cops to most of the people I grew up with and you're asking for a beating - or worse. Wayne then got up and smiled at the dude and said, "Relax. Come on in. I'll go get you your money." The guy stepped in, and my bro closed the door and headed to the kitchen. I immediately thought that's not good.

The taxi guy looked at me and said, "I saved him. He tried to jump off ferry boat. He was on other side of railing and I pulled him back over. He is sick. Not well."

I looked in his eyes and realized this was a good guy who was probably telling the truth. I then asked Shelly, "Is that true?"

She burst out crying and said, "Yes, he did! I couldn't get him back over the railing . He was going to jump. I didn't know what to do, and then Hodgie came out."

The cab driver interjected saying, "I told you my name is not Hodgie." He was getting pissed at this point. Don't blame him but I was thinking, WTF! I decided it was best to close the door so the neighbour, a cop, wouldn't call his buddies or just walk over and check out the noise.

No sooner had that brass door latch clicked into place on the old solid wood door, my brother came charging out of the kitchen with a butcher knife and lunged at the terrified taxi driver as Shelly and I looked on like an RCMP-Taser-stunned Polish immigrant at YVR. It happened so fast that I didn't even react. Thankfully the cabby did, managing to raise his arm up to protect himself from the downward strike of the blade. It cut his arm, not deeply, but sliced it nonetheless. My bro pushed him into the door and tried to bring the ten-inch knife up for a second strike, but Mr. Cabby, in full self-preservation mode, hung onto his arm and did a spider monkey move on him, wrapping his legs around W.A.W.'s waist. They both fell to the dirty and soon-to-be-blood-stained carpet.

I start yelling, "What the fuck are you doing? Stop this shit! Stop, you fucking psycho! You're going to kill him!" Shelly was screaming, but neither of us jumped into the fray, knowing that means getting cut for sure. To Hodgie's credit, he put all his focus and energy into the arm that held the blade ("Always watch the hands," as my sensei, E.C., taught me). They rolled back and forth, my brother punching him wherever he could get a shot in with his free hand, over and over. I somehow snapped out of it and kicked my brother in the back with my bare feet yelling once again, "Stop it! Stop! Stop!"

His reply as he was gasping for air was, "It's okay. I'll just kill him and we 'll bury him in the root cellar."

Ah! Wow! That was it for me. I knew Hodgie had about one minute. My bro was not going to stop nor run out of drug-enhanced power. He would kill this man in front of us, and I would be an accessory to murder. At that realization, I leapt over them as they smashed into the small coffee table and sent my movie-of-the week cup of Earl Grey airborne in a single bounce. I made it to the kitchen and my bedroom trapdoor, pulled it up in one motion and dropped down without using the stairs before it slammed on my head. I hit the cool cement, the moldy familiar smell of my lair reminding me of sleep. I rolled once, came up, and grabbed the two-pound ball-peen hammer that was sitting one a wooden shelf above the wringer washer machine that used to clean our clothes. There were a few empty mason-type jars there that probably held homemade preserves in a more civilized time (if there ever had actually been one). The hammer felt good in my grip. I spun around and was back up the wooden-ladder stairs, pushing the heavy trapdoor open with my head and left arm with all my might. The door hit the wall and crashed back on my arm, the adrenaline rush making it seem like it was made of balsa wood. I flashed my eyes to the death scene in my little theatre and was relieved to see they were still in a death struggle. The hundred-and-forty-pound cabby was one tough little motherfucker, that's a given.

I rolled across the stained kitchen floor, as the trapdoor slammed with a bang that sounded like a gunshot, causing Shelly to stop mid-scream and the two combatants to pause and look in my direction just long enough for me scramble on my knees for the ten feet and dive on them, bringing the full force of Thor's hammer down as hard as I could on the side of my bro's knee. It had to be done. He let out a howl that would bring the hair up on the back of a werewolf about to kill a hiker. He yelled at me, "What the fuck are you doing? Hit him in the head! Hit him in the head!" Well, I did hit someone. I hit my brother on the other knee with all the force I could find. That did it. He dropped the Hodgie Blade of Doom like it was on fire and rolled away from his life sentence. I stood there like a sentinel making sure the unsuspecting taxi driver had a chance to get up. He did and was out the door in a shot. My bro was rolling back and forth in obvious pain, repeating over and over, "Why did you do that? Why did you do that?" His girl knelt beside him, sobbing in sympathy for her messed-up boyfriend and her bad choices.

Before I could drop the hammer, sirens were on the wind. A minute later, five police cars came screeching to a stop outside my very own little house of horrors, the door still open and everything seeming to move in slow mo. It actually appeared very peaceful and beautiful to me, I suspect it was because I was in shock, but who really cared? The cops came to the bottom of the stairs, guns drawn and yelling, "Drop the hammer!" I did. A second later, I was on my belly, knee crushing my spine, looking at my bro in the same position. We were both handcuffed and jerked by the cuffs to our feet a few seconds later. By the way, that really fucking hurts! But to hammers, everything's a nail. "It is what it is" as my awesome cuz, J.T., likes to say.

They pushed me onto the small chair and my bro onto the couch. A woman cop, the whites of her eyes as big as saucers, took Shelly by one handcuff-free arm and led her out the door and down the stairs. I saw her delicately cover the top of her head as she put her in the back of one of the cruisers.

To make this long story short, they asked me what happened, and I told them my bro and the driver got into a fight. They were not amused with my succinct answer and told me they would charge me if I don't tell them what happened. I didn't, and my bro, as you guessed, also didn't say anything. Neither did his girlfriend.

Just before they pulled us both out and off to jail, the amazing Hodgie came up the stairs and said, "I just want to get paid. I am not pressing charges." Say what? The cops looked at him in complete disbelief, his arm bandaged by one of the cops, and they said, "Sir, can we talk outside?" To which he said, "Yes, but I am not pressing charges as long as they pay me."

A big grey-headed centurion walked down the stairs with him, and the other two cops asked me again, "What exactly happened?" I just smiled and said, "I already told you. They got into a fight." "Bullshit!" yelled this young bull. "You're going to tell us what happened here or downtown. Your choice." I chose to say nothing.

Then the woman cop came back in. She seemed pissed at me. Here I was thinking I was much a victim as the cabby but she saw me as the perp. Whatever. I looked at her and she knelt down to look me in the eye and said, "Shelly told us the whole story, and it will be easier on you if you just fill in the blanks." I guess she didn't expect my "Hahaha, that's funny" reply, because she got angry and said, "With your record it will be a slam dunk." I didn't say a word.

One of the outside troopers appeared in the doorway and beckoned her to come outside. Two minutes later they came back in with the cabby and he said again, "I am not pressing charges (unbelievable) if I can get paid right now." That worked for me, and I said, "No problem, I have the money." I asked them to take off the bracelets, telling Hodgie, "I'll get it for you." With my handcuffs off, I went to the kitchen and opened the trapdoor so I could get the cash I had stuffed away under the old sink. A cop followed close behind me, and as I started to go down, he asked me, "Are you for real?" I said, "Yeah, just wait here. I'll be right back." He said, "Not likely," and we both headed underground to get my pirate loot

After re-emerging, I paid the driver, rounding it off to $400. He didn't say thank you but simply walked down the stairs and drove away. The cops stayed and watched him leave in disbelief, knowing that there was nothing they could do. The three on the porch headed down the stairs towards their cars and a lot of paperwork, but the woman cop stopped and said to me, "You got off lucky this time, but I'm sure I'll see you again real soon." I smiled, she left, and I closed the door.

I looked at my bro and his girlfriend sitting on my couch like innocent high school sweethearts making up after a sock hop fight, my English Rose tea cup and saucer sitting in pieces in the corner. I simply said,

"I'm going to bed. I'd appreciate it if you weren't here when I get up in a few hours". They weren't. God had given me a Get-out-of-Jail-Free card. Call me a slow learner, but at that moment I decided that would be the last time I'd hang out with W.A.W. or tell him where I lived.

My brother Wayne overdosed and died in bed a couple of years later. It was Father's Day, 1991. He was 28.

Case closed.

Chapter 33

Night on the Town with My Old BFF

"True friends stab you in the front." - Oscar Wilde

Eddy. What can I say? He was my pal on the Projects and one of the Mental Brothers. We had some good times. but he always managed to attract wasps to the picnic table and still have time to eat his cake and smoke a joint. So I stopped hanging around with him because I always seemed to get stung while he got high. This life-changing night happened by so-called accident; as in, I was literally heading to the bar by myself when I ran into him on the street. I hadn't seen him for years, and it was good to see him again, I can't deny. He said "Let's go for a drink," and against my instincts I agreed, so we headed to the Fraser Arms Hotel, a seedy hotel and strip bar near the docks on Southwest Marine Drive in the far south end of the city.

I thought it would be good to catch up with him after so many years. We used to be best friends, but now travelled in separate circles. My intuition that he hadn't changed and was still a shit-magnet was dead accurate, and it took only an hour or so to see it. If I'd known how that one little decision would have changed my life so drastically, I would have turned and run in the other direction as fast as possible. It's easy to see now, but think of it this way: a ship leaves New York harbour heading for London, but for some reason it is off course by only one degree. A small amount, a little mistake that by the end has put the crew and passengers in peril because the ship has missed its destination by thousands of miles.

We had a few laughs, drank and lot and played pool and darts and talked about the good old days (trust me they weren't that good) and then left the bar at closing time which around 2 a.m. I wasn't driving that night, and as luck or fate would have it, the last bus was just pulling away from the curb as we exited the place. I figured I'd walk home and the few miles would sober me up, but he had other plans.

So what did he do almost immediately to solve our transportation predicament? Well, the same thing he did years ago: try to hijack an unsuspecting patron as he is filling his car with gas (he went to jail the first time after the car owner would not let go and ended up with his leg being run over and broken in five places). I wanted no part of it and was thinking, "What a loser!" not realizing I'd soon be painted with the same brush. I turned away and tried to keep ahead of him hoping, stupidly, that no one would make the connection. I turned to witness him having a short altercation with the owner of the car, a big goatee-wearing bald dude who just wouldn't agree to give up his black Camaro. He got punched in the mouth. (Mike Tyson said, "Everyone's got a plan until they get punched in the mouth.") His plan changed as he dropped like the price of oil in 2015 on the gas-stained blacktop. He got up and was smart enough to bolt across the road back towards the bar, but he turned to see if Eddy was chasing him at a very inopportune moment, tripping on the curb, launching himself into the air and landing down an embankment into the middle of a huge thorn-infested bed of horrors, a.k.a. blackberry bushes. "This is stuff of movies, I thought. as I bent over laughing, while his wounded-dog yelps could be heard for blocks. Then nothing. All went quiet. I was thinking, "Is he dead or just unconscious?" No luck on either. The guy stood up, and in the shadows of the night I could still see he was covered in hundreds of scratches with a deep gash above his left eye.

I decided to split before Eddy saw me. The "never leave a man behind" motto only applies to comrades or good friends in my books, and he was neither, just a heat bag from my past. So I took off running across the street, northeast towards home. I hadn't got two steps before he started to yell, "Wait up! Where are you going? I'm coming. I'm fine. Wait the fuck up!" I pretended I didn't know him and ducked into the shadows between two old apartment buildings. Eddy was in hot pursuit, knocking over garbage cans, breaking car windows, and every so often letting out the famous mating or warrior cry of the drunk male: "Whoo! Whoo!" To this day, I have no idea what that means or why we males need to make that noise when drunk, other than signaling to the world you need to be arrested or, in this case, receive a good beating. Too funny.

It crossed my mind, "Why the fuck didn't I bring my car? I'm not that drunk. I could have driven." After a couple of blocks I heard sirens. "Oh shit, what has that fucking loser done now?" I saw flashing lights reflecting off the many three-storey wooden apartment buildings and darted into the comfort of darkness between two of them. I headed for the alley thinking, "Better stay off the streets," and then who do I run into? My buddy screaming, "Whoo! Jake, you dog! Where the fuck did you go, man? I was trying to hook us up with some wheels, bro."

I stared at him for what seemed like ten minutes but was more like a few seconds. I can't believe my luck.

"What are you doing?" I said in disgust.

He actually said to me, "I set fire to a big garbage bin to create a distraction."

"What the fuck!" I said. "You're such a fucking heat bag. You've always been one. You're on your own. Don't fucking follow me. I don't want to get arrested because of your drunken ass."

I quickly turned and headed down a side alley, hoping to leave him and the situation way behind me. Nice idea, but I didn't get fifty feet, my pal stumbling after me, when out of a side alley came three angry looking no-neck, rock crushers who seemed to be on a mission. I knew instantly what that mission was. Eddy.

"Are you the fuckers who broke my car window?"

Thinking as fast as I could, I blurted out, "No man. I was just walking home from the Arms. I don't want any trouble."

"You're a fucking liar, and it's a little late for that now!" said the tallest of the three. Not sure what happened next, other than bam! I saw a flash of light, and then, nothing. I came to as I was being dragged into an underground parkade and of course my chicken-shit buddy was nowhere to be found.

Thud! Someone threw an uppercut to my chest and then a solid knee smashed me in the face, sending me crashing backwards into the cinderblock wall, my noggin making a loud whomp sound that echoed throughout the small dimly-lit underground parking lot. No one would be coming to my rescue, that much I was sure of; how far they would go was something I wasn't.

Two of the goons grabbed my arms and pinned me crucifix-style against the wall. No-neck number one, a.k.a. the Rich Tall Dude, (found out later his family owned hotels), unleashed a barrage of punches to my rib cage and abdomen.

In case you're wondering, No you can't call for help when you can't breathe. Matter of fact, you can't really think about anything other than getting some O2 in your lungs. They let go of my arms to switch off, while one of them went up the car ramp to see if anyone was around. Even they didn't want to get caught. I slowly slid down, I was clutching my stomach, hoping this was enough for them, but before touching the ground, bulk-boy number two a.k.a. Pretty Boy, (turns out later he was an exotic dancer when he wasn't working nights as a vigilante), reefed me by the hair to my feet. I made a wimpy attempt to break free, but bulk-boy number three a.k.a. the Nice One, came back down the ramp just in time for me to get clothes-lined by him. I hit the deck as he laughed, saying "Where do you think you're going, tough guy?" I was fucked! Blood was pouring from my nose and mouth as I gagged on it; Rich Tall Dude sauntered over to my heaving, soon-to-be-dead corpse by the looks of it, and grabbed my Storm Rider jacket lapels for the second time during our short dance, and as he slammed me upright onto my feet, I uncontrollably spat into his face, blood splattering across it like a Jackson Pollock painting. This shocked even me as I temporarily regained my senses long enough to whisper, "I hope I got AIDS, you fuck!"

That pissed him off I guess, and he went wild, lifting me a foot off the ground; then he paused and looked into my swollen, half-shut eyes, and said, "Well then, I guess the only right thing to do is try and return the favour."

The lowbrow meat monkey then spun around, swinging me like a kids stuffy, driving me full-force into the back window of a late model Chevy Impala, which imploded on impact. That was the end for sure, I hoped, as I was blanking in and out of consciousness. Nope, not so lucky this time. His six-foot-five frame with forty-five-inch arms reached in and dragged my semi-conscious carcass out of the back seat and onto the trunk, where he again laid in punch after punch, this time to my head and face. I could hear the muffled voice of Nice Guy saying, "Stop it! You're going to kill him!" That was it! In a kind of out-of-body moment of understanding, I came to the conclusion this guy could be actually intending to end me. So I did what any good street fighter would do when outnumbered and fighting for their life: I used an equalizer, as you should. Unfortunately or fortunately (could have been a .38) for the Rich Tall Dude, my equalizer was a WWII German youth knife, with an always-razor-sharp six-inch blade.

Can't say I recall the rest of our dance, but the knife became an extension of my thoughts and penetrated the right side of the attacker's well-developed pecs. Best way to describe what it felt like when asked by the Viking some months later: "Like a hot knife going through butter." Bulk-boy let out a girlish shriek after the first puncture and started to scream like a teenage girl that just had to open that door in a slasher movie. I quickly landed three more blows, and he stopped squealing about that time, I guess the HGH just ain't what it should be when it comes to bench-pressing knives, or bullets for that matter. He went limp and I used my knees to push his blood-stained body meat sack off me. The bulk boy turned to his buddies with a look of absolute terror in his eyes and cried out, "He stabbed me...he stabbed me..." as he slid sideways off the car, landing face-first on the unforgiving concrete with a smack.

Realizing what had happened, I slowly sat up and asked, "Who's next?" I trying to act fearless through the onset of a mild concussion, but, honestly, to those dudes I must have looked like something out of a Conan the Barbarian movie, with my face smashed up, left eye almost closed, blood smeared across my cheek like a drunk hooker's lipstick, and a huge knife in my hand. To my disbelief, the other two started to walk towards me, and at the time I couldn't make out if they were going to help their friend or attack me. Either way, I knew I would only be able to get one of them, so I'd better make a break for it. I bolted up the garage ramp towards the exit, my double-sole, tractor-tread Dayton boots reverberating off the ground like a Budweiser Clydesdale.

I was totally out of energy and could hardly see where I was going, so it didn't take long for me to realize there was no way to outrun them.

Plan B: get outside and stop as soon as I found a darkened corner to hide behind. Unfamiliar with the neighborhood and just wanting to stop and catch my breath, I looked behind to see only Pretty Boy in hot pursuit. About that time I was thinking, "Do these steroid monkeys have a fucking death wish, or what?" I darted between two apartment buildings back the way I came. Lo and behold, there was my BFF Eddy standing in the alley cross road like a scarecrow. He got one look at the dude chasing me and hightailed it in the opposite direction.

"Back me up you chicken-shit," I yelled as he disappeared into the safety of darkness, never to be seen again. Unfortunately, at the precise moment I learned one of my key pursuit lessons on optical illusions. Not the best time for a teaching moment, I might add, but there it was. It went like this: as I sprinted under the glow of an old forest-green street lamp, you know, the kind that used to shine warm yellow light on you and not the antiseptic white glare of today, I saw Death Wish's shadow literally racing up beside me. "Holy shit, this guy is on me!" I thought. So I jumped up and turned in midair, blood-soaked knife clenched tight, expecting the dude to run right into me and my cold German steel. But no, it was my own shadow tracking around me like a sundial, not his; a bizarre trick of light that seems like common sense to me now, but then I had nothing common and zero sense.

I was actually leaving him behind (always was a fast runner), but it was too late now. Boom! The bodybuilder hit me like a freight train, sending me flying through the air. My knife sliced deep into his stomach. We both hit the ground, my head smashing on unpaved alley. As stupid as it sounds (or not - lots of young males have the three 'I' complex: Immune, Invincible and Immortal). I guess this guy wanted to be the poster child for that movement), he started laying in a flurry of punches, apparently forgetting that his buddy was not acting so tough after his last round with me. I'm not saying what I did was right, but neither was what they did, and like Ron Sitrop taught me, "It's better to be judged by twelve than carried by six", so I laid in my own flurry, every one of them puncturing a hole or cutting a thick red line in his not-so-Man-of-Steel body. For whatever reason, maybe it was God whispering to me, I stopped stabbing him. There was a voice inside my head that softly said he did not feel the razor-sharp blade, and if I kept it up, he would die. Not sure what really happened after that, but he knocked me out, and I woke up to find him slumped on top of me and a police dog trying to drag me by my balls out from under him. I guess it knew or was trained that the guy on the bottom is, as the cop's say, "the perp." I screamed out as the pain of the hundred-and-ten-pound dog's fangs sunk into my groin, its eyes showing white as he bathed in the scent of blood like a fat kid drinking Kool-Aid. Police flashlights were everywhere. Cops yelling at me to not move, as if I could with a half-conscious vigilante on top of me and a blood-crazed werewolf trying to make me a eunuch. They pulled Pretty Boy off me, then, seeing all the blood, called to someone else to get an ambulance. All the time the dog was dragging me backwards. It took two storm troopers to get him to release me from his grip, which I am thankful for, as I am quite found of my sausage and eggs. And yes, they were not damaged, just a bit traumatized; I still have the fang puncture scars on my inner thighs to prove it.

There was no hospital visit for me to fix any injuries. It was straight to jail, without passing Go. They took all my clothes as evidence and asked me for a statement and wanted me to make a drawing of what the knife looked like. I did both, because in my mind it was self-defense: Me and my blade against three Silver Backs seemed fair to me. My girlfriend used all her savings and posted bail.

I was charged with two counts of attempted murder.

Chapter 34

"Do Not Pass Go...Go Straight to Jail."

"Life is not fair, and perhaps it is a good thing for most of us that it is not."

- Oscar Wilde

My lawyer was a well-known attorney, B.K., who, I was told specialized in helping clients who shared similar brotherhood-type codes, value systems and hardware - sometimes known as at-risk youths or highwaymen or, to put it more bluntly, prospective or current gang members. I'm not sure why this matters, but he looked like the actor John Hurt's identical twin brother. I was thankful he was on my side and had plenty of experience dealing with cases like mine. His office was in a heritage-style building, old from the outside but totally uptown on the inside, and conveniently located kitty-corner from the Main and Powell police station that I had visited so often. He was sharp and articulate as expected, and he seemed to have an unusual empathy for the marginalized as indicated in the article below; or perhaps it was just as simple as "if you could pay he would play." No question, he stayed within the confines of the law, but he worked the grey and pushed it, not to mention that he seemed to be connected to a lot of the right people. He is now a judge. He guided me in everything, including how we should pick the jury, what to wear, facial expressions and who should and shouldn't be in the courtroom, as in drunk or high buddies chirping at the jury and judge. One of the most important things he said was "You need to get a job. it looks better to a judge and jury if you're working. "

So I took it to heart and started looking, but with no post-secondary schooling at the time, and being in one of the worst downturns in the economy since Black Monday in 1929, the pickings were slim to say the least. Then, as usual, my big sister (camp leader girl), stepped into the gap with a job offer of working on a fishing boat that she had just been on and had quit. I should have clued in and asked her why she quit. So they were short a person or, as it turned out, they were always short a person or twelve. Why? Well, if you haven't worked on a fishing boat, then it's like trying to explain the taste of chocolate cake to the chief of a lost Amazonian tribe: you just gotta taste it. The job was brutal! Regardless, I not only took to it but actually excelled at it. Looking back, I guess I had nowhere else to go but jail for ten or fifteen years.

So a few weeks after getting bailed out of jail and Bill saying, "Get a job," I was pulling out of port on that boat. Huge change for me, no more fucking around and working under the table for cash while collecting welfare cheques. I guess it didn't register when the captain said, "You're hired. We ship out for twelve days tomorrow at 6 a.m., we'll be back in for three days, then back out for twelve." It wasn't a 9-to-5 situation. Oh, no. It was sixteen hours on and eight hours off for twelve days. Plus no pay, just a crew share, as in "whatever we catch and sell, you get a cut." That was fine because everyone was basically on that payment plan whether they accepted it or not. We all "sang for our supper," as my friend C.P. Wilson once told me. My life was upside down, and that is exactly what was needed. One thing I did do was ask if they were looking for any more crew. As it turned out, if you had a pulse they would hire you.

So my buddy the Viking came along on the second tour of duty, so to speak. And it was one hell of a tour at that. This was not the Love Boat, we understood that real quickly even though it was a big new fishing boat. That could have been because it was owned by a few investors including big-time singer at the time Linda Ronstadt (think Denzel Washington's song Blue Bayou in the 2007 movie Man on Fire, one of my favourite movies of all time). The boat was a pleasing sky-blue colour on the bottom and white on top, but the rust was already starting to show; that doesn't mean much, as most fishing boats need to be pulled and painted each year, unless they are aluminum that is. This boat had a crew of about twenty-plus, which sounds big until I tell you it was over a hundred and fifty feet long. That's big for a West Coast Canadian ship, but small compared to the giant foreign ships off the two-hundred-mile limit that go out for six months or even a year and catch everything including the kitchen sink. It was what they called a dragger-factory ship (I think), which basically meant they could process the catch, gut, clean, filet, package and fast-freeze on board.

This one fished as a dragger. It dropped this huge net that looked like a plastic shopping bag over the bow, keeping the mouth wide open with two massive steel whale-fin-looking doors. The goal was salmon, but they would catch anything, and I believe they had a contract for whitefish, a so-called bottom feeder that is used as the primary ingredient in a fish burger for a world famous fast food chain.

The captain cruised up and down the coast, hoping the fish-finder would stumble upon a school of fish. It was a total hit and miss (like drilling for gold) and to be frank, we missed a lot, which seemed unsettling for the real fishermen on the boat. This was the early eighties, and even then they said they had not seen it like this before. There were just far fewer fish than they had seen in their past. The days were long, and after the sixteen-hour shift, I did not want to do much but eat, take hot saunas (yes, they had a sauna on board; come on, the boat was built in Finland and a few of the key crew were Finnish), and sleep for as much of the eight hours off as I could. The old hands and drunks that were on for one voyage seemed to never sleep. They played cards and drank every night and then worked the next day, and they did this over and over. No wonder there were just a few accidents like the one that happened to the dude who was the third in command; he lost a finger at the end of my seventh or eighth trip. That turned out to be good for me, because they asked me take his job on the next tour. I was flattered, and, truly, being able to work under those conditions is not easy for anyone, especially if you're not from the Maritimes or a classic fishing family.

What happened to the Viking you ask? Well, he got sea sick on the second day out, which is totally normal, especially since you're working most of the time below deck; the smell was enough to remind any university or college grad of their worst hangover. No question, it's tough to recover from seasickness when you're still at sea. He did not return to work for the remainder of the trip. The captain, who he asked to drop him off, was not going to make a special trip for anyone who was not bleeding out, but as luck would have it, he got dropped off at a small coastal fishing town due to the need for some supplies. The captain gave him bus fare back to the city. Anyway, I guess I had proved I could take it, even though I was sick many times myself, as was much of the so-called "Shanghai crew," most coming from skid row bars of my fair city's fabled DTES.

Back to the boat: When we came in to port, let's just say I can somewhat relate to how the Navy boys feel after being at sea for weeks or months. The anticipation of getting on dry land with money is intoxicating, and it kicks in a day or two before you hit shore. Money in your pocket and lead in your pencil - what else could a guy need or want? We all got handed our cheques, then went and cashed them at a bar on Granville called the Yale. Not sure how they did it or why, but I guess back then the fishing and logging industries were killing it, so whenever the boys came to town, the bar had lots of cash available. I mean even then my crew-share cheques would be two or three thousand bucks, and I have no idea how they kept all that cash on hand for the likes of us. Anyway, like I said, I stuck it out, and not just because I had to but because I decided that I was going to buy a chopper and this shit job was going to get it for me, and it did. That was another early lesson in goal-setting, as in, care more about the outcome than the method.

Court dates and lawyer meetings came and went until the first real one, jury selection. For those who haven't been charged, it means I had to basically interview a jury of my peers (not really my peers at the time) to pick the ones most likely to like me. How could a jury of my actual peers be allowed in the court room with handcuffs, never mind being part of a time-honoured judicial system? I went through the process, which took a day or so. Once we had chosen the best from the many, we set a date for trial. That was about the time I started thinking this was no movie, and the butterflies in my stomach turned to razors which means you start shitting razor blades daily.

I was pleading not guilty, of course. I mean, no one in jail is guilty. Everyone knows that, right? I spoke with Bill many times prior to the trial, and we came to the conclusion that I would do better if I changed the deal to trial by judge with no jury. He thought a jury would have trouble not finding me guilty, since the list of my past altercations would be very front and centre and used as a club to beat me into a ten-by-ten cell for so long I would end up thinking it was a mansion. So we switched it up, which had the serendipitous effect of speeding up the trial date. I guess having that hanging over my head any longer than it had to be was not a good idea because I kept thinking about skipping bail, and I came close to doing that the night before the trial. While me and the Viking were sipping on Lemon Hart Rum at the base of a lighthouse in Stanley Park, I decided not to do like one of my favourite songs Ride Like the Wind by Christopher Cross and head south to Mexico and basically never come back.

I was mostly drunk during the trial, so there wasn't a whole lot of thinking going on. What was the point anyhow? I put my fate in what I would like to say was God's hands but truly, I wasn't on speaking terms with Him at the time. So it was more a matter of fate and a shrewd, talented lawyer than anything else. And possibly some behind-the-scenes help from a rock-solid uncle on my mother's side, but he never admitted to that.

I didn't know what the outcome was going to be. Would I get five years? Ten? I tried not to think about it because the thought could make me do something crazy. Then, on the day before the trial, I met with Bill, and he said if I pleaded guilty on two counts of aggravated assault causing bodily harm, they would drop the two counts of attempted murder. I said, "No fucking way!" Yeah, right! I jumped on it because it was a good deal.

One thing I'm grateful for is that Bill kept some of the details of what was going on and what could happen away from me. Later he told me the closest precedent to what I was involved in was that of an apartment manager who used a baseball bat on some guy and got seven years. Mine was a lot worse.

I got a one-year sentence. That was unbelievable, but as good as the sentence was, I was still shocked when I heard it.. There were about a hundred people in the courtroom, and I guess I was the only one that thought it was bad. Just before the sheriffs cuffed me, I pulled my car keys from the inside pocket of my Storm Rider and tossed them over about five rows of onlookers to the Viking. He gave me a nod, and I was handcuffed and led down through the bowels of the courthouse to the holding cells.

First night is always the hardest they say, and it was. As a matter of fact, even the first few hours in the tiny courthouse holding cell were hard when all I had was my hangover and thoughts to comfort me, or should I say torture me.

Processing included meeting a number of people who asked many questions including, "do you know where you going from here"? Uh…prison perhaps? Really, what kind of question was that? Hours later, I was loaded, along with about thirty other guys, on a prison bus and off we went. An hour later, our happy little crew pulled up to the big gates of the maximum security facility called Oakalla, where I had visited my brother many times and brought him drugs of all sorts tightly sealed in double-wrapped balloons, of course, where he would either "suitcase" them (put them up his ass) or tie a piece of dental floss to it, fix it to one of his back teeth and swallow it, and then pull it back up his throat later. It is a common belief that all prisons and jails are dangerous, frightening places, and most of our communities simply will not consider hosting one. Yet there have been less than a half dozen prisons in all of Canadian history that truly deserve to be labeled infamous. The American penal history has its Alcatraz, its Leavenworth, Sing-Sing, Folsom and San Quentin. In Canada the most feared institution was the super-maximum called Millhaven, situated outside of Kingston, Ontario. Here on the Pacific Coast, no prison was more notorious than Oakalla in Burnaby.

The prison closed in 1991 and is now the site of luxury condos overlooking Deer Lake Park, a place now used for tranquil summer concerts. See below pictures of prison.

Upon arriving, we were stripped, washed and checked for hidden (how you say?) items. (Can you say, "I'm allergic to latex"? You get the picture.)

Well, as it turned out, not only did I have a great lawyer, I also had that influential uncle working in the prison system, whom I had not seen since I was a kid. Regardless, the combination of God, my lawyer and my uncle was an unexpected factor in why I only got a one-year sentence, and as it turned out, I spent only two nights in Oakalla before being moved to a minimum security mountain prison work camp. In retrospect I probably wouldn't have done well in Oakalla or should I say, I may have done too well and had time added to my sentence for getting into who-knows-what? No question that someone at some point, probably one of the guards (no kidding) would have made sure certain people knew my uncle was connected and that just couldn't have been good, no matter how I played it.

The mountain jail/camp, Stave Lake where I ended up was, as I said, a minimum security setup, which means no twelve-foot high fences and razor wire. It was for all intents and purposes a wilderness retreat for first-time offenders and non-violent criminals; basically those who should not go (but used to go) into the general population of a medium or maximum security prison, where they were given a baptism of fire no matter how much they protested. It was also a destination for those well-connected enough to be given the country club sentence.

As for the location of the prison camp? Well it was like being smack dab in the middle of Whistler Mountain Village (for the view, that is; no restaurants, or never-ending Asian and Aussies tourists). It was situated in the middle of the mountains; you could walk away any time you wanted, and some did, but the consequences of that just keep on escalating. Don't kid yourself, Johnny Law will accelerate to lethal levels any chance he gets. So, unless you have a death wish, put on your big boy pants, suck it up and do your time. Get out and change your association, location, vocation, and that will change your situation. If not, then you deserve what's coming. After all, you were the architect of the whole thing.

I started off carrying the oil and gas for another guy who ran a chainsaw (the person actually cutting down the trees), I didn't like that much and made friends with this odd cat who ran the shop. He even eventually made me one of his handmade stainless steel bracelets that only his "special" friends had. A few of the real young guys who had the bracelets were trading some oral interaction with him for other stuff he could get in, like weed and booze. I was never that friendly and turned down more than one of his offers for relaxing back massages (go figure) but I did accept a bracelet. Anyway, he liked me enough to sign me up to run one of the big chainsaws replacing one of many who got injured logging. Remember, we were not professional loggers - just inmates doing time.

The Bulls, as you would expect, were less stressed out than their counterparts who were stuck behind cement and wire walls like prisoners themselves. So, for the most part, they did not get in your face unless you gave them a reason, and then of course they jumped to it with a gusto that they probably learned from movies as opposed to fight training or growing up on the mean streets.

The watching-your-back part was nothing like the medium and maximum jails, but it is always a good idea to have friends, which usually translates into belonging to a group or gang of some sort. In this case, work crews became your gang. You spent ten- plus hours a day with this crew, so you got to know them well, sometimes too well. All I can say about getting into fights is that it's inevitable. Act tough and get into fights; act meek and get the shit kicked out of you daily, or worse. I did get into a couple of altercations, but they did not go far. One was with a buffed black dude. He had not been around long but knew who I was and that I had a reputation of a guy who you probably did not want to fuck with. This was regardless of the fact I had not created any trouble thus far while inside. It is the going into jail for acts of violence that sets up this persona; that is not to say that some other Mother Fucker a.k.a mofos aren't way tougher, but considering I was not that big, it did help me. The fact is, I wanted to get out of that place and that life, and escalating a fight to satisfy my hunger and that of the others was not going to do it. So, fuck them. They could think what they wanted.

As for visiting days, that was every Sunday and I usually had someone come to visit in the beginning. My girlfriend Rochelle came a few times, but that stopped once my buddy, the General, started doing her. That ended both those relationships. The boys came a few times, which was enough, and always had a shot of JD for me just outside the door of the old country hall where the prison had arranged for the visits as they left. I worked out most days and read books, wrote some poetry and thought about the small things we take for granted, like having an alarm clock that you set and decide if and when you get out of bed. I would sometimes get so mad at myself, I would spit in disgust. To break out of one life and into another, I knew I had to change everything, and that depressed the crap out of me. It was the only life I had known, and I liked it.

Interesting that (call it what you want; I'll call it "The other hand of God.") is that years later when I went to apply for a pardon, it was not listed on my record that I'd been charged with two counts of attempted murder or assault causing bodily harm. No, it was listed as a stay of proceedings, which means that my lawyer convinced the judge to go easy on me for the time being. Unbeknownst to me, this could have been reopened without any new charges and I would have been screwed.

As for my release, well, I had a parole hearing four months into my one-year sentence and I guess it went well, because a week later I was told I was being released on the Friday. The Friday came and I was told it was now not going to happen until the Monday. Then early Saturday morning, one of the guards walked into my room and said, "Pack your shit. You're out of here in an hour." Apparently this is a safer way to go for both the inmates and the guards. No final retribution, making plans etc. I walked out into the hot sun hoping no one had made a mistake and would yell, "Hold it a minute, buddy." Freedom, freedom, freedom! Like the feeling of Christmas morning to a kid.

I walked out of the gates and there waiting for me was the Viking. He handed me my car keys, black leather vest and boots, then cracked a couple of cold beers. We leaned against my '68 Mustang, took a long gulp, then jumped in the car and did the classic burnout, leaving that place in my dust. Felt good to be free, but with some chains attached in the form of a parole officer. Beginning on the first day, I was supposed to have a curfew and not leave the province, never mind country. Yet the Viking had other plans. I violated parole within two hours by crossing the border into the U.S.A. and partied hard that night with a fresh selection of drugs and young impressionable ladies just dying to meet me and read some poetry.

> "Little girls fall asleep like a dimmer switch; boys, like a light switch."- JLH

> "There is a fine line between a strong woman and a bitch, a great mother and a shitty wife." - JLH

> "When you come to a fork in the road, take it." - Yogi Berra.

> "I recently read that women are the high income earners in forty percent of American households. Not taking away from that incredible historic change, I can't help but wonder how that stat compares to the national average when it comes to divorce." - JLH

Epilogue

It's Been a Long Road

"When there are no dreams, there is no future." - JLH

It's been a long road to where I am today, and I can't say it was easy, but I also can't say I would change it. Only God knows how changing one event, mistake or commitment, would have altered my trajectory for good or bad. I have tried and failed at more opportunities and jobs than I care to remember or forget for that matter. They fell into a few categories like the classic "no capped income" (it's always capped, don't kid yourself; just earn more than your boss or his boss and give me a call) and some offering nothing more than a hourly pay cheque and the promise of a bulletproof pension (simple, secure but boring; think Government worker who has opinions on everything but hates their life and always wants you to pay), or the entrepreneur type (as my longtime friend and realtor extraordinaire, C.P. Wilson called it, "eat what you kill" i.e., straight commission scenarios, which I have always done best at because in reality, I am difficult to manage because I want to manage you if you are a poor leader - weak, take credit for others' work, lazy, incompetent, but have your boss or parents convinced you walk on water).

So here I am still alive at 54 with three daughters aged 23 and 19 who still think I am Superman, or at least they pretend to. I've either set up or helped launch several mining technology companies in the Americas and Australia as the GM or VP. For this I am humbled, grateful and forever indebted to M.W. and G.S.T. who gave me that opportunity and welcomed me into the mining club despite my lack of mining experience. Make no mistake, the "harder you work, the luckier you get" saying is how I got the opportunity. That, along with cutting out all those (including family members, BFFs and girlfriends) who I made uncomfortable during my fight for freedom: meaning time, money and no debt.

If you can cowboy or cowgirl up long enough to break free from negative company, then all you really have to do is (like Jim Rohn taught), work harder on yourself than you do at your job, gym or school. Also remember the brain is a computer (crap-in, crap-out), so put what you want in, not what they want in. If not, then don't be surprised if you're not seeing progress. Change input and change output, and that includes what you read, movies you watch and humans you associate with.

Don't take shit from anyone standing between you and the goals you have written on paper (not computer).

Some of this I may have written about, but when I look back at a few events and people that changed my trajectory and/or gave me the confidence that I could be someone else, it looks like this:

1. Comments from a stone cold killer who said, "You're not like us ... you and your buddy are hoods ... smart guys who do this stuff for a reason..."

2. High School teachers letting me walk in shoes that were too big for me and believing I could fill them: Mr. Bolding and Mr. Mullan.

3. Steve Morrison, my grade nine and ten math, English and science tutor and friend who was the teacher in the saying, "When the student is ready, the teacher appears."

4. Getting out of jail and finding myself back being charged for assault not long after. Guy didn't show up for his court date.

5. Getting job selling vacuum cleaners door-to-door and learning I could take rejection and be successful, becoming the top salesman in Canada out of nine hundred.

6. Being introduced to the mentors Norman Vincent Peel, Zig Ziglar, Napoleon Hill and Dale Carnegie by my reformed drug dealer sales manager Mark R.

As I sit here by the hotel fireplace, safely nestled in the village of Whistler Mountain, I am hit by a thought triggered by a comment my friend A.K. made when talking about what type of keynote speaking I could do. He said "Mistakes are the message, so don't shy away from them." That made me think that all horizons from a distance look like destinations, yet they are nothing but more horizons. An example would be the realization that when I earned my black belt in Shiki-Jitsu it was not the end I had thought it was…no it was only the beginning:

"In the end you find the beginning." - *JLH*